Major General George B. Duncan

Official History of 82nd Division American Expeditionary Forces

"All American" Division

Written by Divisional Officers
Designated by the Division Commander

1917-1919

INDIANAPOLIS
THE BOBBS-MERRILL COMPANY
PUBLISHERS

PREFACE

THE history of the 82nd Division represents the collaboration of a large number of officers and men of this Division. The undersigned was given the task of preparing in narrative form an account of the operations in which the 82nd Division participated on the western front. To this I have added a brief statement of the organization and early training of the Division. Every "All American" should be informed of the steps which have been taken to make this record accurate in the smallest detail. Immediately after the Armistice, General Duncan directed every Company, Battalion and Regimental Commander to prepare a written statement of the history of his unit. Following the completion of this work, four large parties of officers were taken to the Meuse-Argonne battlefields. The undersigned accompanied the detachments from the Infantry Regiments and joined in the careful study of the terrain which followed. More than two weeks were spent in rechecking the ground covered by the Division in the Meuse-Argonne offensive. One Company officer was present from nearly every Infantry Company in the Division. Consequently, this published record has been authenticated by the men who led the front waves of the attack as well as by higher Commanders with a wider grasp of the general situation. Many of our impressions gained during the great offensive were modified by this study.

Since completing this story of operations the manuscript has been carefully examined and approved in each detail by Colonel Gordon Johnston, Chief of Staff, 82nd Division during the Meuse-Argonne offensive, Colonel Walter Whitman, Commanding the 325th Infantry, and Lieutenant Colonel Moore, Division Machine Gun Officer. In addition the following officers have examined and approved the story of the Meuse-Argonne operations covering the period September 25, 1918 to October 15, 1918.

    Colonel JOHN K. MILLER, 326th Inf.
    Colonel RICHARD WETHERILL, 328th Inf.
    Major EDGAR G. COOPER, 319th M. G. Bn.
    Major OLIN G. SHIVERS, 320th M. G. Bn.
    Major FONVILLE MCWHORTER, 321st M. G. Bn.
    Captain JAMES W. MORRIS, 326th Inf.
    Captain BONNIE HUFF, 326th Inf.
    Captain F. DREW, 327th Inf.
    Captain HENRY E. HACKNEY, 327th Inf.

Weekly historical conferences were held by General Duncan at Division Headquarters from December, 1918, until the middle of April, 1919. All Brigade, Regimental and Battalion Commanders were present at these meetings. Many company officers were invited before the conferences whenever further evidence was required. These discussions covered every phase of our operations. All of this preliminary investigation was completed before the undersigned attempted to write the Division History.

The several contributed chapters were carefully prepared by the officers whose names appear at the head of such chapters.

The statistical Appendixes were prepared from original

sources by Sergeant-Major J. B. Kass, with some assistance from the office of the Division Adjutant.

Several members of the Division have received citations and decorations since the Division was demobilized. To this extent the record is incomplete. Many Appendixes have been omitted because the funds subscribed were insufficient to authorize a larger publication.

      (Signed) G. EDWARD BUXTON, JR.,
      Lieut. Colonel, Infantry, 82nd Division.

Providence,
Rhode Island.

FOREWORD

THE DIGNITY OF THEIR DESTINY

THE 82nd Division has passed into history. It has been mustered into the army of tradition. The crusaders of the Middle Ages died to gain possession of an empty tomb. Yesterday's crusade was fought to preserve a living fire—the spirit of liberty.

The 82nd Division gave itself freely for this purpose. It played its part in the forward line and knew the privilege of deadly peril.

The men who came home are conscious of a very great bond of comradeship. The ties between men who have endured hardship and battles together are not easily expressed in words.

We are glad that the 82nd Division contained men of every blood strain in all the races that make up our nation. This Division has learned that an American is one who is willing to give his life for America.

We are glad that we came from every section of the United States. We can not feel prejudices against states that reared our battle brothers. Together we have blotted out the last mental reservations born of the bitterness of '61. Across the memories of those years our hands have met in something lasting.

This Division has no illusions concerning war. The glamour of peace-time pageantry does not fill the mind of the veteran. He has learned that battles are won by terribly tired men. His worst enemies were thirst, filth, cold and utter weariness.

An offensive suggests an endless movement of sleepless men and animals through countless black nights of rain and mud. It transforms dawn and dusk into a monstrous nightmare of waiting for some new horror. It makes the clean beds of hospitals seem havens of ease and peace.

But the veteran also believes that life without liberty is more hateful than war. He still prefers battle to the loss of country or the betrayal of human institutions which carry the hopes of men.

Most of all we share the memory of those who did not come home. These fallen friends are scattered on all the fronts we held, but most of them sleep in the valley of the Aire, bordering the Argonne Forest. The battalions have sent their representatives to visit each wooden cross. The memorial services are over.

These men we left in France died very young, but we have pondered the words of our chaplains, who told us that old age does not consist of the number of our days nor do gray hairs constitute understanding. We have had a vision of generations of French children who will visit the headstones and memorize the names of those who are forever the symbol of friendship between the two republics.

The Division misses the old comrades but marvels at the dignity of their destiny.

CONTENTS

	PAGE
I. CAMP GORDON TO FRANCE	1
II. THE SOMME AND LAGNY SECTORS	11
III. MARBACHE SECTOR AND ST. MIHIEL OFFENSIVE	17
IV. EARLY DAYS OF MEUSE-ARGONNE OFFENSIVE	30
V. PREPARING FOR THE ATTACK	38
VI. 164TH INFANTRY BRIGADE JUMPS OFF	50
VII. CORNAY AND CHAMPROCHER RIDGE	65
VIII. 163RD INFANTRY BRIGADE ENTERS FIGHT	73
IX. ASTRIDE THE AIRE RIVER	84
X. THE SOMMERANCE-ST. JUVIN ROAD	97
XI. THE MARCQ BRIDGEHEAD	109
XII. CLINGING TO THE SOMMERANCE RIDGE	120
XIII. INTO THE KRIEMHILDE-STELLUNG	134
XIV. THE TAKING OF ST. JUVIN	151
XV. THE ST. GEORGES ROAD AND HILL 182	158
XVI. DEEPENING THE SALIENT	174
XVII. CHAMPIGNEULLE AND EXTENSION OF LEFT FLANK	187
XVIII. A THIN LINE'S POINT OF HONOR	203
XIX. AFTER THE FIGHTING	214

SUPPLEMENTARY MATERIAL

I. LIFE OF GENERAL DUNCAN	223
II. THE ARTILLERY OF THE 82ND DIVISION	225
III. ADMINISTRATIVE AND SUPPLY FUNCTIONS	246
IV. 307TH ENGINEER REGIMENT	258
V. THE MEDICAL DEPARTMENT	264
VI. ADJUTANT GENERAL'S DEPARTMENT	271
VII. 307TH FIELD SIGNAL BATTALION	274
VIII. COMPLIMENTARY LETTERS, ETC.	289
IX. MILITARY SERVICE OF WILLIAM P. BURNHAM	294
X. CRITIQUE OF THE FIGHTING CHARACTERISTICS	295
XI. SECRET ORDERS	302
XII. DECORATIONS, PRISONERS TAKEN, MATERIAL CAPTURED	309

Official History of 82nd Division A. E. F.

CHAPTER I

CAMP GORDON TO FRANCE

AUGUST 25, 1917—DECEMBER 1, 1918

The 82nd Division was assembled, beginning August 25, 1917, at Camp Gordon, fourteen miles from Atlanta, Ga., under the command of Major General Eben Swift, N. A. Lieutenant Colonel Preston Brown was Chief of Staff. Over one-third of the majors and all higher officers were from the Regular Army. With a few exceptions the remaining officers were graduates of the First Officers' Training Camp at Fort McPherson and came from Alabama, Florida and Georgia.

After a week spent in organizing the officers, the Division received by increments the first drafted personnel from Alabama, Georgia and Tennessee, together with a small training cadre of non-commissioned officers, mostly from the 6th and 17th Infantry Regiments.

The progress made toward discipline and morale during the first six weeks was interrupted by a War Department order which transferred the entire enlisted personnel, less training cadre of 783 men, to several Southern National Guard units, some of which were in the 31st Division. The officers of the 82nd Division will not soon forget the regret with which they saw these men depart. The men themselves unanimously wished to remain with their regiments. A real unit consciousness had been created during the days past and every one felt that infanticide was being committed upon newly born regiments. Immediately thereafter, the Division received a continuous flood of replacements from Camps Devens, Dix, Upton, Lee and Meade, until by November 1, 1917, approximately 28,000 men had entered Camp Gordon, including the handful of troops assigned to the 157th Depot Brigade. In a few weeks' time regimental esprit was again developed.

A considerable number, approximately twenty per cent., of these men were of foreign birth, and several hundred were not citizens of the United States. Training was seriously handicapped by a substantial percentage of men who were unable to read and write English. There were those who could neither speak nor understand the common tongue.

The perplexities of the problem were increased by the fact that some of these aliens were of enemy origin. Furthermore, the average American was unable to distinguish between the German or Austrian Pole and the Russian Pole, the Czecho-Slovak or Jugo-Slav and men of the same race from Russia or Serbia. If the soldier was a Greek, he might be a partisan of King Constantine or of M. Venizelos. If an oriental-appearing soldier claimed to be an Armenian, he was possibly a Turk. Hence, every opportunity existed for enemy espionage within the Division, and acts of sabotage seemed a reasonable possibility to the Camp authorities.

This confusion of races and speech was eventually modified by the elimination of confessed enemy aliens, the transfer to the Depot Brigade of suspicious cases, the institution of English language schools throughout the Division under a Committee of Education, and an influx in March, 1918, of 5000 replacements from Camps Dodge, Travis, Devens, Gordon, Upton and second draft men from Alabama, Georgia and Tennessee. Over 1,400 alien enemies were discharged by War Department order.

The occupational classification of the Division's personnel resulted in the withdrawal of 3,000 specialists transferred by War Department order. The loss of these intelligent men, after three months of arduous training, was keenly felt. The Division believed that the War Department had overlooked one important consideration. Although the soldier might be a very good plumber, lumberman, blacksmith or structural iron worker, a great deal of Government time and money had been expended in making him an even more valuable specialist in his present occupation: namely, that of a non-commissioned officer, bayonet instructor, hand-grenade expert or machine gunner.

The training program so far outstripped available equipment that regiments were soon turned out for drills and ceremonies with wooden guns minus all other ordnance property. After a few weeks, the 1917 Eddystone rifle was issued without webb equipment and much energy was concentrated on preliminary training for service practice at the Divisional Rifle Range in Norcross, Ga.

Two features of the early training during General Swift's command will always be remembered by the troops: the emphasis upon road marching and organization singing.

On November 24, 1917, General Swift was ordered overseas and Brigadier General James B. Erwin assumed command of the Division. Major Royden E. Beebe was appointed Chief of Staff. General Erwin was transferred to a command at Chickamauga Park on December 26, 1917, and Brigadier General William P. Burnham succeeded. General Burnham received his promotion to the rank of major general, April 12, 1918.

During the first three months of 1918, the Division was

indebted to a small group of French and English officers who worked with the special units and supervised the first training in offensive tactics and trench warfare as then conducted by the belligerents.

The training of specialists in the United States was necessarily of a theoretical character. The Divisional Automatic Rifle School possessed about a dozen Chauchot rifles; the regiments had none. Colt machine guns were issued to machine gun companies, although this weapon was never to be used in battle. The Stokes Mortar platoons never saw a 3-inch Stokes Mortar while in the United States, and the 37-mm. gun platoons possessed collectively one of these weapons during the last two or three weeks of their stay at Camp Gordon. A limited number of offensive and defensive hand grenades were obtained and thrown by selected officers and non-commissioned officers at the Division Grenade School. The men of one regiment witnessed a demonstration in which four rifle grenades were fired. Everybody was required to walk once through a gas house and remove his mask to sniff the fumes of a light concentration of chlorine gas and endure a mild attack of lachrymose gas. The artillery obtained one battery of American 3-inch guns in November, 1917, and another in February, 1918, and fired several thousand rounds at the artillery range in Marietta, Ga. Marked progress was made, however, in discipline, morale, musketry, bayonet fighting and the normal extended order and security formations prescribed by American regulations and practice.

THE DIVISION SAILS.

The several camps were inspected by the War Department in February and March, and the report upon the 82nd Division was sufficiently favorable to make it the second National Army Division to leave the United States, and the eighth in order of combat Divisions going overseas. Division Headquarters left Camp Gordon, Ga., April 10, 1918, proceeding to Camp Upton, N. Y., the point selected for mobilization and embarkation. The infantry and machine gun units entrained for Camp Upton at the rate of two battalions per day. Division Headquarters sailed from New York City, N. Y., on April 25, 1918, and the last infantry and machine gun units followed on May 3, 1918. These elements of the Division arrived consecutively in Liverpool during the period May 7-17, 1918, and proceeded by battalions after short halts in various English rest camps to embark at Southampton, England, for Le Havre, France.

The 325th Infantry, however, passed through London en route and was reviewed by the King of England in the presence of a large London crowd. This visit of the 325th Infantry is of especial historical significance because it offered the English their first glimpse of the American New Army. It is, therefore, most interesting to preserve here at length the picturesque comment of the London *Times*.

"The war has given London many scenes—some gay, some grave—but few have surpassed yesterday's, when three thousand soldiers of Republican America marched through the capital to parade before the Sovereign Ruler of the British Empire.

"In brilliant sunshine between serried ranks of cheering citizens, these sturdy sons of the New World tramped to the throbbing call of the drums. Very workmanlike they looked carrying their full kit; very happy they looked as they took the salute of their own Ambassador in Grosvenor Square; very proud they were as they marched past the great white statue of Queen Victoria and saw the King of England raise his hand to the Star-spangled Banner that symbolized their homeland.

"It was a wonderful sight, that visible union of the two great English-speaking races. The King and his Queen with their Court stood at the Palace Gates; their subjects swarmed on every vantage point and cheered; and the soldiers of England and America marched past, each with their racial characteristics, each united by one common aim, all impelled by the call of the drum.

The First Greeting.

"From early morning Londoners had waited to pay homage to the men from across the ocean, the 'Sammies' as they familiarly called them—a name, by the way, which, if I remember rightly, was first suggested by Mr. Paul Derrick in *The Sunday Times*. The first contingent arrived at Waterloo Station shortly before eight o'clock, and by half-past nine the York Road approach was dense with a cheering crowd that gave the men their first intimation of the warmth of greeting that awaited them.

"With an admiring escort of civilians they swung down the road to Wellington Barracks, where, with the camaraderie that seems to be the birthright of the fighter, they were soon in laughing converse with British Tommies, many of whom were present wearing hospital blue. It was strange to stand in Birdcage Walk and see, behind the railings, not the familiar scarlet of the Guards of pre-war days, not the flat-topped cap and close-belted khaki dress of war-time, but the somewhat exotic-looking head-dress and canvas leggings that one had usually seen before only on the film.

"Tall they were, clean-shaven almost to a man; and their speech betrayed them. Yet even among themselves it was not difficult to pick out the slow Southern drawl from the clipped speech of the Yankee, while the distinctive profile of the North American Indian was the hall-mark of many faces.

"Every State in the Union had its representative, for these were not men of the Regular Army, such as had 'come across' twelve months ago with General Pershing: they were the vanguard of the New Army, that almost numberless force which America is raising to crush for ever the evil spirit of Prussian militarism.

The Heart of London.

"Suddenly, as we stood chatting, exchanging ideas and the inevitable souvenirs, the bugle called out, shrill and clear, 'Attention.' A few moments of waiting as the bands took up position—the Americans' own band at the head of the long column, the drums and pipes of the Scots Guards to lead the second battalion, the band of the Irish Guards and the drums and fifes of the Grenadiers with the third battalion—and then the procession swept through the gates to the long rolling accompaniment of deep-throated British cheers.

"London in springtime, especially in the Park, is very beautiful; and so thought many of our visitors yesterday, judging by their faces as they gazed from the enthusiastic spectators to the cloud-flecked blue sky, the tender greenery of the trees, the lilacs and bluebells and nodding narcissi. So they marched to the Horse Guards, past the Salamanca Gun beneath the historic window whence an English King stepped to the scaffold, and on to the War Office.

"Here the crowd was even more dense and more enthusiastic, for on the balcony stood England's Prime Minister, Mr. Balfour, Mr. Bonar Law, Sir Eric Geddes, Sir Rosslyn Wemyss, and other famous men; and above their heads fluttered 'Old Glory.' Thence through Clubland and Piccadilly, and on to the one bit of American soil in London—the Embassy in Grosvenor Gardens.

A Veteran's Pride.

"Here stood Dr. Page, hat in hand, with Vice-Admiral Sims on the one side, and General Slocum on the other. 'Eyes Right!' ran the order down the files; and the strains of 'John Brown's Body' were well-nigh drowned in the roar of cheers that seemed never-ending. One little incident here was worth much to a handful of old men who marched gallantly beneath a banner inscribed: 'Not for ourselves, but for our Country.' They were veterans of the Civil War, and as they came abreast of the trio on the Embassy steps, all America, as symbolized by those three men, paid them homage.

"And the white-haired veteran of veterans, who brought up the rear, pluckily marching on by sheer will power, put new vigour into his step and carried his miniature Stars and Stripes even more proudly.

"As the column neared the Palace the crowd grew thicker. Army khaki, Naval serge, hospital blue and civilian drab, all mingled with light and airy feminine frocks, and cheered the marching men.

"The Victoria Memorial was surrounded many ranks deep with a loyal throng that waited patiently for the coming of the King. At first they feared he would watch the parade from inside the forecourt, but shortly before the Americans were due a Guard of Honour of the Grenadiers, accompanied by the band, and carrying the Colours, took up a position facing the main gates.

The Royal Party.

"And then the King was seen, walking across the forecourt and accompanied by Queen Mary and the Queen Mother. His Majesty wore Field-Marshal's uniform, as did the Duke of Connaught. There were also present in the Royal Party Princess Beatrice, Prince Arthur of Connaught in military uniform, Princess Arthur of Connaught, the little son of the Prince and Princess, and the various ladies and gentlemen of the respective suites.

"These included Countess Fortescue, Sir Charles Cust, R. N., Sir Derek Keppel, Mr. Charles Fitzwilliam, the Earl of Pembroke, Lieutenant-General Sir Francis Lloyd, Commanding the London District, Sir Arthur Davidson, Sir Henry Streatfield, the Hon. Henry Stonor, the Hon. Charlotte Knollys, General the Right Hon. Sir Dighton Probyn, V. C., and Sir Malcolm Murray.

"As they waited for the parade the King chatted animatedly with General John Biddle, in command of the American troops, who presented to him a number of staff officers.

"A number of specially invited guests were present also. These included Lord Francis Scott (a wounded officer), Lord Wimborne (who had just previously been received by the King on surrendering the office of Lord Lieutenant of Ireland), representatives of the Diplomatic Corps, and a number of wounded officers.

"The steady roll of distant cheering grew louder, and soon the head of the column was seen approaching. The gates of the forecourt were thrown open, and, to the frantic delight of the hundreds of fortunate spectators in the vicinity, the King and Queen and their entourage stepped out into the roadway to greet the American contingent.

Symbol of Unity.

"With a swing and a clash and a roar of cheering they marched up, steadily tramping onwards, the manhood of the free Republic saluting the ruler of the free Empire and receiving in return the salute of the King and Emperor. Londoners have witnessed many pageants on this historic spot; they have watched the incomings and outgoings of foreign sovereigns, the gorgeous pageants of crownings, and the stately trappings of death; but yesterday's setting was something even greater than these. It was a symbol of unity, of the final healing of an old and well-nigh forgotten wound.

"And that instinctive courtesy which is ever present with English Royalty was noticeable as the King beckoned Colonel Whitman, commanding the regiment, to break away from the column and take up his position beside him while his men marched past.

King and Officers.

"As the Commanding Officer of each battalion reached the saluting point, he, too, broke away, and was presented to the King, who shook hands with each of them. They were Lieutenant-Colonel Wagner, Major Peirce, Major Hawkins and Captain Battey. The Americans marched somewhat more stiffly than our own lads, but exceedingly well, and made not only a very excellent show, but a very good impression on all observers.

"The King warmly complimented General Biddle and Colonel Whitman on the general bearing of the troops and told them how very pleased he was to see so fine a sample of the forces which America is sending to aid the Allied cause.

"And so the Americans saw the King. As they marched back to barracks they were full of the glamour of it all. Officers and men alike were delighted with the cordiality of their reception and spoke enthusiastically of the Londoners who had received them so handsomely.

"Nor was it only Londoners that greeted their American cousins in the presence of their King. Men from almost every part of the Empire were there, and representatives of all the Allies. One saw the slouch hat of the Australian and the 'Baden-Powel' of the New Zealander, the gorgeous turban of an Indian officer and the Kepi of a French infantryman; the tasselled cap of a Belgian, and the flowing cape of an Italian. And, gorgeous in their scarlet and gold, with bayonets glinting in the sunlight, their imperishable colours drooping in the still air, the Guard of Honour of the Grenadier Guards reminded us of the pageants that were in the days before the war.

"Thus England greeted America. And America, realizing more than ever the meaning of cousinship, will send many more such troops as those we saw yesterday, to fight for freedom and justice, and peace—the trinity that holds them fast for evermore."

KING GEORGE'S LETTER OF WELCOME TO AMERICAN TROOPS.

"Soldiers of the United States, the people of the British Isles welcome you on your way to take your stand beside the Armies of many nations now fighting in the Old World the great battle for human freedom.

"The Allies will gain new heart and spirit in your company.

"I wish that I could shake the hand of each one of you and bid you God speed on your mission.

GEORGE R. I.

"April, 1918."

CHAPTER II

THE SOMME AND LAGNY SECTORS

DIVISION HEADQUARTERS opened in Escarbotin, Somme, France, on May 16th. The troops were held at Le Havre only long enough to exchange U. S. 1917 rifles for British rifles and receive helmets and gas masks, when they proceeded by rail to the British training area adjoining Escarbotin. All units were billeted over a considerable area, comprising numerous villages west of Abbéville. Our troops started upon an intensive program of training under the supervision of the 66th British Division, Major General Bethel, commanding. The Infantry was completely equipped with Lewis automatic rifles and the machine gun units with Vickers machine guns. The 37-mm. and 3-inch Stokes Mortar platoons received their weapons and other *matériel*. English horse-transport was issued to all battalions.

Other American Divisions swiftly followed to the various training areas behind the British front, until ten American Divisions were assembled in British support.

Hard training followed for all units of our Division. Many officers and non-commissioned officers attended schools. A British demonstration platoon illustrated the British idea of bayonet fighting, the attack, ceremonies, close order drill and physical training games. The countryside echoed savage shouts of "In—Out—On Guard!" Our troops assimilated those features which appealed to them, especially the games and method of bayonet fighting, and applied themselves to mastering the Lee-Enfield rifle, the Lewis automatic rifle and the Vickers machine gun.

On May 28, 1918, the Division was inspected by Field Marshal Sir Douglas Haig, who talked at length with many company commanders and concluded with an inspection of company kitchens.

On May 30, 1918, the Division was informally inspected by General John J. Pershing, and the troops were required to demonstrate various features of their training schedule.

The battalions were moved each week to a different town in the area to afford practice in road marches and to test the possibilities of their new transport.

Early in June, details of officers and non-commissioned officers were guests of British front-line units in the new trenches before Albert and Amiens, where the lines were becoming newly stabilized after the upheaval which followed the successful enemy offensive of March 21, 1918. It was during one of these tours of duty that Captain Jewett Williams, 326th Infantry, was killed, June 9, 1918, the first casualty in action from the 82nd Division. It was generally assumed by both British and American officers that the American battalions were to be attached immediately to British brigades and share the honors and burdens of redeeming the lost battlefields of Picardy. This assumption was suddenly overturned by an order entraining the Division for destination near Toul. The Lee-Enfield rifles, to which the troops had just become accustomed, and the Lewis automatic rifles and Vickers machine guns were turned back to the British, and the U. S. 1917 Rifle (Eddystone) was reissued. The train movement began June 16, 1918, and lasted two full days. The Division occupied towns and villages north of Toul, and once again addressed itself to the task of obtaining and mastering new weapons.

The Infantry received Chauchot automatic rifles, and machine gun companies were equipped with the French 8-mm. Hotchkiss machine guns. At this time all units of the Division, except the 157th Field Artillery Brigade, joined the Command. The artillery, however, remained in training at La Courtine, France.

FACE TO FACE WITH THE GERMAN.

Orders were received to relieve the 26th U. S. Division, then occupying that part of the Woëvre front known as the Lagny Sector. Reconnaissance was made by the battalion and company commanders of the battalions selected to be the first in contact with the enemy. These units were the 2nd Battalion, 325th Infantry (Major Hawkins), 1st Battalion, 326th Infantry (Major Wells), 3rd Battalion, 327th Infantry (Major Hill), and 2nd Battalion, 328th Infantry (Major Buxton). One battalion from each of the four Infantry regiments was to occupy the front lines or outpost zone, with one battalion each in support and the third battalions in reserve. Relief began on the night of June 25, 1918. All the machine gunners of the Division, together with selected Chauchot riflemen and the 37 mm. platoons, were temporarily detached from the Division and sent to Automatic Arms school at Bois L'Evecque between Toul and Nancy. Here they received a course of training from French officers. The regimental machine gun companies joined the front-line infantry battalions on July 5, 1918, and the machine gun battalions on July 14, 1918. The positions of the artillery of the 26th Division were taken over by French Artillery, and a limited number of French machine guns joined the front-line battalions.

The Division held the left flank of the French 32nd Corps, French VIII Army. The left battalion (328th) of the Division was in liaison with the right battalion of the French II Army. The American unit at once discovered that while the outpost battalions of the VIII Army were ordered to hold in case of attack until the last man, the outpost battalions of the II Army were to withdraw into the zone of resistance a depth of about five kilometers. This fact was brought to the attention of the VIII Army and resulted in a correspondence between the VIII and II Army that was still active when the 82nd Division left the sector six weeks later.

During the days and nights of life in the Lagny Sector, the intensive military education of the Division progressed in marked fashion and the men soon accustomed themselves to the details of existence in trench warfare. Patrolling from the outset was conducted in an aggressive manner and the Division not only maintained an ownership of No Man's Land, but penetrated deeply into the enemy's positions on numerous occasions. Several of these forays without artillery help resulted in collisions, during the course of which numerous casualties were inflicted upon the enemy, and some losses suffered in return.

The battalions in support and reserve were able to accomplish some important training work with automatic rifles, rifle and hand grenades, and finally to hold exercises in the combined use of all infantry weapons on a firing range.

Contemplated maneuvers were prevented by orders from the VIII French Army, requiring the 82nd Division to construct an entirely new defensive system of trenches, especially in the zone of resistance. The outpost battalions were compelled to cover battalion fronts extending from 4000 to 5500 meters. This was done by arranging combat groups echeloned in diamond formation. The support and reserve battalions were also echeloned in great depth. Concrete pill boxes were constructed, new camouflage erected, roads built to the front and additional bands of wiring provided. The Division was cautioned to be ready to repulse a serious attack, and working parties consisting of entire reserve battalions worked nightly in a vain endeavor to have all complete on August 5, 1918, the date set by the VIII Army.

On August 4, 1918, Companies K and M, 326th Infantry (Major Watkins), conducted a trench raid with artillery assistance against a section of the German position immediately in front of that regiment. The officers and men had been carefully trained for this operation by French officers, upon similar works erected in a rear area. The raiding personnel performed this enterprise in very commendable fashion, penetrating 600 meters into enemy territory, killing about a platoon of the enemy and taking three machine guns, numerous rifles, pistols and other equipment. During the raid, one American was killed and four wounded. When every one had returned to the protection of the American trenches, German artillery fire, heretofore silent, opened vigorously and two bays filled with men were hit. Altogether, seventeen men were killed and fifteen wounded by two shells. A Division order was published to the Command on August 8, 1918, citing the troops participating in this operation for their gallantry and soldierly conduct. This raid was supported by the 320th Machine Gun Battalion with overhead fire.

The first week of August was marked by a noticeable increase in the activity on both sides. Artillery fire became more general and German airplane operations became very active, bombing and firing machine guns at combat groups and command posts, attacking observation balloons and engaging our pursuit planes with more numerous fighting planes.

On August 3, 1918, the 30th Engineers effected a gas projector attack of seven and one-half tons of various gases and, as was later ascertained from enemy sources, caused many German casualties. This projector attack provoked enemy retaliation by a severe bombardment of mustard gas shells on the night of August 7, 1918, while a relief of the 82nd Division by the 89th U. S. Division was in progress. All front-line Infantry battalions of the 82nd Division had been withdrawn, and this Division suffered no gas casualties except among the front-line machine gun units, which had seventeen casualties. The 89th Division suffered very heavy casualties.

The total casualties in the 82nd Division during its occupancy of the Lagny Sector were as follows:

	Officers	Enlisted Personnel
Killed in action or died of wounds	1	43
Known Prisoners	0	3
Missing	0	0
Wounded, including "Gassed"	21	306
Total	22	352

The relief of the 89th Division was completed on August 10, 1918, and the 82nd Division moved by marching and 60-centimeter railroad to an area west of Toul, with headquarters at Blénod-les-Toul.

CHAPTER III

MARBACHE SECTOR AND ST. MIHIEL OFFENSIVE

ORDERS were received August 10, 1918, assigning the Division to the American III Army Corps, with further directions to join at once on the Marne salient. Within twenty-four hours this order was revoked and the Division was directed to undertake a course of training in the area where then billeted.

After training two days, the Division was assigned to the IV American Corps for administration and the VIII French Army for tactical control. Concurrently the Division was ordered to relieve the American 2nd Division in the Marbache Sector. The relief began August 15, 1918, and was completed in two days. On August 20, 1918, the 82nd Division was transferred to the command of the American 1st Corps, which became part of the American First Army, August 30, 1918. The Division pursued the same methods of relief by battalions within the regiments as followed in the Lagny Sector. The 125th French Division was on the right of the 82nd Division and the 1st American Division on the left for the first week after the arrival of the 82nd Division, when the 90th U. S. Division relieved the 1st Division.

The Marbache Sector lay astride the beautiful Moselle Valley and included just within its front lines the considerable city of Pont-à-Mousson. The sector had been known after the first year of war as a rest sector for both French and German Divisions. Such was still the status of the sector when taken over by the 82nd Division, but during the last of August a marked change was evident. Considerable artillery activity developed and the enemy was exceedingly aggressive in the air. Patrolling and small ambuscades featured the Infantry activity of both belligerents.

The 157th Field Artillery Brigade had joined the 82nd Division just as the Division was entering this sector. It had received its entire equipment and subsequent training at La Courtine, where it had been stationed since its arrival in France on June 3, 1918. The advent of this brigade was most gratifying to the Infantry, which was quick to perceive the advantage of Artillery support controlled by officers imbued with personal pride in the work of the Division, and with whom the Infantry had established personal relations during the months at Camp Gordon.

An event took place on August 29, 1918, in the 325th Infantry which remained a mystery until long after the Armistice. Lieutenants Wallace and Williams went out on a daylight reconnaissance with Corporals Slavin and Sullivan of Company L, 325th Infantry. This little patrol left Dombasle Château and never returned. When American prisoners were released after the Armistice Corporal Slavin came back to the regiment. The party had pushed across the Sielle River and through No Man's Land to the German wire. On their way back they were ambushed and all the party killed except Corporal Slavin.

A few days before the St. Mihiel offensive of September 12, 1918, it was common knowledge that some major operation was impending and this assumption carried a most stimulating result throughout the Command. For a week before this offensive, civilians were evacuated from the advanced areas.

The tentative plan of attack of the 1st Army Corps, published September 6, 1918, stated the mission of the 82nd Division. The Division from its position on the right flank of both Corps and Army was given "for its special mission the exerting of pressure on, and maintaining contact with, the enemy." It was further stated that no attack was expected from the Division.

In full performance of this mission, all Infantry regiments of the Division pushed to the front strong daylight patrols on the first day of the drive, September 12, 1918. These combat groups gained close contact with the enemy, driving in his outposts and obtaining definite information concerning the location of his supporting troops. This was not accomplished without considerable casualties among the officers and men of the combat platoons. One of the combat groups from the 327th Infantry on arriving at the Bel Air Farm was counter-attacked by a strong German force and compelled to withdraw to our own trenches. The retirement was covered by a platoon of D Company, 321st Machine Gun Battalion, under 2nd Lt. Robert Goodall. The cool and efficient manner in which this detachment handled its guns was worthy of special commendation.

On September 12, three platoons from F Company, 328th Infantry (Captain Foreman), the most advanced unit, were pushed forward on the west bank of the Moselle to ascertain whether or not the German lines had been withdrawn. Lieutenant Cox with his platoon forced an entrance into the Maison Gauthier, a well-known strong point, which covered the southern approach to the town of Norroy. This formidable position was located about one kilometer north of our front-line trench. The patrol forced its way through the enemy wire and drove the German occupants out of the southern trenches and dugouts.

Lieutenant Harrison led his platoon farther to the west against the outer defenses of Norroy.

Lieutenant Gould with his platoon attacked on the left flank of the battalion sector. All three platoons met with heavy fire and numerous casualties, but demonstrated the presence of substantial enemy forces in the long-established German positions.

After gallantly performing his mission, Lt. Charles Harrison was killed while directing the withdrawal of his platoon. The patrols from the 325th Infantry succeeded in reaching Eply. The 326th Infantry patrols operated in Bois de la Tête d'Or, west of Bois de la Voivrotte.

The soldierly manner in which these combat reconnaissances were executed elicited the following telegram from Commanding General, 1st Corps, to the Commanding General, 82nd Division:

"Please convey to the officers and men of your Division my appreciation of the difficult part they had to perform in the highly successful operation of the 1st Corps to-day. This part they performed to my full satisfaction."

Throughout the St. Mihiel operations the 163rd Infantry Brigade was supported by the 320th Machine Gun Battalion (Captain Muldrow) and the 321st Machine Gun Battalion (Major Moore) shared the experiences of the 164th Infantry Brigade.

It was known that prior to this offensive the enemy order of battle in this sector from west to east was the 255th Division, the 84th Landwehr Brigade and the 31st Landwehr Brigade. Corps Headquarters wishing to ascertain whether the enemy had added other units in preparation for a counter-attack, directed that a strong raid with artillery assistance be made against the German strong point, Bel Air Farm, just east of the Moselle. In compliance with this order, Companies E and K, 327th Infantry (Captain Welch), advanced against Bel Air Farm and Bois de la Tête d'Or adjoining, at 18 hours, September 13, 1918. A smoke screen was thrown down in front of the objective and the Division Artillery laid a barrage on the enemy position. One prisoner was taken, from whom was obtained a confirmation of the enemy order of battle. In addition a light machine gun was captured and several of the enemy killed. The German artillery countered by laying a heavy fire upon our Infantry during the entire period of the raid and until the return to our own trenches. The steadiness with which this fire was supported indicated a high order of discipline and morale. During our withdrawal the enemy attempted an infantry counter-attack from the woods east of the farm. This effort was broken down by the fire of Company B, 321st Machine Gun Battalion (Captain Cunningham). Our casualties numbered:

	COMPANY E.		COMPANY K.	
	Officers.	Men.	Officers.	Men.
Killed	1	5	0	0
Wounded, severely	0	9	0	2
Wounded, slightly	1	14	0	15
Missing or captured	0	1	1	8
Gassed	0	15	2	22
Total	2	44	3	47

The decision of the American high command to advance the right brigade of the 90th Division through the famous Bois le Prêtre, drew the 328th Infantry (Colonel Nelson) on the west bank of the Moselle into a series of offensive actions not contemplated in the tentative plan of September 6, 1918.

328TH INFANTRY ADVANCES ALONG MOSELLE RIVER.

On September 12, 1918, the right brigade of the 90th Division remained in place and the 328th Infantry was engaged in the aggressive daylight reconnaissance already described. On the afternoon of September 13, 1918, the 328th Infantry was informed that the right brigade of the 90th Division was attacking north and that our regiment would maintain liaison and protect the right flank of the 90th Division.

In compliance with these orders the 2nd Battalion, 328th Infantry (Major Buxton), in the outpost zone was assembled as rapidly as possible from its scattered positions in a defensive trench sector and placed in attack formation on the most advanced line. Engineers cut gaps in our front wire and E and G Companies moved out just before dusk, followed by F and H Companies and Company C, 321st Machine Gun Battalion (Captain McWhorter). The 328th Stokes Mortar and 37-mm. platoons also accompanied the advance. This was the first battalion of the 82nd Division to go over the top as a complete unit in a general attack.

The raid on Bel Air Farm across the river was in operation and helped divert enemy attention from this movement west of the river. It is certain that two factors alone saved the 328th Infantry from very heavy casualties by enemy artillery. First, the fact that darkness enabled the battalion to advance without hostile observation. The second factor was the careful avoidance of all roads and established trails. The combat groups cut new trails through the heavy bands of formidable German wire, while the enemy continued to shell the usual approaches to Norroy throughout the night.

The battalion jumped off just after the receipt of a message stating that the right flank of the 90th Division

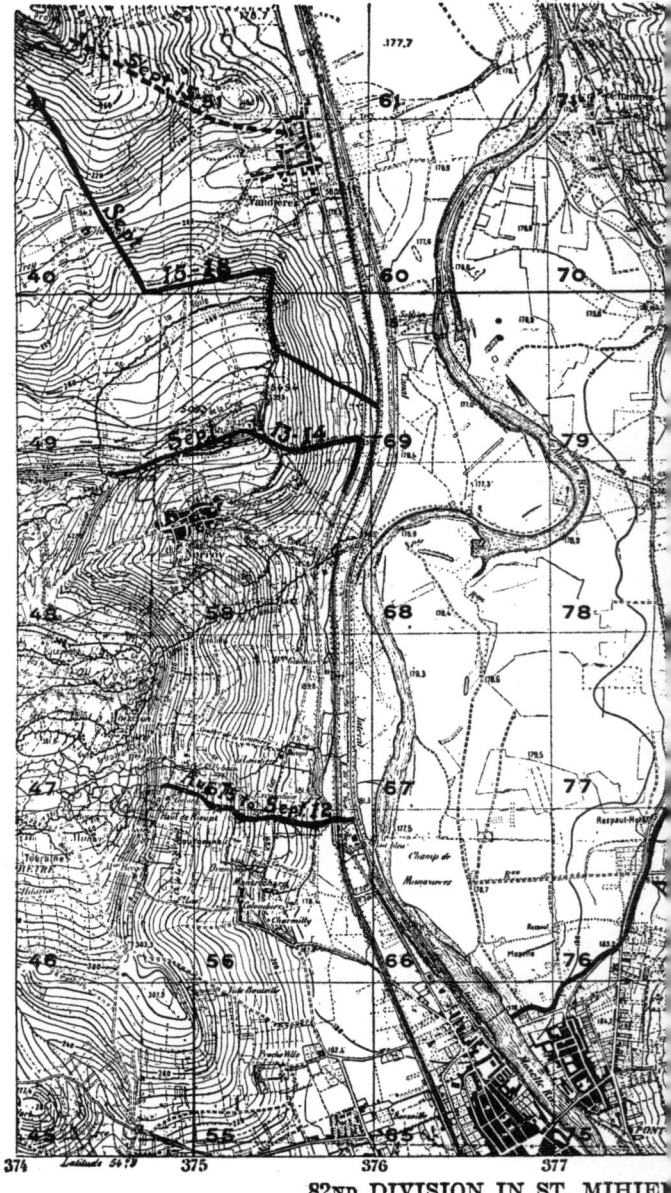

82ND DIVISION IN ST. MIHIEL
---------- Dotted lines indicate temporar
———— Solid lines indicate organized f

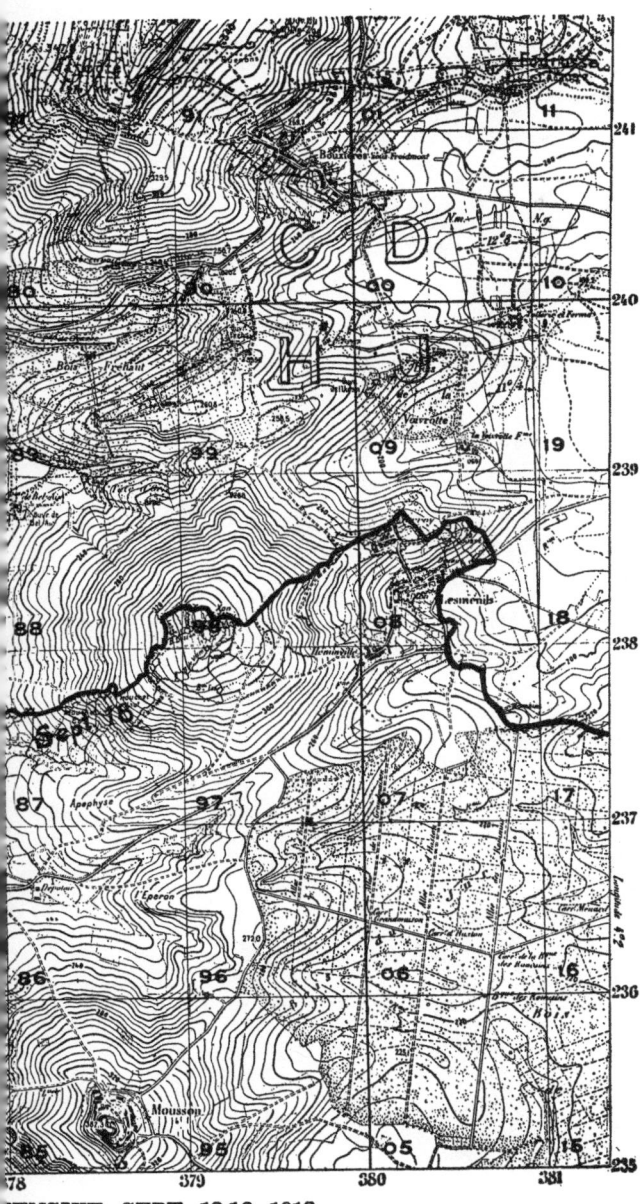

ENSIVE, SEPT. 12-16, 1918
tions of advance units during the day
ine at midnight

had pushed into the Bois le Prêtre and held a line about 600 meters southwest of Norroy.

The expected Infantry resistance did not develop. A battalion of the 68th Landwehr, 255th German Division, had hurriedly abandoned Norroy and the commanding heights north of that village a brief period before the arrival of our battalion. The German positions south of Norroy were strengthened by concrete pill boxes and a huge anti-tank trench in addition to a very complete trench system fortified with an unusual quantity of wire defenses.

When our troops entered Norroy one building was burning as the result of our artillery fire during the afternoon. One German soldier was captured in a sniping post. Seventeen French civilians, mostly elderly women, crawled out from the cellars of their ruined homes and joyfully welcomed "their deliverers."

At about 22 hours* on the night of September 13 the battalion was organized in depth with Companies G, F and E and the Machine Gun Company occupying the shallow trenches on the crest of the ridge north of Norroy. Liaison had been established with the 90th Division whose front line now held the continuation of the ridge to the west. Our battalion had achieved a night advance of more than two kilometers.

The occupation of our new position was accomplished in total darkness by company commanders working from map designations given them in the jumping-off trench. Two platoons of E Company were placed facing east along the river canal. Since the units of the 82nd Division east of the Moselle River did not advance, the 2nd Battalion, 328th Infantry, was now nearly three kilometers in advance of any support on that side of the river. The Bat-

* Our army adopted the French military practice of using 24-hour clock designations instead of the usual 12-hour system, and thus avoided the necessity of using A.M. and P.M.

talion had been given the mission of protecting the right flank of the 90th Division, but the right flank of our own Battalion had no protection whatever, except by a river fordable in many places. Furthermore, the 328th Infantry was now placed some two kilometers nearer than the 90th Division to the direct enfilade fire of the German batteries on the hill across the river east of Norroy. In addition to the possibility of a frontal attack by enemy infantry our unit was compelled to guard against any force which might come down the open valley of the Moselle and attempt to encircle our flank between Norroy and Pont-à-Mousson.

The prisoner captured the evening of September 13 stated that his own Battalion was probably entrenched at Vandières, two kilometers north of Norroy. This prisoner had been told by his officers that the Americans killed all captives.

The civilians found in Norroy had just escaped from a thraldom endured for four long years. They testified to the destructive character of the initial American bombardment during the early hours of September 12, 1918. Some civilians and several German soldiers had been killed in Norroy during this barrage. These civilians testified that the Germans left Norroy very hurriedly just before their evening meal on September 13, 1918. This was evidenced by the untouched food found upon the mess tables, the complete battalion records and a large quantity of military equipment abandoned. Great numbers of Belgian hares about the village indicated one prolific source of fresh meat for the resourceful Germans. Further statements made by the rescued population of Norroy may be found in the report of the lieutenant commanding the French military police attached to the 82nd Division. The following is an extract from the report:

"The population of NORROY during the German occupation consisted of 330 individuals according to the list of rations which were distributed by the Priest.

"On the 11th, 12th and 13th of Sept., the Germans evacuated the inhabitants to VANDIÈRES, telling them that NORROY had been mined and that they had the intention of destroying same following their withdrawal. Only 17 individuals who had hidden themselves in cellars were found at the time of its occupation by the American troops.

"STATEMENTS MADE BY THE INHABITANTS: The German Battalion Commander made himself particularly conspicuous by his brutal ways. He plundered houses and confiscated everything, according to his desires. During the day the 12th inst., the Priest having refused to leave with the Germans was carried away by force. Several persons saw the Priest bareheaded, being taken away by four soldiers. The Mayor was taken away under similar conditions on the 13th inst.

"The inhabitants received for the month of September, 13 pounds of flour, 1 kilogr. (about 2 pounds) of fat, 1 kilogr. of preserved meat and 400 grammes of dried vegetables. The distribution of the foregoing had not been completed; the Priest had received same from the American Aid Committee. Inhabitants with means paid for their rations. The sum of 3,000 Francs which had been collected was carried off by the Germans in spite of the protest of the Priest. It appears that a stock of food exists at the Presbytery.

"A supply of grenades is said to have been placed by the Germans in cellars of houses bearing the numbers of 40 and 42.

"According to statements made by several individuals, the enemy is suffering from a lack of foodstuffs. For some time past no meat rations had been distributed.

"The inhabitants of NORROY were aware of the presence of American troops in the sector opposite, having been so informed by the Germans. The Germans, it appears, were in great fear of them."

Despite our expectation the enemy did not attempt any counter-attack on the morning of September 14 nor during the day and night following. Enemy aeroplanes were continually over the town. Furthermore, German artillery bombarded the town from the north and east with a mixture of mustard gas and high explosive shells throughout the day and night of September 14, 1918, causing a number of casualties in that period. Six men in E Company were injured by the explosion of one shell alone. A heavy concentration of mustard gas collected in Norroy during the afternoon and troops in the town were compelled to wear gas masks continuously for about four hours until it was possible to remove the men to high ground relatively free from gas.

The Attack on Vandières

The 3rd Battalion, 328th Infantry (Major Johnson), was ordered to relieve the 2nd Battalion during the night of September 14-15, 1918, and the last platoons effected the relief just at daylight.

On September 15, 1918, the 90th Division pressed forward to ground west of the village of Vandières, and the 3rd Battalion, 328th Infantry, with Company C, 321st Machine Gun Battalion, made a daylight advance to extend again the flank of the 90th Division. The heights from which they jumped off sloped away into a level valley which held the small village of Vandières, and because of the open nature of the country, the advance was necessarily made in full view of all enemy artillery flanking the position from the east. The battalion was required to proceed through almost continuous shell fire, and suffered approximately 275 casualties in a few minutes. Vandières was entered and some units of the command seized high ground north of Vandières, from which points all troops were later withdrawn. The battalion dug in just south of the village, refusing the right flank and connecting up with the 90th Division on the left. This advance still further exposed the flank of the 328th Infantry to enemy artillery fire and constituted a tempting invitation for a German infantry counter-attack.

The terrible punishment inflicted upon this battalion was caused almost exclusively by enemy artillery, which was able to use direct fire at a murderously close range. Casualties inflicted by enemy infantry were slight. No unit of the Division had thus far been subjected to a test approaching in severity the experience of the 3rd Battalion on this afternoon. That the platoons continued to advance in many instances after losing their accustomed leaders reflects the highest credit on this unit. Among other officer casualties, Captain Rumph, of I Company, and Captain Cooper, of M Company, were severely wounded. The units of the Machine Gun Company were also conspicuous for great gallantry. The gunners were well forward in the advance and sustained heavy losses with unbroken spirit. One very gallant and dramatic part was played by the drivers of the machine gun carts. These men drove their mules at a gallop through the barrage and up to the outskirts of Vandières. Even after the new front had been organized, enemy artillery continued to bombard the new line with gas shells and high explosives.

The 1st Battalion, 328th Infantry (Major Boyle), which had been in support of the 3rd Battalion during this operation, relieved the 3rd Battalion after dark the night of September 15, 1918, and held the new line under constant harassing fire supported by the 328th Infantry Machine Gun Company (Captain Carr) until in turn relieved September 16, 1918, by a battalion of the 90th Division.

The 1st and 3rd Battalions of the 328th Infantry were cited in Division orders for splendid conduct in taking Vandières under very heavy artillery fire.

A Division citation at the same time was given Lieutenant Colonel Emory J. Pike, Divisional Machine Gun Officer, who died from wounds received during advance of 3rd Battalion upon Vandières. Colonel Pike was voluntarily assisting some Infantry units when struck down by a shell. During the advance in the St. Mihiel drive the forward battalions of the 328th Infantry were under the tactical supervision of Lieutenant Colonel Richard Wetherill. Among officer casualties in the other regiments of the Division during this offensive was Captain Arthur E. Hamm, Company M, 326th Infantry, who was killed in an outpost position by a bomb dropped from an aeroplane. The 327th Infantry suffered many officer casualties, among which were 1st Lieutenant Robert R. Forrester of Company L and 2nd Lieutenant Leo D. Sheridan of Company E, both severely wounded by shell fire. 1st Lieutenant Joe N. Neal, Jr., died from shrapnel wounds received September 13th. Another loss in the 327th Infantry was that of Captain James E. Welch, Jr., commanding the Third Battalion. About dark on the afternoon of September 14, 1918, Captain Welch took two soldiers and went into No Man's Land to search for some members of his command who had been missing since the raid on Bel Air Farm the previous afternoon. After going a short distance they were fired on by German machine guns. Captain Welch told the soldier nearest our lines to "go back in if you can." This soldier reported several hours later. Neither Captain Welch nor the second soldier were ever seen again. After the Armistice the Regiment sent a searching party back to this sector, but no crosses were found marked with the names of the missing pair. It is believed that they were killed and buried by the enemy who failed to mark their graves.

The 82nd Division was relieved by the 69th French Division, the movement being completed September 21, 1918, and all units were camped in the woods around Marbache and Belleville. Division Headquarters moved to

OFFICIAL HISTORY OF 82ND DIVISION 29

Liverdun. At this time, Lieutenant Colonel Royden E. Beebe was transferred to General Headquarters, and Colonel Raymond Sheldon became Chief of Staff.

The total casualties of the Division during its tour of duty in the Marbache Sector numbered:

MARBACHE SECTOR—*August 17-September 10.*

	Officers	Enlisted Personnel
Killed in action or died of wounds	0	11
Known Prisoners	0	4
Missing	2	2
Wounded, including "Gassed"	4	56
Total	6	73

ST. MIHIEL BATTLE—*September 11-September 20.*

	Officers	Enlisted Personnel
Killed in action or died of wounds	4	74
Known Prisoners	0	6
Missing	1	8
Wounded, including "Gassed"	38	819
Total	43	907

The Division was ordered to embuss September 24, 1918, for the vicinity of Clermont, west of Verdun. The horse transport and artillery preceded the Division by marching. The Division was directed to report to the Commanding General, American First Army, as Army reserve. The Division arrived in the new area on September 25, 1918, and pitched shelter tents in the woods west of the Clermont-Bar-le-Duc Road. Division Headquarters was established in Grange-le-Comte, an old French farm-house.

CHAPTER IV

EARLY DAYS OF MEUSE-ARGONNE OFFENSIVE

SEPTEMBER 25, 1918—OCTOBER 5, 1918

WHEN the long French bus trains, driven by hundreds of uniformed Annamites, debarked the last unit of the 82nd Division south of Clermont-en-Argonne on September 25, 1918, the Division stood ready for any emergency as Army Reserve in rear of the 1st Corps area. The total strength of the 82nd Division mustered 934 officers, 25,797 enlisted men and 5646 animals.

The vast concentration of troops, transport and *matériel* convinced all ranks that the day of an important military effort was at hand. When, at 1 hour, September 26, 1918, the bivouacked thousands were awakened by the thunder of massed artillery in a barrage obviously extending from the Meuse River west across the Argonne Forest, along the front of the French Army on our left, we knew that the hour had come.

The following three days proved a trying period. Repeated warnings from the higher command kept all units on a continuous alert. In Division Headquarters it was known only that the Division could expect two hours' notice prior to a definite movement. Liaison officers from the Division with the 1st Army and 1st Corps Headquarters kept the Division in touch with the progress of the attack along the entire front. Liaison was also maintained with the 92nd Division in 1st Corps Reserve near Clermont.

The Advance P. C. of the 82nd Division was located at Grange le Comte Farm, about three kilometers northwest from Rarécourt, the Headquarters of the 1st Corps. The 2nd Echelon of Division Headquarters was established at Passavant. The regiments and separate battalions were bivouacked in the woods west of the main army road to Clermont and extending from the vicinity of Grange le Comte Farm to the region west of Froidos.

The nights were cold and periods of rain were sufficiently frequent to keep all ranks in an uncomfortable condition. Animal transport and trucks mired in the forest mud, and green, drenched wood seriously handicapped the efforts of cooks and kitchen police. Most of the men of the Division had now been in continuous bivouac in rain and cold weather since September 16, at the end of the St. Mihiel Drive. As a result of this exposure, many men were suffering from diarrhœa, and hard colds were general. Notwithstanding this situation, the morale of all units was of the highest type and the attitude of the troops indicated both resolution and an earnest desire to meet the enemy. During the occasional periods of sunshine, regimental bands played lively airs. As far as practicable troops continued the usual training schedule.

327TH INFANTRY (SEPTEMBER 29—OCTOBER 1, 1918)

The period of waiting and of fruitless "alerts" continued until 16:25 hours, September 29, 1918, when the following telephone message was received by the Chief of Staff, 82nd Division, from the Chief of Staff, 1st Army:

"You will cause the 82nd Division to stand at the alert at once and to load on the Supply Trains of the Division one regiment of Infantry with two days' rations, to be at the disposal of the 1st Corps."

The First Corps followed immediately with instructions

to embuss the 327th Infantry and send it to Varennes by main road. Upon arrival, Colonel Ely was to report with his command to the Commanding General, 28th Division.

"Men to take two extra bandoliers of ammunition and two days' rations. Don't lose any time about it. The other regiment to be alerted."

These orders were communicated to the 164th Infantry Brigade and at 16:33 hours, Brigadier General Lindsey telephoned the details of the order to the 327th Infantry.

At 17 hours, the 1st Corps amended the order by telephone stating that the regiment would embuss without machine gun company, combat trains or supply company. This last message reached the 327th Infantry at 17:10 hours. The regiment moved out and embussed at 17:53 hours, arriving at Varennes in spite of traffic congested roads at 23:00 hours that same night. This highly creditable performance of both regiment and supply train caused Brigadier General Craig, Chief of Staff, 1st Corps, to comment next morning that

"the 327th Infantry reached its destination last night in good time under considerable difficulty."

Colonel Sweeney, the Chief of Staff, 28th Division, directed that the regiment bivouac in the woods two kilometers west of Varennes.

On the morning of September 30, Colonel Ely was given a statement of the situation in the following terms:

"The 28th Division was holding the ridge of hills just northwest of Apremont. The line of the 35th Division had extended from Gesnes to Montrebeau Woods and connected with the 28th Division near Apremont. At the present moment, however, Colonel Sweeney was informed that the 35th Division was falling back and that the men were straggling badly."

Colonel Ely was directed to send the 2nd Battalion, 327th Infantry (Major Blanchard), to proceed at once along the army road toward Baulny and occupy the ridge northwest of Baulny no matter what troops of the 35th Division might still be on the ridge. This battalion was "to pick up all stragglers, using extreme measures if necessary."

Colonel Sweeney stated further that an attack would probably be ordered for that afternoon (September 30) at 14 hours, with Montrebeau Woods, the objective. The 1st Battalion, 327th Infantry (Major Blalock) received orders to follow the 2nd Battalion in support, and to take up a position extending from St. Quentin Mill through Charpentry.

The 3rd Battalion (Captain Davis) was ordered to La Forge Farm, where it remained for two days. The 2nd and 1st Battalions moved out at once, taking up battle formations when coming under shell fire. The movement was made under complete enemy observation and, in consequence, shelling was heavy throughout the advance. Some troops belonging to the 35th Division were found on the Baulny Ridge. They were in a disorganized condition and many units were without officers. An outpost was established at Chaudron Farm. The attack planned for 14 hours that afternoon was postponed, but Colonel Sweeney sent a warning that an attack was planned for 5 hours on the following morning, October 1. The enemy appeared to anticipate an attack, for the Baulny Ridge was constantly searched by his artillery.

At 3 hours, October 1, 1918, the 327th Infantry was informed that the 35th Division would be relieved immediately by the 1st Division, and that upon completion of this relief the 327th Infantry would withdraw to Varennes. Relief was completed by the 1st Division at 4 hours, October 1, 1918, and our regiment returned to Varennes, where it bivouacked. The 1st Division attacked at 5 hours that morning. The 327th Infantry was highly complimented by the Chief of Staff of the 28th Division for the manner in which it had discharged the duty assigned the regiment. Our men suffered during this period from a shortage of food, as the regimental trains were unable to reach the troops until after the reserve rations were exhausted.

In this action, Captain W. K. Meadows, Company G, and Second Lieutenant Preston A. Love, Company D, were severely wounded and evacuated. There were 117 casualties among the enlisted personnel.

Meanwhile the swift march of events on all fronts of the World War may be measured by the announcement from the 1st Corps Headquarters on the night of September 30, 1918, to the effect that "Bulgaria accepts peace on the Allied terms, which includes disbanding of the Bulgarian Army and occupation of Bulgarian railroads by the Allies."

307TH ENGINEERS

Immediately upon their arrival in this area, the 307th Engineers and 307th Engineer Train had been temporarily detached from the 82nd Division and ordered to proceed by marching to Clermont-en-Argonne, where they reported to the Chief Engineer, 1st Army, for work on the Route Gardée. The Army order effecting this assignment authorized the Commanding General, 82nd Division, to recall the Regiment and Train to duty with the Division whenever the Division received an order to enter the action or to leave the vicinity of the Clermont-Varennes-Fléville Road. In consequence, on the day following the drive, our Engineers were at work preparing roads, rebuilding demolished bridges and filling in mine craters.

In compliance with orders from the 1st Corps, D Company, 307th Engineers, reported before daylight on the morning of September 30, 1918, to Brigadier General Nolan, commanding the 55th Infantry Brigade, 28th Division, in Apremont. At daylight, 50 men, under Lieutenant Sam H. Andrews, Jr., were sent to an old quarry about four hundred yards north of Apremont. This position was organized as a strong point, and in addition to the Engineer Detachment, was garrisoned by a platoon of machine gunners with four guns and two squads of Infantry. At six o'clock on the morning of October 1, the enemy laid down a heavy rolling barrage and made a counter-attack in the direction of Apremont with a force estimated to comprise twelve companies of Infantry and one company of machine gunners. Following is a summary of the report made by Lieutenant Andrews:

"Immediately after the barrage, the enemy in large numbers were seen approaching from the north in the direction of Châtel-Chéhéry and from the west along the edge of the woods in a formation resembling platoon columns. They sent five men forward with grenades to take the quarry which they evidently considered to be no more than a sentry post. These five men were put out of action with our rifle fire and the enemy continued their advance sending forward a machine gun crew, which was put out of action by Sgt. 1st Cl. William L. Eilhardt with hand grenades. Fire was not opened from the quarry until the enemy had advanced well abreast of it, at which time all four machine guns, all automatic rifles and riflemen opened fire from both flanks, inflicting very heavy casualties. The enemy succeeded in surrounding the quarry, but the garrison continued to fire from all sides. The enemy deployed on passing the quarry and attempted to gain admission to the town by infiltration, but were also repulsed in this attempt."

Eleven prisoners were taken by the garrison at the quarry and casualties inflicted upon the enemy estimated to approximate five hundred men. Two hundred of this number were accounted for by the American force in the quarry. The engagement lasted about an hour. The other elements of D Company were on the firing line immediately in front of Apremont. Casualties in D Company were comparatively light, sustaining none killed and nineteen wounded. Following this action, General Nolan informed the company commander of D Company, Captain G. P. Donnelan, that he had "a damn good company." On October 3, this unit returned to road work.

82ND DIVISION IN CORPS RESERVE

Conditions remained unchanged with the Division until October 3, 1918, when the 82nd Division passed into 1st Corps Reserve. At the same time the 164th Infantry Brigade, less the 327th Infantry Regiment, was ordered to proceed at once by marching to the woods west of Varennes for bivouac. The 327th Infantry was already located west of Varennes. The 164th Brigade moved on the afternoon of October 3 north by way of Les Islettes to the vicinity of Loshères, where it bivouacked for the night. The march was resumed at 7 hours on the morning of October 4, 1918, and covered a distance of 12 kilometers to a position east of Champ Mahaut in concealed bivouac along the road. This march took our troops through the territory occupied by the 77th Division at the beginning of the drive and across a No Man's Land where, for four years, friendly and hostile artillery had torn up the forest and blasted the ground into a desolate mass of wreckage and shell craters.

Following the order of October 3, moving the 164th Brigade, a second order came from the 1st Corps directing the 82nd Division, less artillery and the 164th Brigade to proceed by marching at 6 hours, October 4, 1918, to the woods west of Varennes for bivouac. This march was completed in two days with a bivouac on the night of October

4th at Camp Mahaut, about three kilometers east of Les Islettes.

On October 4th, Major General W. P. Burnham was relieved from duty with the 82nd Division and left at once to become Military Representative of the United States in Greece. The command of the Division was at once assumed by Major General George B. Duncan.

An order received October 4, 1918, from headquarters 1st Corps completed preparations for the concentration of the Division west of Varennes by setting in motion the 157th Field Artillery Brigade. The Brigade was directed to leave its area near Futeau at 8 hours, October 5, and proceed via Les Islettes, La Fille Morte, to junction with the Four-de-Paris-Varennes Road, and thence to bivouac near the Infantry brigades. Camp Mahaut, two kilometers northwest of Clermont, was indicated as the staging point for the night October 5-6. In consequence of these successive movement orders, the Division was chiefly occupied in road marches and bivouacs from October 3 to October 6.

CHAPTER V

PREPARING FOR THE ATTACK

THE 6th of October, 1918, is one of the fateful days in the life of the 82nd Division. All combat units in the Division except the artillery were concentrated in the woods about three kilometers west of Varennes. The artillery had spent the preceding night at Camp Mahaut and was then a day's march from Varennes, where the Division P. C. had been established since October 3. General Duncan's headquarters was located in a dilapidated cellar, which afforded slight protection from the elements, and none from the shell fire which fell at intervals upon this historic, but now almost obliterated, community. There was a feeling in all ranks that the moment of supreme testing for the Division was at hand. With this attitude of expectancy went a quiet confidence, born of the experiences endured in the weeks before Mont Sec and astride the Moselle River, and the important task accomplished in the St. Mihiel offensive.

On October 1, the Division had watched the elements of the 35th Division withdraw slowly down the main highway from Clermont toward Bar-le-Duc. We had listened for days to the ceaseless uproar of battle. Men must be tiring. Fresh Americans must be needed to replace the appalling wastage. Heart and mind the Division was ready. On the 6th of October, two of the three divisions which had jumped off in the 1st Corps on the morning of September

26, 1918, were still in the line—the 77th on the left and the 28th in the center.

As previously said, the 1st Division had, on October 1, replaced the 35th Division on the right of the Corps. The gallant drive of the 1st Division had resulted in the formation of a salient which placed that unit at least one and one-half kilometers north of the 28th Division on its left, and also in advance of the 5th Corps, on its right. The line of the 1st Division extended from Bois de Moncy and Ariétal Farm to Montrefagne Hill. From this point the left flank ran back to the right of the 28th Division, which had pushed up the Aire River as far as the southern outskirts of Châtel-Chéhéry. The 1st Division had sent patrols to Fléville but found it unprofitable to attempt any occupation of that fiercely shelled and exposed area. Small units from the right brigade of the 28th Division had occupied La Forge and vicinity on the east bank of the Aire River. Thence the line of the right brigade of the 28th Division swept in a southwesterly direction along the edge of the steep ridges west of the Aire Valley to the neighborhood of Le Ménil Farm. The left brigade held the line from this point southerly to and along the Chêne Tondu Ridge, where it connected with the right of the 77th Division which, in turn, continued the line westerly through the Argonne Forest toward Binarville. Contact with the 38th French Corps on the left of the 77th had been lost and the enemy, taking advantage of the densely wooded terrain, had infiltrated behind this flank, cutting off six companies of the 77th Division in the Charlevaux Ravine. Contact with these companies was not regained until the night of October 7-8.

The upper valley of the Aire River was a No Man's Land between the 1st and 28th Divisions, penetrated by small patrols during the night by both enemy and American forces. The country to the east of the Aire afforded a certain amount of cover from due north, the ravines having in general an east and west direction. These ravines, however, were enfiladed from the west of the valley, where the eastern edge of the Argonne Forest rose in a continuous echelon of rugged hills. No more formidable natural fortifications are to be found on the entire battle front than the precipitous ridges extending from Châtel-Chéhéry and west of Cornay to the town of Marcq. It was this enfilade fire of both machine guns and artillery which was inflicting very serious losses on the left brigade of the 1st Division. Further progress on the entire Corps front was almost at a standstill, for the enemy had rallied his full resources to prevent further American progress at this vital front in the battle line.

Our high command determined upon a bold and hazardous expedient. A surprise attack must be driven into the enemy flank west of the Aire and north of Châtel-Chéhéry. Troops making such an attack would be exposed to counter-attack and concentrated artillery and machine gun fire from west and north, northeast and southwest. If the thrust accomplished its purpose, the forest would be cleared and the way opened for a substantial American advance with slight losses by troops now struggling four kilometers south of Châtel Chéhéry in the heart of the forest. If this plan of attack failed, very great disaster might befall the battalions which presented an open flank to a vigilant enemy, but if the assault succeeded, two-thirds of the mission of the 1st Corps, as stated in Field Orders 17, September 25, 1918, would be brilliantly accomplished. This mission was stated:

"(a) To reduce the Forêt d'Argonne by flanking it from the east.

(b) To assist in cutting off hostile artillery fire and observation from the eastern edge of the Forêt d'Argonne.

(c) Upon arrival at the Corps objective, the 1st Corps will advance to the American Army objective in conjunction with the 5th Corps."

In selecting the 82nd Division to perform this thrust into the flanks of the Argonne Forest, the 1st Corps had honored this Division with a heavy share of its expressed mission toward which it had been bending every resource for eleven terrible days.

Long Awaited Battle Order Arrives.

At 12 hours on October 6, the following telephone message was received by the Chief of Staff, 82nd Division, from G-3, 1st Corps:

"General Rhodes will move his outfit at once, from his present camp by way of the two-way road through La Fille Morte to the junction of the Four-de-Paris-Varennes road, thence along that road, to Varennes. The movement to start at once. The ultimate destination is the vicinity of Charpentry. General Duncan and General Rhodes will report at once to General Liggett at his advance P. C. They will be accompanied by a suitable officer to carry orders to General Rhodes' outfit for the continuation of its march beyond Varennes. Reconnaissances will be at once made of the route prescribed from the present camp to Varennes so that the movement will not be delayed."

A copy of this order was given to General Rhodes at Varennes, who dispatched a message to his brigade directing it to complete the final stage of the march directly to Varennes and with all possible haste.

General Duncan proceeded with Colonel Sheldon, Chief of Staff, to the Advance P. C. of the 1st Corps, located in dugouts behind the ridge three or four kilometers southeast of Varennes. General Duncan found that General Rhodes had already been notified and had preceded him.

General Duncan was informed that Major General McAndrews, Chief of Staff, G. H. Q., and Brigadier General Drum, Chief of Staff, 1st Army, were in conference with Major General Liggett, commanding 1st Corps. After a considerable period, these officers left and General Duncan was informed by General Liggett that Brigadier General Craig, Chief of Staff, 1st Corps, would give him certain instructions affecting the 82nd Division. General Craig stated that the 82nd Division would make an attack on the following morning, October 7, 1918. The attack would be made across the Aire in a westerly direction between Châtel-Chéhéry and Cornay. The 28th Division would give ground permitting the 82nd Division to take up the territory between the Aire and the 1st Division. The attack would be made by one brigade supported by the artillery of the 82nd Division and the 6th Field Artillery from the 1st Division. General Craig stated that this assault was a military necessity and General Liggett was very positive in his purpose to have the attack driven through on the following morning. A written order would be communicated later to the Division, but meanwhile all necessary preparation and reconnaissance must be made.

General Duncan telephoned to Division Headquarters directing that brigade, regimental and battalion commanders be assembled in Varennes. He then returned with Colonel Sheldon to Divisional P. C. at Varennes, arriving shortly before 16 hours. A majority of the battalion commanders of the Division were present in addition to regimental and brigade commanders. The Division commander repeated the orders received from the Corps and named the 164th Infantry Brigade (Brig. Gen. Lindsey) to make the attack. He further directed that immediate reconnaissance be made of both maneuver ground and objective before darkness. General Lindsey with several of his officers proceeded to the Baulny Ridge and eastern edge of Montrebeau Woods, from which point he examined the terrain to the north and west. Before leaving the Divisional P. C. General Lindsey had sent word to the units of his brigade to make preparation for an immediate move. Reconnaissance was incomplete when night fell and all officers returned to Varennes. General Lindsey remained at the Division P. C. while regimental and battalion commanders went at once to their commands. General Duncan sent General Lindsey about 18 hours to the P. C. of the 1st Division located at Cheppy, to arrange cooperation with Major General Summerall, commanding. General Lindsey returned to the Division P. C. about 19:30 hours. Colonel Sheldon had meanwhile returned to Corps Headquarters to await the completion of the Corps order. Between 21 and 22 hours, Colonel Sheldon came to the Division P. C. with the written Corps order. Lieutenant Colonel Wainwright, G-3, at once drafted Division Field Order No. 20, and General Lindsey worked simultaneously upon his Brigade order. Both orders were then submitted to General Duncan and approved. The written Brigade order was given to the Regimental Intelligence Officers about 23:25 hours.

"The leading elements of the brigade will be crossed over the Aire River via the bridge at La Forge and improvised foot bridges between La Forge and Fléville and formed along the railroad track running along the west side of the Aire River before the hour for attack, covered by active patrols. Rate of advance of infantry units from position of departure, 100 meters in three minutes. Front line infantry battalions will not be reinforced but will be passed through by support battalions when they are definitely slowed down by enemy resistance. Combat liaison detachment consisting of one company of infantry and one machine gun platoon will maintain combat liaison with 28th Division on our left; one company of infantry and one machine gun platoon will maintain combat liaison with the liaison detachment of the 1st Division on our right near the bridge at Fléville."

The order further provided for a rolling barrage to start at 5 hours, 200 meters west of the railroad track, and to advance in a westerly direction to the Division and Corps objectives.

164TH INFANTRY BRIGADE MOVES FORWARD

Meanwhile the 327th Infantry, 328th Infantry and 321st Machine Gun Battalion had been moving in the face of every conceivable difficulty. The 327th Infantry marched out from camp at 18 hours 10 minutes. Their route was the Varennes-Baulny-Fléville Road to the Dépôt de Munitions at point 183, which had been designated as Brigade P. C. Here the regiment was to receive its final orders for the morrow's attack. The regiment moved out in the following order:

> 1st Battalion,
> Machine Gun Company,
> Stokes Mortar and 1-pounder platoons,
> 2nd Battalion,
> 3rd Battalion.

The 321st Machine Gun Battalion (Captain Holloway) followed the 327th Infantry. The 1st Battalion of the 327th Infantry reached point 183 at 22 hours and waited until Captain Drew, the Regimental Intelligence Officer, arrived from Varennes with the attack order for the brigade. It was then 1 hour 10 minutes, 7 October.

Colonel Ely held a conference with Major Blalock (1st Bn.) and Major Blanchard (2nd Bn.). They managed to contrive sufficient light to decipher the attack order, in pursuance with which Colonel Ely made his dispositions. Major Blalock with the 1st Battalion would proceed to La Forge, cross the river and deploy for attack along the railroad east of Hill 180. Major Blanchard was sent to Pleinchamp Farm with the 2nd Battalion in support of the attack and with the further mission of meeting all enemy counter-attacks down the Aire Valley from the direction of Fléville. Captain Davis with the 3rd Battalion remained at the Dépôt de Munitions in Brigade reserve. Major Blanchard moved out shortly thereafter and at 2:30 hours Major Blalock led his battalion down the road toward La Forge.

328TH INFANTRY

The 328th Infantry had been ordered to follow the other units of the Brigade. It left camp on scheduled time at 20 hours in the following order:

1st Battalion (Major Boyle),
2nd Battalion (Captain Tillman),
3rd Battalion (Major Johnson),
Machine Gun Company (Captain Carr).

After leaving the forest and entering the little valley west of Varennes, the regiment was ordered by the Chief of Staff to halt and permit the Artillery Brigade to take the right of way into Varennes. The 1st Battalion dropped full packs and made up combat packs.

At midnight the Chief of Staff directed that the regiment filter through the Artillery. This resulted in the most intense traffic congestion. The route of the 328th Infantry lay through Varennes, thence along the west bank of the Aire River to Montblainville, where it crossed the river to the east and came out upon the main army Varennes-Fléville Road. The Regiment was compelled to thread its course in small detachments and maintained organization only by admirable discipline.

General Lindsey, while making his way on foot to Brigade P. C. at the Dépôt de Munitions, passed the 328th

Infantry on the main road east of Montblainville shortly before 3 hours. From the camp in the woods west of Varennes, the distance by road to the Dépôt de Munitions was approximately ten kilometers, with the bridgehead at La Forge, jus east of Châtel-Chéhéry, some two kilometers farther.

Lieutenant Colonel Wetherill, commanding the 328th Infantry, had been informed that guides from the 28th Division would wait in the vicinity of the Dépôt de Munitions to conduct the assault battalion to the jumping off line. These guides were never encountered and it is presumed that one of the two men from the 28th Division who met the 1st Battalion of the 327th Infantry on the cross-road to La Forge was intended as the guide for the assault battalion of the 328th Infantry.

In consequence, the head of the column of the last named regiment proceeded past the Dépôt de Munitions to the cross-road running to Pleinchamp Farm, without finding any one from the 28th Division. Colonel Wetherill, convinced that he had proceeded beyond his objective, countermarched the troops on the main road until he personally met an officer, who led him to General Lindsey at the Dépôt de Munitions. Captain Holloway, commanding the 321st M. G. Battalion, was sent with Colonel Wetherill to identify the cross-road leading to La Forge. The 1st Battalion at once deployed in attack formation in the woods Des Granges, about one kilometer east of La Forge. This last movement was accomplished about 5 hours 30 minutes, October 7.

An Extraordinary Maneuver

The events of the night of October 6-7 can not be judged by any ordinary standards, nor can an adequate opinion be formed of the merits of this maneuver unless there

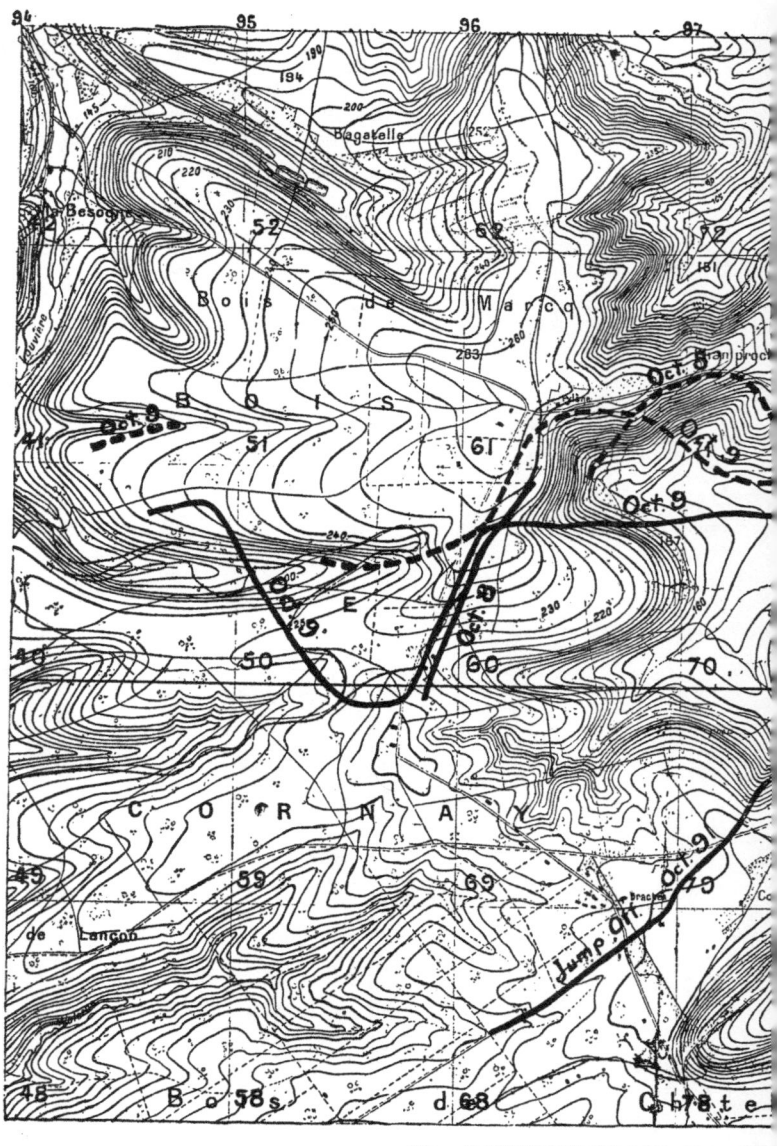

82ND DIVISION IN MEUSE-ARG
---------- Dotted lines indicate temporar
——————— Solid lines indicate organized f

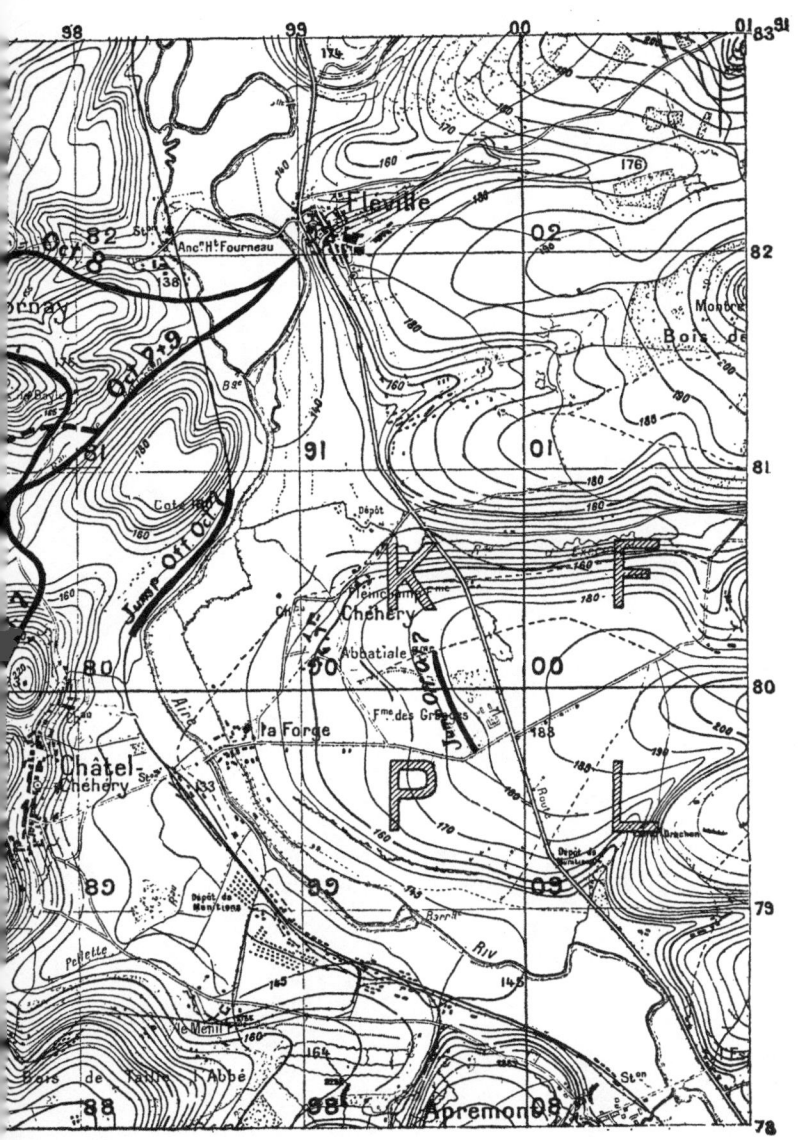

E OFFENSIVE, OCT. 6-10, 1918
sitions of advance units during the day
line at midnight

is some understanding of the physical difficulties which made the movement a nightmare for those who participated. A drizzle of rain started at nightfall October 6 and continued throughout the night. Rains of previous days had converted all routes into a mire of heavy mud. Before a vehicle or a truck or a gun or a man of the 82nd Division debouched upon the highway, the congestion of traffic had reached a point prohibitive of anything except the most painful progress. This road was one of the main arteries for ammunition, food supplies and other traffic for both the 28th and 1st Divisions. It was essential that traffic should be uninterrupted by the movement of the 82nd Division. It will be remembered that the 157th Field Artillery Brigade, pursuant to orders received at midday, October 6, was during this whole day and night moving across the No Man's Land bog in the Argonne Forest, through Varennes, to the vicinity of Charpentry. Our artillery was therefore mingled with a mass of moving trucks and horse transport of the 1st Division and the 28th Division. To this swollen stream was added two regiments of Infantry and a battalion of machine gunners. The night was black beyond the power of any human eye to penetrate more than a short pace ahead. The Infantry was compelled to move in the gutters on both sides of the road. Machine gun carts slipped into such gaps and intervals as presented themselves. For a half hour at a time, the whole struggling mass would be at a halt, until officers and M. P.'s could find the center of the jam and unravel the tangle. Once Colonel Wetherill and Captain Tommasello at the head of a column pulled a dead man and his dead horse off the road to enable our vehicles to proceed.

In addition to these appalling difficulties it must be considered that our troops were moving up the Aire Valley into a No Man's Land between the 1st and the 28th Divisions over a road, every yard of which was familiar to the enemy by four years of occupation. Enemy flares and star shells lighted the valley at intervals and made the succeeding darkness more intense. German gunners pounded the entire terrain throughout the night with shell fire, searching the east and west ravines for hidden artillery and harassing the road without cessation. This was endured with fortitude by troops in totally unfamiliar country and in darkness which made it impossible to seek cover or retaliate against an enemy firing from some distant ridge. Almost every unit suffered some casualties. Nothing but discipline and cooperation of the highest order could prevent absolute disintegration. As a peace-time maneuver, it was obviously a problem impossible of solution. That it was attended by so considerable a measure of success was due to the fact that all ranks were imbued with the conviction that the movement was of paramount necessity.

In telling the story of this Division, it must not be forgotten that troops from the 82nd Division were face to face with the enemy before midnight on the 6th of October, 1918, and that any record of days spent in continuous contact and action in the Meuse-Argonne operations must accept the 6th of October as the entry of this Division into the conflict.

A detailed description of the kaleidoscope events of the next few days will be less confusing if a paragraph is given to outline the first phase of the Division's operations in this offensive, namely the period October 6 to October 10, 1918, inclusive.

The attack of the 164th Infantry Brigade on October 7, 1918, won the first objective assigned. This success placed the 327th Infantry on Hill 180, the right of the Brigade sector, and the 328th Infantry on Hill 223, the left of the sector. On October 8, the 327th Infantry was unable to enter Cornay during daylight, but did seize and occupy the town during the night of October 8-9. On this same day, the second day of the attack, the 328th Infantry advanced west two kilometers to the Decauville railroad. The formidable ridges west of Cornay to Pylône remained in enemy possession.

On October 9, the Germans counter-attacked the 327th Infantry in Cornay, and captured the town with heavy casualties on both sides. We retained possession of Hill 180. The 328th Infantry attacked north along the railroad toward Pylône and gained ground, which later in the day was retaken by the enemy, and the Regiment stood at night on the same line from which it had jumped off in the morning. The 326th Infantry from the 163rd Infantry Brigade relieved the 28th Division west of Châtel-Chéhéry on the morning of October 9 and advanced northwest, forming a line that night in liaison with the 328th Infantry and extending southwest.

On October 10, the 325th Infantry, relieving the 327th Infantry, and the 328th Infantry, attacked north in conjunction with the 326th Infantry, clearing the enemy entirely from the eastern half of the Argonne Forest, and seizing all territory south of St. Juvin and the Aire River.

CHAPTER VI

164TH INFANTRY BRIGADE JUMPS OFF

ATTACK OF 1ST BATTALION, 327TH INFANTRY, OCTOBER 7, 1918

THE incident of missing guides and the condition of traffic conspired to prevent a coordinated attack by the assaulting battalions of the two regiments. Major Blalock reached the vicinity of La Forge with the 1st Battalion, 327th Infantry, at about 3 hours, 7th October. Roads leading to this point and the buildings in the vicinity were under harassing shell fire. The bridge crossing the river had been destroyed and the majority of the battalion crossed by fording the river, which was between two and three feet deep at this point. Passage of the river began at about 4 hours. Major Blalock personally stood upon the west bank and assisted man after man to clamber up the sharp slope. A detachment of divisional engineers had laid boards from stone to stone and some of the men crossed on them in single file. The Battalion marched north a short distance along the west bank of the river and formed for the attack on the railroad track just east of Hill 180.

Promptly at 5 hours the assault was made by C and D Companies, supported by Companies A and B, the 327th Infantry, Machine Gun Company, 37 mm. and the Stokes Mortar Platoons. A heavy mist hung over the entire valley and the enemy appeared to be completely surprised by the advance of this battalion.

Hill 180 is a hump of land about a kilometer in length in a north and south line. It rises close to the river bank and dominates the flat marsh land east of the river. The assaulting companies found some wire on the east slope and picked up a detachment of prisoners. Captain Harrison (Co. C.) sent the following message to Battalion Headquarters:

"Going good. Captured 39 prisoners and 3 machine guns. No casualties yet."

The entire hill was in American possession by 8 hours 30 minutes, including the Ravin de Boulasson west of the hill. Eighty-one prisoners and four machine guns were captured. At this point the advance was subjected to very heavy artillery and machine gun fire which swept the crest of the slope. Enemy fire came from the northeast near Fléville, northwest from the heights of Cornay, west from the cliff-like ridges that bordered the Argonne Forest and southwest from Hill 223. Heavy casualties were suffered and the battalion was without support on either flank. The battalion dug in and returned the enemy fire with all available weapons. Later in the day Company H, 327th Infantry, and a platoon from Company A, 321st Machine Gun Battalion, joined Major Blalock, pursuant to orders. Lieut. W. P. Pinnell, commanding this machine gun platoon, received wounds from which he later died. It was on this hill that Lieutenant Schiller of the same machine gun company was severely wounded.

ATTACK OF 1ST BATTALION, 328TH INFANTRY, OCTOBER 7, 1918

The story of this day's events now turns to the operations of the left regiment of the brigade—the 328th Infantry—against Hill 223, about one kilometer southwest of Hill 180. This formidable position rises in a steep cliff on its eastern side just north of Châtel-Chéhéry and about one-half kilometer west from the Aire River. The west slope of the hill is relatively less steep but a sufficient obstacle to take the breath of a strong man in a steady climb. From the crest of this hill one may see the Aire Valley, both north and south. From such an observation point the road from Varennes to Fléville is visible at many points. A partial trench system with wire ran lengthwise on the hill and two concrete emplacements for large mortars had been located by the enemy on the western slope. The enemy artillery itself had been withdrawn some time before the American assault and German artillery positions were located on the semicircular ridge running from northwest of Hill 223 to Cornay.

When the 1st Battalion of the 328th Infantry formed for the attack in the woods Des Granges, one kilometer east of La Forge, it was already daylight. Companies A and C moved out as assault companies and marched about half way to La Forge. Companies B and D were in support in the woods named. A heavy fog which rested on the valley rendered it quite impossible to see more than one hundred meters in front. The enemy put down a heavy shell fire extending from the ford at the river along the road east to the woods Des Granges. Colonel Wetherill, under these conditions of visibility, could not see his objective or determine how far the movement of events in the two hours elapsed since zero-hour had altered his mission. Furthermore, he felt that artillery support would be required. The advance was halted and the men of A and C Companies secured what slight protection was available in the ditches on each side of the road and in small folds of the ground in the fields on either side.

In order to make a clearer estimate of the situation the Regimental Commander proceeded to La Forge and established the Regimental P. C. in a culvert which was occupied jointly with a small detachment of signal troops from the 28th Division. Considerable time elapsed in these movements and in attempts at reconnaissance and investigation of the assigned objective. For a time it was thought that the steep slopes of Hill 244, southwest of Châtel-Chéhéry, might be the Hill 223 for which they were seeking. As the mist lifted later in the morning, men who proved to be from the 28th Division, were seen clinging to the lofty east bank of Hill 244 just west of the town. A steady stream of machine gun fire came from the plateau which crowns Hill 244 and swept from time to time the vicinity of La Forge and the road running east of La Forge. It was finally determined to make the attack with B and D Companies, still located in the woods Des Granges, passing them through A and B Companies, which had been subjected to heavy shell fire for several hours. Major Boyle went forward with B and D Companies, and established his P. C. at La Forge in conjunction with the Regimental P. C.

Capture of Hill 223

Simultaneously H Company advanced on the left flank as the liaison unit between the 82nd and 28th Divisions. The advance of these three companies was performed in the most gallant manner under artillery fire of barrage-like intensity. Men fell and survivors filled the gaps. The line swept to the river and struggled through the water to the opposite bank. The conduct of these troops was observed by men of the 28th Division in Châtel-Chéhéry and a report commending their bearing was made by Brigadier General Nolan of the 28th Division, in Châtel-Chéhéry, to the Headquarters of the 28th Division. This assault started from the woods Des Granges at 11:15 and reached the river at 11:55. After crossing the river, B Company and two platoons of D Company advanced northwest enveloping Hill 223 from the long spur jutting out north of the hill. Captain Lewis of D Company with two platoons made for the gap at the south end of Hill 223. The purpose of this maneuver was to pinch out any forces on the hill by a simultaneous assault from the north and south. The hill was completely occupied by these two companies at 13 hours.

Shortly after reaching the hill Captain Douglass of B Company was wounded and the same fate shortly befell Lieutenants Cabaniss and Edens of B Company. Lieutenant Day then took command of B Company. Lieutenant Brown had meanwhile reported with H Company to General Nolan at his dugout in Châtel-Chéhéry, the latter town having been occupied in force that morning by the 28th Division. H Company was held for a time in Châtel-Chéhéry and that evening a part of the Company reinforced Captain Lewis.

Since the armistice it has been stated by some officers of the 109th Infantry (28th Division) that Hill 223 was occupied by their forces prior to the arrival on the hill of the 328th Infantry.

A painstaking inquiry in this connection reveals the following situation: Companies B and D, 328th Infantry, received machine gun fire from the north slope of Hill 223 during their advance. Lieutenant Cabaniss' platoon (B Company) took some twenty German prisoners on the north slope of Hill 233. Lieutenant Candler of D Company proceeded with two platoons of D Company up the north side of Hill 223 and organized a position on the military crest on the western side of the hill. Lieutenant Candler did not see any men from the 28th Division. Captain Lewis (D Company), who had gone with two platoons to the south slope of Hill 223, went up to the crest of the hill a few minutes after Lieutenant Candler had arrived from the opposite slope. Captain Lewis found a lieutenant and not over a squad of men in fox holes on the extreme peak of the hill near the cliff which overlooks the river to the east. The lieutenant stated that he had arrived at about 11 hours that day but had seen no Germans and had not fired a shot. About the same time Lieutenant Brown of H Company came on the hill from Châtel-Chéhéry and saw this little detachment of the 28th Division. Hence it is apparent that no attempt had been made to occupy or organize the hill in sufficient force to hold it and that Germans and Americans were simultaneously in possession. It is especially significant that German prisoners captured on the hill were more than double the number of the patrol from the 28th Division.

Liaison was established with a detachment of the 28th Division located south of Hill 223 on Hill 244 and it was agreed that an attack would be made at once in the direction of the Corps objective—the Decauville railroad, two kilometers farther west. At about 14 hours Companies B and D started forward and advanced about two hundred meters into the valley west of Hill 223. At this point they were met by machine gun fire from the front and both flanks, heavy fire coming from the southwest in front of the 28th Division. This was followed by an Infantry counter-attack from the west and north under cover of a machine gun barrage. Our men withdrew up the slopes of Hill 223 behind the wire on the crest, where hard fighting followed at close range. The Americans succeeded in pushing back the enemy line from this point, and when darkness fell both sides were dug in at close range, the Americans on the crest and the Germans on the upper slopes of the hill.

Severe casualties were suffered by both companies in repelling this counter-attack. In fact, the German assault was so nearly successful that a runner coming into the Regimental P. C. at La Forge reported on his own authority that the hill had been lost and both companies wiped out. A written message from the hill shortly afterward gave evidence that such was not the case. This counter-attack fell also upon the 1st Battalion of the 327th Infantry on Hill 180. Here, too, the attempt was repulsed. Many casualties were caused in both of these American regiments by the barrage which fell along our front at about 17 hours. While the objective assigned by the Corps had not yet been reached, a foothold had been obtained by the 164th Infantry Brigade on two strong natural positions from which future assaults could be launched at the heart of the German stronghold in the upper Argonne Forest.

Attack of the 164th Infantry Brigade, October 8, 1918.

About 23 hours, October 7, Brigade Field Order No. 2 reached the regiments directing that the attack be resumed the following morning, October 8, at 5 hours. H hour was later changed to 6 hours. Information from higher authority was as follows:

"The enemy is reported retreating generally towards the northwest. French are attacking northeast from Lancon. The Commander-in-Chief directs that a powerful thrust be made to cut off the ridge and railroad due west."

The plan of attack for the Brigade stipulated that the Corps objective should be taken by noon. The attack was to be preceded by harassing fire by our artillery on Hill 151, Cornay, and the ridges east and southwest of Cornay. In addition a rolling barrage at the rate of one hundred meters in three minutes was to be laid until the objective was reached. The 319th Machine Gun Battalion was placed at the disposal of the Commanding Officer, 327th

Infantry and reported at Pleinchamps Farm during the night Oct. 7-8. In addition, the 3rd Battalion, 328th Infantry, was transferred from Brigade Reserve and placed at the disposal of Colonel Ely, commanding the 327th Infantry. Throughout this entire flank operation, the higher command anticipated the probability of enemy counter-attacks upon the exposed right flank of the brigade.

In the 327th Infantry, Colonel Ely directed that the 1st Battalion should resume the attack at H hour, supported by the 3rd Battalion, 328th Infantry (Major Johnson). The 2nd Battalion, 327th Infantry, less F Company (held to meet possible attacks from the vicinity of Fléville), would be the reserve battalion. Major Johnson reported to Colonel Ely at about 2 hours, 8th of October, and received his orders. As the 3rd Battalion, 328th Infantry, approached Hill 180 just before daybreak, a heavy enemy barrage caught these troops while the column was fording the river and continued with such intensity that L and M Companies were dispersed for the time being and did not arrive upon the hill in time to participate in the attack, which was launched promptly at 6 hours.

During the night, orders from Headquarters, 1st Corps, changed the compass direction of the assault units, ordering an attack to be directed north rather than in a northwesterly direction. This change reached the front battalion of the 327th Infantry at about 6 hours 30 minutes and the correction was effected with some difficulty. I and K Companies, 328th Infantry, were on the right flank of Companies D and A, 327th Infantry. The change of objective, however, was not known to the assaulting battalion of the 328th Infantry until about 10 hours 30 minutes that forenoon, when the information reached the battalion commander under very dramatic circumstances. A runner from the battalion noted a dead runner near the dugout south of Hill 223, which constituted the regimental P. C.

He felt in the upper left-hand pocket of the dead runner's coat and discovered the order which directed an attack to the north. The assault battalion of the 328th Infantry had at that time been fighting its way ten degrees north of west for four and one-half hours, with both flanks wholly unprotected. The flanks of the 327th Infantry were similarly exposed.

The 327th Infantry continued its struggle all day against continuous machine gun and artillery fire from the front and flanks. The line, however, was unable to advance beyond the eastern and southeastern borders of the town of Cornay. During the day the 2nd Battalion, 327th Infantry (Major Blanchard), crossed the river and took up a position in support on Hill 180. That same forenoon, Major Johnson, 328th Infantry, was evacuated and the command of the 3rd Battalion, 328th Infantry, passed to Captain Clarkson. Major Blanchard was joined on the reverse slope of Hill 180 by a platoon from the 319th Machine Gun Battalion.

Attack of 2nd Battalion, 328th Infantry, October 8, 1918

In the 328th Infantry, the 2nd Battalion had moved west across the Aire River with orders to pass the lines of the 1st Battalion on Hill 223 and jump off at 6 hours, October 8, 1918, with a compass direction ten degrees north of west. Their objective was the Decauville railroad, two kilometers away. The 328th Infantry Machine Gun Company and the one-pounder and trench mortar platoons, also of the 328th Infantry, were moved to Hill 223 and Châtel-Chéhéry for the purpose of supporting the attack.

The 2nd Battalion of the 328th Infantry assaulted with E Company on the right and G Company on the left, and with F and H Companies in support respectively at six hundred meters. The record of this battalion on that day constitutes a very splendid page in the history of the division. Under steady and intense machine gun fire from the northwest and southwest, this battalion maneuvered down the long western slope of Hill 223, crossed the five hundred yards of open valley, fought its way through a kilometer of heavy woods which covered the precipitous spur protruding into the center of the valley from the west and dug in along the Corps objective, the Decauville Railroad, at 17 hours that afternoon. It had no liaison with the troops attacking to the north of Hill 180, over a kilometer away. For most of the day it was without contact with units of the 28th Division, also attacking in a westerly direction from Châtel-Chéhéry. By nightfall this battalion had taken some 270 prisoners and left more than one hundred dead Germans on the ground. It had captured the astonishing total of 123 machine guns, a battery of four field pieces, two trench mortars, a set of electrical field signal equipment complete, four anti-tank guns and a quantity of German small arms and ammunition of several varieties.

As the result of a day spent in charging and outflanking machine gun nests and crawling across an exposed valley, the battalion had suffered about 350 casualties, of whom forty-five were killed. Among the dead was 2rd Lt. K. P. Stewart, G Company, who, when shot in the leg, continued to pull himself along, waving encouragement to his men until a second bullet crashed through his head and robbed his platoon of a very gallant leader.

One exploit in this day's work will always be retold in the military tradition of our country. It is entitled to a place among the famous deeds in arms of legendary or modern warfare. Early in the attack of this battalion, the progress of G Company on the left was seriously impeded by heavy machine gun fire from a hill directly southwest across the valley from Hill 223. Although this territory was south of the zone of action assigned the 82nd Division, it was necessary to reduce this fire or suffer disastrous consequences.

A force of four non-commissioned officers and thirteen privates was sent from the left support platoon of G Company to encircle the hill and silence the enemy guns. This detachment, under Acting Sergeant Early, encircled the hill from the southeast and by a very skilful reconnaissance passed through the heavy woods on the east crest and descended to the wooded ravine on the west side of the hill. The detachment in working through the underbrush came upon a German battalion estimated to contain about 250 men, a considerable number of whom were machine gunners. Orders taken later from the pocket of the German battalion commander proved that the mission of this battalion was to launch a counter-attack against the left flank of our attack at 10 hours 30 minutes. About seventy-five Germans were crowded around their battalion commander, apparently engaged in receiving final instructions. A force of machine gunners and infantrymen, however, were lying in fox holes fifty yards away on the western slope of the hill. Other machine gun detachments were located on the north and northeast slopes of this same wooded hill.

The handful of Americans, led by Corporal Early, appeared as a complete surprise to this German battalion. The large body of Germans surrounding the German battalion commander began surrendering to our men, whom the enemy supposed to be the leading element of a large American force which had enveloped their position.

German machine gunners on the hillside, however, quickly reversed their guns and poured a hail of bullets into the bottom of the ravine, killing six and wounding three of the American detachment. All of the non-commissioned officers were killed or seriously wounded except Corp. Alvin C. York of Pall Mall, Tenn. With Corporal York were seven privates, four of whom were mostly occupied in covering with their rifles the large group of German infantrymen who had thrown down their arms at the first surprise. A few shots were fired by the remaining three Americans, but the chief burden of initiative and achievement fell upon Corporal York.

Crouching close to the huddle of German prisoners, he engaged in a rapid fire action with the machine gunners and infantrymen on the hillside. The return fire struck just behind him, due to the fact that careful shooting from the hillside was necessary by the Germans to avoid injuring their own men a few feet in front of Corporal York. The American fired all the rifle ammunition clips on the front of his belt and then three complete clips from his automatic pistol. In days past, he had won many a turkey shoot with the rifle and pistol in the Tennessee mountains, and it is believed that he wasted no ammunition on this day. Once a lieutenant on the hillside led a counter-attack of a dozen gunners and infantrymen against this extraordinary marksman, who shot the lieutenant through the stomach and killed others before the survivors took cover. German morale gave way entirely and the battalion commander surrendered his command. Corporal York placed himself between two German officers at the head of the column and distributed the seven Americans on guard along the flanks and in rear of the hastily formed column of prisoners. On his way back over the hill he picked up a considerable number of additional prisoners from the north and northeast slopes of the hill. When he reported at the Battalion P. C., Lieutenant Woods, the Battalion Adjutant, 2nd Battalion, 328th Infantry, counted the prisoners and found that they totaled three officers and 129 enlisted men. The prisoners proved to be part of the 45th Reserve Division. The three wounded Americans were brought in with the column. The six dead Americans were buried later where they had fallen. During the forenoon Lieutenant Cox passed the scene of this fight with a portion of F Company. He estimates that approximately twenty dead Germans lay on the hillside.

After the armistice, Corporal York received the personal thanks of Major General Duncan, the Division Commander, Major General Summerall, Commanding 5th Corps, and General Pershing, the Commander-in-Chief. He also was given the Congressional Medal of Honor and the Croix de Guerre.

Throughout the day the assaulting battalions of both regiments received a continuous and costly fire from the ridge named Champrocher, running generally west from Cornay to Pylone, the latter an enemy observation station. The sides of this ridge rise up like the walls of a tower and the summit was strongly held with men and machine guns. One platoon of E Company and a platoon from F Company, both 328th Infantry, during the day endeavored to scale this ridge and silence the fire. Both thrusts were staunchly made, but were totally inadequate to gain and maintain possession of this natural fortress.

3RD BATTALION, 327TH INFANTRY, OCTOBER 8, 1918

The 3rd Battalion of the 327th Infantry (Captain Davis) had meanwhile been held as Brigade reserve at the Dépôt de Munitions. About midday, the 8th of October, 1918, this battalion was ordered forward to Hill 223, to report to the Commanding Officer, 328th Infantry. Colonel Wetherill directed Captain Davis to assault the Ridge Champrocher and to hold the road on the summit. This attack was made at 16 hours the same afternoon. After I and M Companies had jumped off from Hill 223, orders

Sgt. Alvin C. York, Co. G, 328th Infantry
Scene of the memorable exploit

were received that K and L Companies would be held at Hill 223 as Brigade Reserve.

The assault was made without an accompanying barrage. Officers and men of the 328th Infantry who witnessed the attack of these two companies from the other regiment describe its gallantry with unmeasured praise. I and M Companies advanced in perfect waves like men at drill. As they crossed the valley, men went down like ten-pins before a ball, but the survivors gained the crest of the hill. There were approximately sixty men left in each company, and this number was not sufficient to retain a footing upon the ridge against the great numbers of Germans that swarmed the entire length of the road to Pylône. The enemy succeeded in creeping about the flanks of these units and many of our men were shot down by machine guns from the right and left rear. When darkness came, it was necessary to withdraw the survivors to prevent their being completely cut off. The remnants of these companies were placed in support in trenches on Hill 223.

In the afternoon of October 8, D Company, 328th Infantry, was ordered forward to support the 2nd Battalion, 328th Infantry, and was assigned by Captain Tillman to a position on the left of the battalion front, where it participated in the last stage of the advance to the Decauville railroad. The American troops along this little 60 cm. railroad were confronted by German machine gunners and infantrymen dug in only a few yards west of the railroad. During the night both sides sniped back and forth in the brush with little intermission.

All through the night, however, the Americans could hear the rumble of the German transport moving north out of the heart of the Argonne Forest where the enemy had been holding up the advance of the 77th and the left of the 28th Divisions between three and four kilometers south of the ground gained by this successful thrust of the 82nd Division. It was during the night of October 7-8 that Major Whittlesey's "Lost Battalion" of the 77th Division was relieved on the left flank of the 77th Division. The center of the Argonne Forest had been made untenable for prolonged German resistance, and the enemy was making haste to withdraw invaluable equipment and supplies.

CHAPTER VII

CORNAY AND CHAMPROCHER RIDGE

As has been said, the 327th Infantry was engaged through the 8th of October in driving north from Hill 180 toward the Corps objective, Fléville exclusive to Cornay inclusive. The attack was unable to surmount the machine gun nests situated near Fléville as well as on the knoll north of point 176 and the ridges west of Cornay. Shortly after dark, however, the assaulting companies entered Cornay. Patrols were sent in different directions throughout the village and from one German dugout to another. In addition to the companies which had been attacking during the day, elements of L and M Companies, 328th Infantry, under Captain Sisson and Lieutenant Walton respectively, entered Cornay and took part in the business of mopping up during the night of October 8-9. While this was in progress, the town was heavily shelled by artillery, necessitating the withdrawal of most of our force to the southern edge of the town. Upon the cessation of this fire just before dawn the town was reentered. A considerable number of prisoners captured in the town were being conducted out of the village before daylight when the party encountered a strong American patrol who at once challenged. One of the German prisoners answered in German and the patrol fired, killing and wounding several Germans and wounding one American guard.

Brigade Field Order No. 5 directed that the attack be

resumed that morning, October 9, H hour being set at 8 hours 30 minutes. Companies K and L, 327th Infantry, in Brigade Reserve at Hill 223, had been ordered to report on the night of October 8 to the Commanding Officer, 327th Infantry. L Company was sent to Major Blalock on Hill 180, and K Company to Captain Brown at Cornay on the morning of October 9. Both companies, however, were caught in heavy shell fire during these moves and reduced by casualties.

CORNAY RETAKEN BY THE ENEMY

During the early morning German troops began to infiltrate into the woods and orchards surrounding Cornay, apparently coming from a northeasterly direction. A heavy fog prevented our troops from perceiving enemy movements until German detachments were at short range. The Americans endeavored to advance through the town and drive out forces closing in upon the village. Considerable bodies of the enemy were immediately encountered and driven back.

A section of the 327th Infantry Machine Gun Company, under command of Lieutenant Gilmore, which had just arrived, rendered valuable assistance. Again about 9 hours 30 minutes, the Germans counter-attacked from the orchard east of Cornay and the ridge west of Cornay. This time the enemy came in greatly outnumbering force and compelled a gradual withdrawal of our men to the south edge of the town. Some prisoners taken during the mêlée asserted that large numbers of fresh German troops had been brought up for the purpose of recapturing the town. These new troops were from the German 41st Division, a first-class division. Captain McCall was now the senior officer in Cornay since Captain Brown, also of the 1st Bn., 327th Inf., had been severely wounded. Captain McCall decided to take shelter in the buildings near by, where he hoped to maintain a foothold until expected reinforcements arrived from Hill 180. Consequently he organized one building with some thirty or forty Americans and an adjacent house was occupied by Lieutenant Gilmore and his detachment. Lieutenant Shipp, 328th Inf., in command of a patrol numbering a dozen men operating in the center of Cornay, was driven back and after reporting to Captain McCall, took up a position in a third building. About this time the enemy was guilty of the following violation of the Red Cross insignia:

A machine gun was carried forward on a litter covered by a Red Cross flag into the orchard east of the town. The men accompanying the litter wore Red Cross brassards on their arms. The gun was placed in a shell hole and two Red Cross flags stuck in the ground on each side of the shell hole. One member of the party waved a Red Cross flag. Lieutenant Gilmore would not permit his men to shoot, but Lieutenant Shipp, deciding that the proceeding was a trick, directed his detachment to open on the party. The German waving the Red Cross flag was finally shot down, whereupon the enemy immediately opened fire with the machine gun from the shell hole, killing some of our men in windows and apertures.

From this time on our troops were constantly subjected to heavy machine-gun fire under cover of which the enemy endeavored to envelop the American detachments. About 11 hours 30 minutes, the enemy opened with trench mortars from the ridge. This fire soon knocked holes in the walls of the occupied houses, killing and wounding numerous men. About 12 hours 30 minutes, the enemy made his final counter-attack. He sent troops forward from the orchard east of the town; others from the north end of Cornay and very considerable forces down the steep ridge on the west, thus surrounding on three sides the

Americans, whose fire by this time had been practically silenced.

Captain McCall permitted a number of men to attempt to escape by jumping from a window and running down the road to the south. These men were shot down almost immediately. At least half of the surviving Americans were wounded. Captain McCall decided to surrender and ordered his men to cease firing. Lieutenants Shipp and Lingo, both of the 328th Infantry, and one private obtained permission to make a break for Hill 180.

A German prisoner was sent out of the house to wave a towel and all enemy fire was stopped. Lieutenant Shipp and his two companions then ran from the house, and when opened upon by rifle and machine-gun fire, took refuge in a shell hole outside the town, where they remained until darkness permitted escape to Hill 180.

After a time, the American remnants were picked up by the enemy and, carrying their own wounded, proceeded under guard towards Martincourt Farm, Marcq and Buzancy, where they arrived the following morning. On their way back from Cornay, while on the sunken road running up the steep ridge west of that town, an American barrage, striking the sides of the cliff, killed and wounded many Germans at the base. That the American prisoners escaped injury at this point is most remarkable.

HILL 180 THREATENED

About 13 hours reports began to arrive at the Battalion P. C. on Hill 180 that Cornay had been recaptured by the enemy. This was made further apparent by the appearance of enemy forces in the vicinity of Hill 180. Machine guns could be seen pushing forward from the orchard east of Cornay. Enemy fire on Hill 180 increased in intensity.

Previous to this time, the command of the troops on Hill 180 had devolved on Major Blanchard, 327th Inf. Major Blalock had reported back to Regimental Headquarters, where he collapsed and was evacuated. Information of the loss of Cornay and the threatening counter-attack on Hill 180 was sent to Colonel Ely, who requested a barrage. Our artillery responded promptly and broke up the enemy concentration, causing substantial losses to the Germans. The following messages sent to the Brigade P. C. by Colonel Ely indicate the existing conditions:

"Large force of Boche counterattacked and captured Cornay just before 13 o'clock. My forces there killed and captured. Some escaped. Shall counterattack at 18 o'clock with remaining men available, organizing on Hill 180, and have called on artillery to shell Cornay between parallels 81.6 and 82—from meridian 97 to 98 until 18 o'clock, then jump to NW of Cornay. Our success may be doubtful. Fresh troops should reinforce us by ford southeast of Hill 180 and participate in attack.
(signed) ELY."

"Capt. Drew reports enemy seem to be attacking Hill 180—advises a barrage. No word from Blanchard but observers here report our men going up reverse slope Hill 180. Will you please telephone for barrage north and west of Hill 180.
(signed) ELY."

"Find my men exhausted and gassed. Probably 200 can be mustered for counter-attack, but these practically exhausted and nearly worthless. Fresh troops imperative for success. Machine Guns from NE and west playing on all approaches to Cornay with constant shelling Hill 180 all day. Blalock collapsed, but here. Fourteen officers lost in his Bn. before losing Cornay. Heaviest possible Art. should shell Cornay and surroundings for hours before assault which must be by dark. Under cover of darkness for success. Early morning probably best hour for assault.
(signed) ELY."

"Escaped men report Capt. McCall after terrific barrage stopped his further progress, gathered all available men in buildings at edge Cornay, established observation posts in upper windows:—Observers reported some 50 enemy advancing under Red Cross flag and our men hesitated to fire until enemy opened on all sides. Our men fought with rifles and m. guns and Chauchots from doors and windows killing great number and suffering heavy losses. Corp. Gallup, Co. 'E,' 327th Inf. and Pvt. Levine, Co. 'L,' 328 Inf. reported that finally Capt. McCall said: 'We have done all we can, men; we shall all be killed if we stay,' and the men laid down their rifles and went out; a number of men broke and ran, escaping under fire. Capt. Brown, 327th Inf., wounded in leg during fight and either captured or killed. All my Regt. have been in continuously gassed area since midnight, 6th October. About six gas alarms last night. All of us more or less gassed and ineffective.

(signed) ELY."

General Lindsey placed this situation before the Division Commander and was soon afterward informed that the 325th Infantry, which had been in reserve, would be placed at his disposal that night. The counter-attack planned for 18 hours, 9th of October, was countermanded and orders issued for an attack on the morning of October 10th by the relieving regiment. The troops on Hill 180 organized the position and patrolled throughout the night awaiting the expected attack, which did not come.

Unsuccessful Assault on Ridge Champrocher

While these large events were taking place in the vicinity of Cornay on October 9 the 328th Infantry was continuing its attack against a new objective and the 326th Infantry from the 163rd Brigade of this Division relieved the 28th Division and jumped off from the line held by the exhausted and depleted units of that hard-fighting Division

Town of Cornay

Shortly after dark on the night of October 8, C Company, 328th Infantry, moved forward from Hill 223 and endeavored to maintain combat liaison between the 2nd Battalion, 328th Infantry, on the Decauville railroad and I and M Companies of the 327th Infantry on the rim of the ridge Champrocher. Captain Weaver commanding C Company found that the survivors of the two 327th Infantry Companies had been withdrawn and sent a runner to Colonel Wetherill with this information. He was ordered to withdraw to Châtel-Chéhéry. Also during the night, A Company, 328th Infantry, was moved from Châtel-Chéhéry to reinforce the 2nd Battalion, 328th Infantry, whereupon Captain Tillman placed it in support of E and H Companies. At about 4 hours on the morning of October 9, A Company was again withdrawn to Châtel-Chéhéry.

The mission of the 328th Infantry for October 9 required an attack due north against the Champrocher from Pylône east of Cornay. At 7 hours 30 minutes, October 9, the 2nd Battalion received orders to attack north. The wagon road running east into Cornay was given as the first objective. During the early morning hours, the following change in dispositions was made pursuant to orders directing a resumption of attack in a northerly direction. F Company was turned from the west to north with its left flank on the Decauville railroad. E Company was moved from the railroad to the right flank of F Company. H and D Companies were turned north and placed in support of E and F Companies. G Company was extended along the railway, still facing west to protect the open flank for the entire depth of the battalion. In conjunction with this attack, A Company and two platoons of C Company were ordered to assault the ridge east of the 2nd Battalion's objective.

At 8 hours 30 minutes October 9, under cover of a fog,

the assault was launched. F Company proceeding up the Decauville railroad obtained a footing on the highway running east from Pylône. E Company was compelled to descend into the deep valley south of ridge Champrocher and struggled up the north perpendicular side of that position. A storm of rifle and machine-gun fire dislodged the precarious hold of Company F and drove it slowly back in liaison with E Company, which had succeeded in reaching the southern edge of the plateau that crowned the ridge. The two companies together did not muster more than one hundred men and they were opposed by the fresh troops from the 41st German Division which was at this time enveloping Cornay. It was found necessary to draw back from the ridge and valley, to the hill from which the attack had started and there await the arrival of additional troops adequate to the task. Many losses were suffered from machine-gun and artillery fire and the valley south of the ridge was smothered by the enemy with gas shells. A Company and the detachment from C Company had meanwhile reached the foot of the ridge farther to the east and nearer Cornay. At this point the enemy opened fire, and in addition hurled grenades upon the assaulting party. Our men held their positions throughout the day, sniping back as opportunity offered. Lieutenant Coston of A Company and several men of his platoon were killed early in the day.

About midday, our artillery strafed the ridge and materially assisted our infantry. D Company relieved E Company on the front line at 13 hours 30 minutes and later was in turn relieved by two platoons of C Company, which had been held in reserve.

CHAPTER VIII

163RD INFANTRY BRIGADE ENTERS FIGHT

THROUGHOUT October 7-8, while the 164th Brigade was driving at the east flank of the upper Argonne Forest, the units of the 163rd Infantry Brigade (Brig. Gen. Cronin) in Corps reserve, were expecting hourly the orders which would place them beside their comrades from the other brigade. During this period and throughout the drive the 163rd Infantry Brigade was accompanied by the 320th Machine-Gun Battalion (Captain Muldrow). It will be recalled that on the afternoon of October 6, 1918, both infantry brigades were bivouacked west of Varennes. On the night of October 7-8, the 326th Infantry (Colonel McArthur) was ordered to Montblainville. The march began about 22 hours 30 minutes through a black night filled with hard, driving rain. Here again this night maneuver was made over roads blocked by moving artillery and transport and through ankle-deep mud. Montblainville was found to be a mass of ruins upon an exposed hill, still subjected to constant enemy shell fire. The 1st and 2nd Battalions with the Regimental Machine-Gun Company bivouacked in the woods west of the village. The 3rd Battalion and Headquarters Company camped in the grove at Farm La Forge. Regimental Headquarters was located on the Montblainville road near this farm.

The first intimation received at Division Headquarters of the early employment of the reserve brigade appears in the Division dossier as a telephone message received October

8, 1918, at 11 hours 40 minutes from Chief of Staff, 1st Corps, to Chief of Staff, 82nd Division.

"The Corps Commander directs that the reserve of Lindsey's brigade be stationed somewhere south of Cornay so as to be able to function properly after our final objective is reached. In case of an advance on the Cornay-Fléville line to the north, a portion of the brigade in Corps reserve will be placed at the disposal of the Commanding General, 82nd Division, but not now. The 163rd Brigade will probably come in to-night, either to extend your front or into your own sector. It is of the utmost importance that the whole area in rear of your lines should be thoroughly mopped up by the tanks and by the infantry. If you have not already told him about this, notify Lindsey."

At 15 hours 45 minutes, 8th of October, 1918, the following order was sent to the Commanding Officer, 326th Infantry:

"Move one battalion of your regiment at once to La Palette Ravine, approximately ½ km. south of Châtel-Chéhéry. Carry reserve rations. Field trains remain at present location. Combat Trains accompany battalion. This movement is urgent. Expedite departure of battalion. This battalion remains in Corps reserve. No change is supply arrangements. By Command of Major General Duncan—Raymond Sheldon, Chief of Staff."

The following telephone message was received at 19 hours 20 minutes, October 8, at Division Headquarters, from Chief of Staff, 1st Corps:

"The 82nd Division will take over sector of the 28th Division before 4 A.M. to-morrow. Orders are now on the way. The Commanding General, 28th Division, will have supervision of the relief and will furnish the necessary guides, etc. This does not include the 28th Artillery, which will remain in place for the present. The 28th, on being relieved, will pass to the Corps reserve and will assemble in the vicinity of Montblainville. The General thinks we had better confine the relief to one regiment. That will leave one regiment for Division reserve. The orders for to-morrow are just the same as they were to-day.''

The order to despatch one battalion to La Palette Ravine just south of Châtel-Chéhéry reached Headquarters, 326th Infantry, at 16 hours, and at 17 hours the 3rd Battalion (Major Watkins) started its march from Montblainville. About 20 hours, Colonel McArthur was called to Headquarters, 28th Division, at Farm La Forge. Here an extended conference was held in which Brigadier General Cronin, commanding the 163rd Infantry Brigade and Colonel Sheldon, Chief of Staff, 82nd Division, were present, together with Col. Sweeney, Chief of Staff, 28th Division. As a result of this conference, the 326th Infantry was directed at midnight to move the two remaining battalions forward and relieve the entire 28th Division in time to jump off in attack at 8 hours 30 minutes, October 9, 1918.

After another night's march through mud and rain, the 1st Battalion (Major Barrett) and the 2nd Battalion (Major Jones) arrived just before daybreak west of La Palette ravine on the main forest highway to Pylône. Regimental P. C. was established in one of the abandoned German dugouts on a slope of this ravine. The 1st Battalion proceeded with the relief of the left brigade of the 28th Division, which occupied fox holes on a road running southwest from Châtel-Chéhéry and crossing the forest highway. This jump off line is about 2 kilometers due southwest from Châtel-Chéhéry.

The terrain which faced the 326th Infantry is of different character from that which confronted the 164th Infantry Brigade. While it does not consist of precipitous ridges like those which overhang Cornay, it presents difficulties quite as troublesome. The objective assigned required a turning movement in a general northwesterly direction to La Besogne, on a front which extended about 2 kilometers west from the Decauville railroad, to which the 328th Infantry had driven on the previous afternoon.

It will be recalled that the advance of the 328th Infantry on October 9, 1918, had been halted by very determined resistance from enemy machine guns and infantry. The high command suspected at this time that the enemy was withdrawing generally toward the heights north of the Aire Valley. This is clearly evidenced in a telephone communication from the Chief of Staff, 1st Corps, and inserted in the 82nd Division dossier under date of October 8, 1918. Subsequent events proved the accuracy of this surmise. Nevertheless, the quantities of enemy *matériel* which remained at this time south of the Aire River, as well as general tactical considerations, compelled the Germans to make a desperate rear-guard resistance.

West of the often mentioned Decauville railroad, the Argonne Forest stretches for 6 kilometers toward the town of Lançon. This country is a desolate jungle of tangled underbrush and forest, cut by ravines and small watercourses, with here and there a farm-house and an open patch of cultivated ground. Occasionally the ground rises to an eminence of considerable height. Near La Besogne, the rolling land falls away into a sharp valley, at the bottom of which clusters a few buildings, which the map dignifies as La Besogne.

3RD BATTALION, 326TH INFANTRY, OCTOBER 9, 1918

When the 3rd Battalion, 326th Infantry, arrived just south of Châtel-Chéhéry during the early night of October 8-9, Major Watkins reported in Châtel-Chéhéry to Brigadier General Nolan, commanding the right brigade of the 28th Division. In compliance with the plan of relief, the 3rd Battalion spent the remaining hours of darkness in La Palette Ravine. At 8 hours 30 minutes it climbed the north slope of the ravine and, moving northwest across Hill 244, passed through the elements of the right brigade of the 28th Division along the cross-road running southwest from Châtel-Chéhéry. It was this same cross-road which served as the jump off line for the 1st Battalion about five hundred meters still farther to the southwest.

The advance of the 3rd Battalion was made with Companies I, K and L as assault companies and Company M in support. The compass direction was northwest to the Decauville railroad, and thence north with the right flank on the forest highway leading to Pylône. The advance to the narrow gauge railroad covered a distance of about 2 kilometers and was uneventful save for light, intermittent shell fire. The advance north along the forest road, however, brought the battalion in contact with enemy machine-gun elements, which gave considerable difficulty in this extremely wild and wooded country. After forcing a way north for nearly a kilometer, enemy machine-gun fire increased in volume and a number of casualties were suffered. Lieutenant Owens of L Company was killed while leading his platoon forward. The battalion was not in liaison with the battalion on its left, and fearing the possibility of an enveloping movement, which would cut off the battalion, Major Watkins ordered a withdrawal for several hundred meters to the railroad. Here the battalion dug in on the left flank of the 328th Infantry and formed a line which followed the sharp bend in the Decauville railroad to the southwest, a distance of five or six hundred meters. Here the 3rd Battalion remained until the attack of the following morning.

1ST BATTALION, 326TH INFANTRY, OCTOBER 9, 1918

The 1st Battalion, 326th Infantry with Company D, 320th Machine Gun Battalion in support, jumped off at 8 hours 30 minutes on the morning of October 9 on the line previously described where it had relieved the left brigade of the 28th Division. At this time the 1st Battalion was in complete liaison with the right elements of the 77th Division, which formed a line to the southwest along the same cross-road. The barrage which preceded this advance was excellent, but too rapid for the character of the terrain, and A and C Companies, the assault companies of the 1st Battalion, were compelled to run from time to time to keep close to their barrage. This resulted in these companies gaining some distance upon the two support companies of the battalion and getting completely ahead of the corresponding elements of the 77th Division. Practically no enemy opposition aside from desultory shell fire was met during the first stage of the advance. This situation was one of the factors which opened a gap between the 1st and 3rd Battalions of this Regiment. The 3rd Battalion maintained liaison with the 328th Infantry on its right and the 1st Battalion worked with the 77th Division on its left.

After the front line had proceeded about two kilometers northwest, some machine gun resistance was encountered. In spite of this opposition, a farther advance was made and a platoon of A Company, under Lieutenant Patton, succeeded in penetrating eight hundred meters farther north than the advance of the other elements of the Battalion. This platoon won a foothold on the slopes of a small ravine about 1 kilometer due south from La Besogne. Enemy infantry and machine gunners started to envelop this platoon, and Lieutenant Patton was compelled to withdraw a few hundred meters, where he joined the other forward elements of his battalion. Here A and C Companies dug in and held their ground until the following morning. Late in the afternoon the leading elements of the 77th Division again came abreast of the 1st Battalion, 326th Infantry. They remained in liaison throughout the night. The 2nd Battalion in support moved forward during the day and took up a position for the night on the line occupied by the 1st Battalion that morning. At about 23 hours, October 9, 1918, a conference was held at the regimental P. C. and battalion commanders were given instructions for a resumption of the attack on the following morning.

325TH INFANTRY, OCTOBER 10, 1918

The attack of October 10 was made in the Divisional sector by the 325th Infantry (Colonel Whitman) and the 326th Infantry (Colonel McArthur). For the time being the 325th Infantry was placed in the 164th Infantry Brigade and the 328th Infantry transferred to the 163rd Infantry Brigade. The 325th Infantry had, up to this point, been held in reserve and was therefore at full strength. Its men were relatively in much better physical condition than the two regiments which had been engaged continuously for three desperate days.

On October 6, Colonel Whitman had made a reconnaissance in the vicinity of La Forge, opposite Châtel-Chéhéry, under the supposition that he would assault at that point the following morning. Plans were changed, however, and on the night of the 7th, the 325th Infantry moved from the camp west of Varennes to the valley of Charpentry. The march was the usual night maneuver in a rainstorm on overcrowded roads and under some shell fire. The regiment sat in the mud for the balance of the night and during all of October 8. Early on October 9, the 325th Infantry was moved west across the Aire River to the vicinity of Chêne Tondu.

At 18 hours on October 9 Colonel Whitman was directed to report to the P. C. of the 164th Infantry Brigade at Châtel-Chéhéry. General Lindsey prepared a Brigade order for the attack on the following morning. This order stated in part:

"1. A hostile counter-attack succeeded in driving our troops off the Corps objective from Fléville to railroad west of Cornay. The enemy occupied Fléville, Cornay and the ridge to the southwest. On our right is the 1st Division and on our left is the 326th Infantry, now on the Corps objective. The 325th Infantry with artillery support will counter-attack on 'D' day, 'H' hour and regain the Corps objective, which runs generally along the 82nd meridian from Fléville on the east (exclusive) to north and south railroad, west of Cornay. One battalion of the 325th Infantry will attack from Hill 180 the line Fléville (exclusive) Cornay (inclusive). One battalion will attack from the ridge extending from point 97.0-80.5 to 96.5-80.5, that part of the objective between the line Cornay (exclusive) to the north and south railroad west of Cornay. These battalions will pass the line of the 328th Infantry located in that vicinity. One battalion of the 325th Infantry as reserve will be posted under cover south and west of Hill 223.

"2. Stokes Mortars and one-pounders will be placed as directed by regimental commander.

"3. A machine gun company will be attached to each attack battalion. The commanding officer of the 321st M. G. Battalion has designated Companies B and D to be reported to commanding officer 325th Infantry for duty.

"4. For artillery plans, see Annex 'A.'

"5. Immediately on reaching the Corps objective, the position will be organized in depth as the position of resistance, and exploitation patrols will be sent to the woods and terrain north as far as the Aire River, which will be the limit of the outpost position.

"6. The 327 Inf. on Côte 180 and in Pleinchamp Farm will remain as now organized until further orders. The 328th Inf. on the hill to the north and west of Hill 223 will likewise remain as now organized until further orders. All elements of whatever nature north of the Côte 180 or of the hill northwest of Hill 223 will be withdrawn by 'H' hour.

"7. 'D' will be Oct. 10th. 'H' will be 5.00 hours.

"8. All elements must be in place to jump off at 'H' minus 1.

"9. Posts of Command: 82nd Division, La Forge Farm; 164th Inf. Brigade, Châtel-Chéhéry; 325th Inf., Châtel-Chéhéry.

"Annex 'A': Annex to Field Order 6, 164th Inf. Brigade. All artillery of Division will support the attack of the 325th Inf.; interdiction fire will be kept in front of infantry; harassing and destructive fire as ordered by Commanding General, 157th Field Artillery Brigade. Upon arrival of the Infantry at their objective, all artillery will be available for harassing and searching fire north of the final objective. This fire must be so regulated by infantry commander and artillery liaison officer as to best protect their troops and exploitation patrols."

By 4 hours, October 10th, the 325th Infantry had moved up from the Chêne Tondu and was ready to relieve the two infantry regiments in accordance with the above order. The 2nd Battalion (Major Hawkins) was in rear of Hill 180; the 1st Battalion (Major Lott) was in rear of the 328th Infantry along the Decauville railroad, and the 3rd Battalion (Major Pierce) was in rear of Hill 223 as support. B and C Companies constituted the assaulting waves in the 1st Battalion and E and F Companies in the 2nd Battalion. The 321st Machine Gun Battalion was at this time concentrated at the following points: Companies B and D near Hill 244; Company C at Hill 223; and Company A on Hill 180. From these positions they assisted the infantry attack. H hour was advanced to 7 hours, October 10. Although furious resistance had been anticipated, the 325th Infantry advanced on approximately a two-kilometer front without substantial opposition. Cornay and the ridge Champrocher were shortly occupied and the 1st and 2nd Battalions pushed strong groups forward as far north as Martincourt Farm, Marcq and the Aire River. A few casualties had been inflicted by enemy shell fire and an occasional sniper. About forty prisoners were taken from Cornay and the western ridge. Captain Brown, 327th Inf., and several other wounded men belonging to the 327th Infantry were recovered in the vicinity of Cornay and Martincourt Farm. The enemy's counter-attack of the previous afternoon proved to have been his final effort, and during the night October 9-10, he withdrew his forces to the heights north of the Aire.

326TH INFANTRY, OCTOBER 10, 1918

The advance proceeded with equal success in the sector occupied by the 326th Infantry. The 3rd Battalion supported by C Company, 320th M. G. Battalion, jumped off with Companies K, L and M in assault and advanced in a northerly direction along the Decauville railroad and the forest highway on a front of about five hundred meters. The observation station known as Pylône was captured and the attack drove due north of Pylône for another one and one-half kilometers to the Corps objective. This placed the right of the 326th Infantry on the heights one kilometer south of the town of Marcq and overlooking the Aire River and St. Juvin to the north. Some casualties were caused by enemy shell fire during the day's progress.

The 1st Battalion, 326th Infantry, moved out at H hour October 10, with Companies A and C in assault and in complete liaison with the 77th Division. Prior to the attack a platoon of C Company, 326th Infantry, sent a patrol to the outskirts of La Besogne and were the first American soldiers to enter that village. The main forces of the battalion entered La Besogne with troops of the 77th Division. At this point they were met with heavy enemy shell fire.

Another incident of this advance was the automatic explosion of German mines near La Besogne on the road which runs from La Besogne to Pylône. A large crater was blown in the road, but no troops were injured by the explosion. Companies A and C were then sent forward to Marcq, arriving there at about 23 hours. Company A remained during the night in Marcq. Company B was held at La Besogne with the Battalion P. C. and Companies C and D outposted between Marcq and La Besogne. After four years of continuous occupation, the enemy had been finally ejected from the Argonne Forest and the first phase of the Division's operations was successfully terminated.

CHAPTER IX

ASTRIDE THE AIRE RIVER

Up to this time, the Division had been fighting west of the Aire River. The second phase of the Division's participation in the Meuse-Argonne offensive required the 82nd Division to fight astride of the Aire River, and it was not until the night of October 14, 1918, that all of the combat units had again recrossed that tributary to the east bank. After October 14, the river was placed once and for all at the backs of our fighting men.

Reference to the map will show that after flowing in a northerly direction to a point about three kilometers north of Cornay, the river turns sharply to the west and makes a twisted passage toward Grand-Pré for six kilometers in a direction north of west. Still farther west, it effects a junction with the River Aisne. This western bend to Grand-Pré marks the north boundary of the Aire Valley. The little towns on the banks of this brief six kilometers are now historic names: St. Juvin, Marcq, Chevières and Grand-Pré. The same is equally true of the villages which dot the river's northerly progress from Varennes to St. Juvin. The names, Montblainville, Baulny, Apremont, Châtel-Chéhéry, La Forge, Cornay and Fléville will forever recall the valor of the American soldier.

The river is, during six months of the year, an uninteresting stream, forty to fifty feet wide and varying from two feet to perhaps five feet in depth. In the winter months it is a muddy flood which inundates the entire Aire Valley and assumes the attributes of many well-known American rivers.

North of the Aire Valley the terrain is very different from that of the Argonne Forest. The country runs north to Sedan and the Meuse River in a series of ridges, which have the regular appearance of an ocean swell. These ridges are for the most part bare, save for isolated large patches of woods like the Bois des Loges and the still larger Bois de Bourgogne due north from Grand-Pré. Many small islands of trees and thickets stand here and there, and provided concealment for enemy artillery and machine gunners.

THE KRIEMHILDE STELLUNG

Much is said of the Kriemhilde Stellung. Those who have not seen it will probably imagine a highly organized German defensive position with a complicated network of deep trenches and many bands of heavy barbed wire. The American soldiers who assaulted and cut the Kriemhilde Stellung know that such was not the fact. This line was a series of natural positions, hills, ridges and woods which gave the enemy unrivaled opportunities for coordinated defense by artillery and cross-fire barrages with machine guns. Some shallow trenches were of course prepared and wire obstacles set up, but neither trench nor wire constituted the barrier which held the American army from the German throat during the critical days from October 11 to November 1, 1918. In front of the 82nd Division, the elements of the Kriemhilde Stellung were, first, a powerful outpost line comprising St. Juvin and Hill 182 immediately north of that town, and the ridge between St. Juvin and Sommerance known as Ridge 85.5. North of this outpost line stand the natural fortresses Champigneulle and St. Georges. The Kriemhilde Stellung was, however, the last partly organized defensive barrier south of the Hirson-Mézières-Sedan railroad. This railroad was of fundamental importance to the Germans, running from the big center at Metz to Mézières, parallel to the front of the battle line. Its importance was greatly increased by the fact that north of the railroad lay the Ardennes Forest with few roads and no railroads. Therefore, the retirement of a very large part of the German army must necessarily be effected along this one railroad. It was imperative that the German should hold his last defensive position south of Sedan. In the light of these facts, it is easy to understand why every prisoner captured during the month of October stated that his organization had been ordered to hold its position "at all costs." The will of the American was equally resolute to break through.

Price Paid by 164th Infantry Brigade

On the morning of October 10, 1918, when the 325th Infantry attacked through the 327th Infantry and 328th Infantry, the two last-named regiments had been in continuous heavy fighting for three days and nights. The men had been without hot food or coffee, and no water had been available for drinking except the polluted water of the Aire River. The wounded had been evacuated by stretcher bearers working under continuous heavy fire, and many of these stretcher bearers had themselves become casualties. The losses in both regiments had been severe. Many dead were buried during October 10, and for forty-eight hours thereafter parties of pioneers worked at this melancholy task. In the 327th Infantry the following officers had been killed in action or later died from wounds: 1st Lt. Jerome E. Kemmerer, Co. D; 1st Lt. Walter H. Levie, Co. I and Lt. James E. Cantwell, unassigned. Nineteen officers were wounded, six were gassed and evacuated

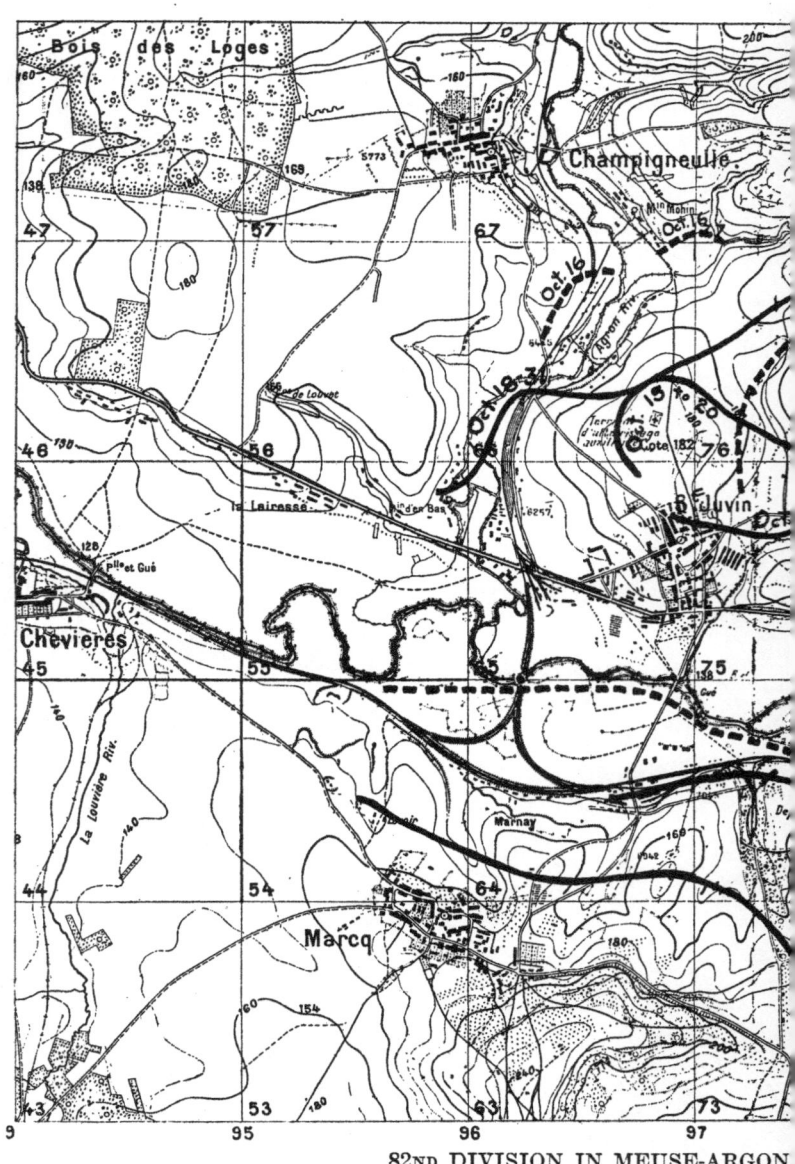

82ND DIVISION IN MEUSE-ARGON
- - - - - - - - - - - Dotted lines indicate tempora
——————— Solid lines indicate organized

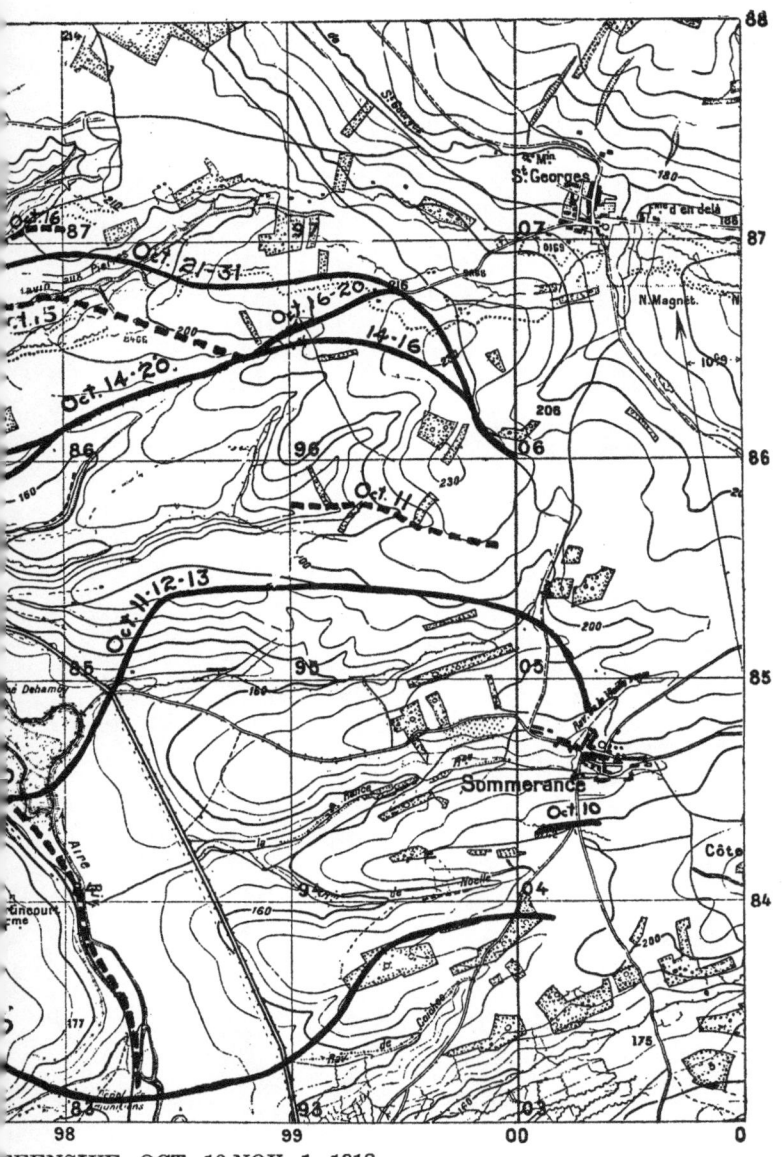

FENSIVE, OCT. 10-NOV. 1, 1918
tions of advance units during the day
ine at midnight

and three were evacuated sick. Six officers of the regiment were captured in the German counter-attack at Cornay and one of these officers, Capt. Charles H. Brown, Co. A, who had been severely wounded and captured, was later recaptured at Martincourt Farm by the 325th Infantry. Of the enlisted men of the 327th Infantry 115 were killed in action or died of wounds; 90 were captured or classified "missing in action"; 675 were wounded or gassed and 100 were evacuated, sick.

In the 328th Infantry, the following officers were killed in action during this flank attack: 2nd Lt. Kirby P. Stewart, G. Co., 2nd Lt. O. M. Coston, A Co., and 2nd Lt. Carl Goldsmith, M Co., 328th Inf., who died at the outskirts of Cornay leading his platoon in an attack. 2nd Lt. Walter M. Little, Supply Co., 328th Inf., died later in the hospital of wounds received October 7. Twelve officers of the regiment were evacuated wounded; 9 evacuated gassed; 3 evacuated sick, making a total of 28 officer casualties. One hundred and twenty-nine enlisted men were killed or died of wounds; 387 evacuated wounded; 130 evacuated gassed; 52 evacuated sick; 20 captured, making a total of 718 lost in this operation.

The importance of this flank attack and the measure of success achieved is indicated by the telegram sent on the late afternoon of October 7th by direction of General Pershing:

"Headquarters, 1st Army Corps—Oct. 7th, 1918
C. G., 82nd Division, G-3, 1095 period The Commander-in-Chief directed me to congratulate General Julian R. Lindsey, on the success of his thrust in which I heartily concur. (sgd) Liggett—4:30 P. M.

* * * * *

Dear General Lindsey: It gives me great pleasure to transmit this to you. (sgd) G. B. Duncan, Maj. Gen., Comdg. 82nd Div."

October 11, 1918, a Day of Testing

In many respects, the 11th of October, 1918, tested the qualities of the 82nd Division more than any day in its history. The 325th Infantry, 326th Infantry and the 327th Infantry were all three plunged into an exceedingly desperate fight for a footing in the outpost positions of the Kriemhilde Stellung line. The 326th Infantry, west of the Aire, attacked from Marcq in an effort to cross the Aire River, where it bends toward Grand-Pré, just south of St. Juvin. The 325th Infantry and 327th Infantry, east of the Aire, attacked the ridge between St. Juvin and Sommerance. The 326th Infantry failed, but with a gallantry which will be a source of boundless pride to this Division. The other two regiments were tried to the utmost, but eventually achieved the ridge.

It will be necessary to consider the operations of each regiment separately and to examine the special situation with which each was confronted. The dossier of the 82nd Division shows the receipt of the following messages, which resulted in the relief of the left brigade of the 1st Division by the 327th Infantry.

"00:05 hours, 10 Oct. 1918, Col. Montgomery, G-3, 1st A. C. called at 12 o'clock midnight and asked if we had received our Field Order. When told 'No,' he stated as follows: 'General Duncan will continue to-morrow morning 1½ hours earlier than to-day (7 a.m.). Your right boundary extends from Baulny north practically in a straight line along the western edge of Bois de Boyon to Sommerance. You will relieve the elements of the 1st Division west of that boundary. The 1st Division line extends from Fleville, running northeast to Côte de Maldah. You will be responsible for the part of the line west of your eastern boundary. You must effect relief of the elements of the 1st Division on this line before daybreak.' "

* * * * *

"10 Oct. 1918, 2 hours, 22 minutes—from General Duncan to Major Scott. Tell General Lindsey when he comes in that in sending that one company to his right that he must send it to arrive by 5 hours if possible to the line between Fléville and west edge of Bois de Boyon to relieve the elements of the 1st Division at that point."

In accordance with the above message, K Company, 325th Infantry (Capt. Melton), proceeded before 5 hours, October 10, to a point one kilometer south of Fléville, where the main Fléville road is crossed by an east and west road to Exermont. No elements of the 1st Division were encountered, but a German patrol was met and captured. Captain Melton outposted the Exermont Road for a distance of some 500 meters from the main Fléville road. This company remained in the assigned position until October 12th.

"11 hours 5 minutes 10th Oct.—message to C. G., 164th Brig. Send one Major and one company from your reserve to the east of the River Aire to back up the company which relieved the elements of the 1st Division between Fléville and Bois de Boyon. The Major will be in command of these two companies and will push forward to the general line Sommerance (exclusive) to the west, where they will relieve the elements of the 16th Inf. now on that line. I believe that there is very little in front of you. Corps is very insistent that they should have exact location of your front lines and perhaps you can send some officers down to get location. The Division Commander directs that you push forward to the line indicated and report the location of your front line—By direction of the Division Commander—Raymond Sheldon, Chief of Staff."

* * *

"12 hours 25 minutes 10th Oct. 1918—Message from Col. Ely: I have message dated 10 A.M. from C. O. 16th Inf. as follows: C. G., 1st Brig. informs me that your Division is to relieve our lines from Sommerance west. We are advancing on that line this A.M. and are about there now. Please advise when you intend to make relief for we will have to move on the east of Sommerance in support. (sgd) Koppeck."

     *   *   *   *

"Bonehead 7 (G-3, 1st Corps) reported at 13 hours 5 minutes Oct. 10, 1918, a large concentration of enemy troops 1 km. east of St. Juvin. Wants to know if he can fire upon them. Albany 1 (C. G., 82nd Div.) replied 'Yes' to above question. Same information had been received from 1st Division by Albany 7 (G-3, 82nd Div.) and same reply."

Relief of a Brigade of 1st Division.

Shortly after 11 hours, Companies E and F, 327th Infantry, under Captain Conklin, were sent to relieve the front line of the 16th Infantry north of Fléville. Early that afternoon the two remaining companies of the 2nd Battalion and Companies I, L and M of the 3rd Battalion moved to complete the relief. The 2nd Battalion (Major Blanchard) took over the positions of the outpost battalion, and the 3rd Battalion (Captain Davis) relieved the support line. The movement was started at 16 hours, 10th of October, and was completed an hour later. At 17 hours, the following telephone report was received at Division Headquarters from the 164th Infantry Brigade:

"Mr. Ely reported at 16 hours: Operations Officer reconnoitered and reports much gas in Fléville with constant shelling. Am running telephone lines forward. Blanchard will assume command of the advance lines. May establish ammunition dump north of Fléville to-night and will push our advance. Observation and intelligence work being established. Men in excellent spirits. (sgd) Ely."

After the relief had been completed, the 18th Infantry informed the 327th Infantry that the 18th Infantry also was to be included in the relief. The depleted companies of the 327th Infantry therefore extended their lines to the east until they had covered in addition the position occupied by the 18th Infantry. The most advanced outpost groups of the 1st Division were relieved by similar groups from the 2nd Battalion, 327th Infantry, in little patches of woods or thickets scattered along the small ridge 00.0-84.3 to 99.0-84.2. This outpost line is about 500 meters south of an east and west line through Sommerance. The main body of the forward battalion of the 1st Division was relieved on two lines, the 1st of which was 500 meters south of the outpost detachments.

The 164th Inf. Brig. Field Order No. 7, issued during the forenoon of October 10, had stated:

"The new position will be simply occupying a defensive sector."

This interpretation of the relief was not reversed until late on the night of October 10. At 18 hours, October 10, 1918, the following message was received at Division Headquarters from Chief of Staff, 1st Corps:

"Operations for 1st Corps to-morrow will be continued at 7 o'clock. Line of direction is Sivrey-lez-Buzancy (exclusive)-Briquenay (exclusive)-the heights northwest and southwest of Le Morthomme. Liaison with 38th Corps on eastern edge of Bois de Bourgogne-Grand-Pré."

(Answer.) "General Duncan to Chief of Staff, 1st Corps: 'I will have to push forward all the artillery to-night.'"

At about 21 hours, the orders for attack reached the 327th Infantry.

The east boundary of the 82nd Division sector was now Sommerance (exclusive)-Sivry-lez-Buzancy (exclusive); the west boundary Marcq (inclusive)-St. Juvin exclusive)-Verpel (exclusive)-Thénorgues (exclusive)-Harricourt (inclusive). The intermediate Corps objective was the line Imécourt-Champigneulle-Grand-Pré. The Corps Order called for a halt of one-half hour on this line for the purpose of reorganization and movement forward of artillery. The first objective was Sivry-lez-Buzancy (exclusive)-Verpel (inclusive). The 1st Corps directed that divisions advance to the first objective independently, prepared to advance farther to the Corps objective at 13 hours. The 1st Corps objective was Sivry-lez-Buzancy (exclusive)-Thénorgues (inclusive). When this line was reached, it was directed that exploitation be carried out to the front and contact kept with the enemy. Five tanks were ordered to support the attack of the 82nd Division. The artillery was to keep harassing and interdiction fire in front of the infantry with one accompanying gun for each front line battalion. C Company, 321st M. G. Battalion, was ordered to support the attack. The jump-off line designated was the Sommerance-St. Juvin road.

Colonel Ely directed that the 3rd Battallion, 327th Infantry, (less K Company) act as assault battalion, supported by the 2nd Battalion, with the 1st Battalion (plus K Company) as Divisional reserve. During the night of October 10, B Company, 321st M. G. Battalion (Captain Cunningham), relieved machine-gun elements of the 1st Division at the cross road, 300 meters south of Sommerance. Later in the night Captain Cunningham sent a patrol forward into Sommerance to make a reconnaissance. This patrol was fired on from the center of the village.

Capt. McWhorter with C Company, 321st Machine Gun Battalion, moved into a support position, just north of Fléville. During the heavy shell fire which took place during this change of position, Lieutenant Dutton was severely wounded and died shortly afterwards in the hospital.

Col. Gordon Johnston came to the 82nd Division as Chief of Staff at 2 hours 20 minutes, October 11. Colonel Sheldon was relieved and went to the 77th Division.

It will now be necessary to turn back to the 325th Infantry and follow their progress through the night of October 10. At darkness on that day, Regimental Headquarters was established on the Cornay Ridge with the 3rd Battalion on the slope in reserve. The 1st and 2nd Battalions were scattered from that point north to the Aire River doing patrol work over a large territory. During the day, the battalions of the Regiment had been in close liaison with the regimental commander. This is evidenced by the numerous messages in the regimental dossier of which the following are of special interest:

To Capt. Marshburn, Co. G, 2:50 P.M. "No Germans found on this side of the River Aire. Point 84.5-96.8 is covered by M. G. fire from Boche trenches. Able to locate M. G. at 86.5-97.8. No Germans seen in St. Juvin, but about 100 seen to east of St. Juvin in trenches from 85.5-97.4 to 85.4-98.2. The R. R. tracks along river could not be patrolled on account of M. G. fire. We did not cross river on account of so many guns opening fire. R. R. dump at 8.45-96.8 was fired on by our artillery and a few buildings are on fire. The Germans threw two barrages and we had to advance toward St. Juvin slowly. We could only observe St. Juvin, but did not draw fire. (sgd.) Fawcett."

* * * * *

To C. O., 325th Inf. "No report of river crossings have been received from our patrols. (sgd.) Hawkins."

* * * * *

To C. O., 325th Inf., 17 hours. "Patrols sent toward Aire River have reached Hill 240 at point 96.3-83.3 and extend west from there to point 97.4-83.3. Patrols report they have been held up by enemy and our own artillery. No sign of enemy infantry. (sgd.) Lott."

* * * * *

Note to Regimental Commander: "There has been slight shelling of Cornay by enemy artillery. Our patrols received very severe shelling at times. Men in Cornay have received fire from Boche plane twice during the day. This fire they returned. One Lieut. and 10 men from 164th

Brig. were found wounded in enemy territory and evacuated. The Lieutenant and three men were found 3 km. from our present line by patrol from Co. G. This Lieut. states that Germans retired about 10 P.M. 9th-10th Oct. and left them in dugout with three other men. There seems to have been a relief to our front as about 500 troops were exchanged in region to right of St. Juvin on Oct. 10. (sgd) Bettes."

In addition to these messages, the following despatch was received by the division commander from Headquarters, 163rd Infantry Brigade:

At 19 hours 5 minutes: "326th Inf. reports that they learned from five prisoners that the enemy is evacuating St. Juvin."

Between midnight and 1 hour, night of October 10-11, Colonel Whitman received Field Order No. 8, 164th Inf. Brig., attached to which was 82nd Division Field Order No. 23. The substance of these orders have already been outlined in the statement of orders received by the 327th Infantry during the night of October 10-11. Some further details not previously covered and contained in both orders are as follows:

"For this attack, the 164th Brig. is composed of the 325th and 327th Inf. Regiments. Each regiment will have one battalion in front line; one battalion in support and one battalion in reserve. Reserve Battalion, 327th Inf., will be the Division reserve and will follow the support battalion, same regiment, at 3 kil. The reserve battalion, 325th Inf. will be the brigade reserve and will follow the support battalion, same regiment, at 3 kil. The Machine Gun Co., 325th Inf., will be attached to the advance battalion of that regiment, and B Co., 321st M. G. Bn. to Advance Battalion, 327th Inf. The remaining machine gun companies constitute the brigade reserve and will be maneuvered and commanded by the C. O. 321st M. G. Bn. Field and combat trains will accompany their units."

The Brigade order stated that information of the enemy and our own troops is as set forth in Par. 1 of the Divisional order, which reads:

"(a) The enemy has been driven north of the line Sommerance-St.Juvin-Grand-Pré. St. Juvin is reported evacuated.
(b) The 1st Corps attacks at 7 hours, 11th Oct., 1918, on its present front."

The Division order further provided that:

"Battalions that are to lead the attack in each brigade will be moved north of the Aire River before daylight. Crossing will be covered by strong patrols."
"The 163rd Brig. will attack between the west boundary of the Division and Meridian 98.5 and the 164th Brig. between the same meridian and the east boundary of the Division."

Colonel Whitman was confronted with the problem of getting to the jump-off at 5 hours, October 11th, from his extended positions north of Cornay. The distance from Cornay Ridge to the St. Juvin-Sommerance road was about 4 kilometers. No fords had been found by the patrols and the 1st and 2nd Battalions were extended over a front of two kilometers. The night was dark and the time was short. It was decided not to waste valuable hours hunting for fords under such unfavorable conditions. It was known that the engineers were constructing a foot bridge at Fléville. This was selected for the point at which to cross the river. The 3rd Battalion on the Cornay Ridge was ordered to start immediately. Rush orders were sent to the 2nd Battalion to assemble and follow. The 1st Battalion was put in Brigade reserve with orders to follow at three kilometers. The leading companies felt their way to the river and waded it in single file, using the foot bridge as a guide. Daylight found the 3rd Battalion, 325th Infantry, about 1½ kilometers from the St. Juvin-Sommerance Road and moving with all possible speed in column of twos up the river road from Fléville to St. Juvin. It was apparent to Colonel Whitman that he would not be in position by 5 hours, but he felt confident that his dispositions would be complete on the jump-off line by 6 hours with a full hour remaining for final instructions before attacking at 7 hours.

CHAPTER X

THE SOMMERANCE-ST. JUVIN ROAD

THE story of events now returns to the 327th Infantry. Before daybreak the three companies of the 3rd Battalion moved forward from the lines on which the 2nd Battalion had relieved the 1st Division and advanced about 500 meters to the St. Juvin-Sommerance Road. As these companies advanced they found themselves in immediate contact with the enemy who retired slowly fighting as he fell back. Our men were in position on this jump-off line in accordance with orders at 5 hours. The battalion was extended along this road to cover a kilometer of front. The right flank was about 250 meters west of the first building in the western outskirts of Sommerance. After arrival on this line, machine guns and artillery fire continued to harass our troops. A heavy mist hung over the entire country. The battalion appeared to be alone on a desolate road. Liaison groups could find no evidence of support on either flank. At 7 hours the battalion advanced followed by the 2nd Battalion in support. Captain Cunningham placed his machine gunners with the support waves and advanced with the infantry. On reaching the top of the ridge 85.5, a few hundred meters from the initial point, enemy fire became very intense. Captain Davis, commanding the 3rd Battalion, was severely wounded less than twenty minutes after jumping off. Captain Henley of M Company took command of the battalion, but was himself shot down shortly afterward. All the remaining officers of this battalion became casualties within a few minutes after the advance was commenced, and the men went forward led entirely by non-commissioned officers. No tanks had appeared; no troops had come up on either side; no friendly artillery barrage was apparent and bands of wire met the leading wave on Ridge 85.5, northwest of Sommerance. As the men struggled through these entanglements, they were subjected to terrific enfilade fire along the wire and from both flanks. They were also under a continuous rain of missiles from the front. Major Blanchard, commanding the leading and support battalions, saw that the 3rd Battalion was melting into disorganization and took forward the 2nd Battalion to continue the attack. The 2nd Battalion, E and F Companies leading, arrived abreast of the remnants of the 3rd Battalion and endeavored to carry on from this point. During the advance of the 2nd Battalion to the Sommerance Road, 1st Lt. G. H. Byrd, Adjutant, 2nd Bn., was killed by a fragment of shell at Major Blanchard's side.

When the assault had proceeded for about a kilometer north of the St. Juvin-Sommerance Road, Major Blanchard perceived that groups of the enemy were filtering south from one thicket to another and out of the various small patches of woods that dot this open country. Already the enemy had collected in considerable numbers in rear of his right flank. He could see no American troops coming to his support from any direction. It was now about 9 hours 30 minutes. Major Blanchard sent Lieutenant Hackney to Colonel Ely, who had established an advance Regimental P. C. in a gully just south of the Sommerance-St. Juvin Road. Lieutenant Hackney explained the present situation to the regimental commander, who sent word to Major Blanchard to use his own judgment and fall back if he found it necessary. About twenty minutes after receiving this message, Major Blanchard directed retirement to the Sommerance Road. This movement was covered by the machine gunners under Captain Cunningham. The Infantry was withdrawn in orderly fashion by groups, each retirement being covered by our fire. Captain Fowle, Regimental Operations Officer, and Lieutenant Hackney, 2nd Bn. Intelligence Officer, personally placed each detachment in position on the St. Juvin-Sommerance Road. Outposts and observation posts were established 300 meters north of this road. Through this screen, the last of the Infantry and finally the machine gunners leap-frogged to the rear. A brave effort was checked, but the 327th Infantry had pierced and held for a time the outpost of the Kriemhilde-Stellung. The following officers of the 327th Infantry died that morning: 1st Lieutenant Byrd (already mentioned), 1st Lt. John W. Anderson (Gas Officer, 3rd Bn.) and 1st Lt. Walter B. Saddler, Co. E. Captain Conkling, F Co., received wounds from which he later died. Many officers were wounded and a large number of enlisted men were killed and wounded. During this engagement Lieutenants Rowell, Grainger and Moylan, all of Company B, 321st Machine Gun Battalion, were evacuated for wounds. 1st Lieutenant Fitzpatrick, Co. E, and 2nd Lt. Theodore H. Smith, Co. L, with a little handful of men were so far in front that when the retirement came they were unable to get back before being cut off by the enemy. Lieutenant Fitzpatrick was not captured until that night and Lieutenant Smith until the next morning. A number of the enemy were in turn captured by our troops during this attack. All prisoners taken were from the 37th German Division.

THE 325TH INFANTRY ON OCTOBER 11, 1918

The story of the 325th Infantry left that unit at about 6 hours on the Fléville-St. Juvin Road, hastening to get in position on the St. Juvin-Sommerance Road. Colonel Whitman, Captain Wright, his adjutant, and Major Pierce were at the head of the column consisting of Companies M, I, L and the Regimental Machine Gun Company, in the order named. About 300 meters south of the junction formed by the Fléville-St. Juvin Road with the Sommerance-St. Juvin Road, a burst of machine-gun fire from the right flank swept the column. Several men fell and our men moved into the ditch on the east side of the road for protection. This fire came from the crest and slopes of the hill 200 or 300 meters east of the river road. This hill was south of the Sommerance-St. Juvin Road. Fire also came from the slopes of Ridge 85.5 to the north and from the direction of St. Juvin. Colonel Whitman and Major Pierce worked forward to the Sommerance Road for a personal reconnaissance. A survey of the situation showed no friendly troops in sight, but many enemy snipers and machine gunners on the high ground immediately ahead. Artillery now opened on the road on which the regiment lay. It was 6 hours 45 minutes. To get into position for the Corps attack, it was necessary to deploy to the right front and extend for a kilometer in width from the road junction to the east. No deployment, however, could be made until the enemy was dislodged from the hill on the immediate right of our column. Orders were sent to the two rear infantry companies (I and L) to break off to their right and send a skirmish line with its left flank on the highway to sweep the enemy north of the St. Juvin-Sommerance Road. This was successfully done and the regiment extricated for the moment from the peril of close range flank fire. In this preliminary action, Capt. Charles A. Fowler of Company M was killed as he leaped to the top of the bank to direct the deployment of his company.

As the line passed the jump-off road, Company M joined on the left flank, and at 7:20 the attack moved forward and started up the slopes of Ridge 85.5 under a heavy fire which ran along the crest clear to St. Juvin. The ridge was found to be heavily protected by enemy wire. Along the top of the crest was a sunken road which ran due west into St. Juvin. No American troops appeared on the left flank of the regiment, but St. Juvin was obviously full of Germans who kept up a continuous raking fire.

The promised tanks had not appeared and no 75 mm. accompanying gun had reported. There was no friendly barrage preceding the advance. One platoon of the Machine Gun Company supported the advance of I Company and another platoon cooperated with M Company. The 3rd Platoon used indirect fire over the heads of our advancing troops. The machine gunners moved forward with this assault battalion and lost heavily. Our men tore through the wire, charged and maneuvered against the German machine gunners and killed and were killed until the top of the ridge was in our possession. This was accomplished at 8 hours 5 minutes. This success could not have been achieved except by troops of the highest morale. The right flank company could see no American troops on the right, but the thick mist did not permit a far view. At 8 hours 30 minutes, liaison was established along the 85.5 Ridge with the 327th Infantry. Colonel Whitman, accompanied by Captain Wright, proceeded along the fire-swept road half-way to Sommerance and talked with Captain Fowle, Operations Officer, 327th Inf.

The opposition of the enemy to our advance beyond

the sunken road on the crest of the ridge became so intense and the fire from the left flank assumed such proportions that the 325th Infantry was unable to make further progress. Indeed, it became a very serious question whether the regiment could cling to the position won without suffering virtual annihilation. Colonel Whitman sent a runner back on the road toward Fléville with a message to Major Hawkins, commanding the 2nd Battalion in support, and directed that reinforcement be sent up. F Company was immediately ordered forward, reporting to Colonel Whitman at the crossroads at about 9 hours. This company was used to cover the left flank of the regiment by filling in the gap between the crossroads and the Aire River to the west. The Brigade Order had given meridian 98.5 as the western boundary of the brigade. This gave a front of 500 meters immediately east of the Aire River to the 163rd Infantry Brigade. No troops appeared, however, to fill this gap and Colonel Whitman made the disposition already indicated.

About 10 o'clock, Capt. Parley B. Christensen of I Company was killed on the ridge. The regiment had now lost two of its company commanders.

325TH INFANTRY ALONE ON SOMMERANCE ROAD

It will be remembered that at 10 hours, Major Blanchard had withdrawn from his point of farthest advance and was organized on this same ridge between the 325th Infantry on the west and Sommerance on the east. Both regiments were now in liaison and Major Blanchard, going to Colonel Ely, told him that he considered the position a good one, although very heavy fire was coming from the front and right flank. At 10 hours the following message was sent to the C. G., 164th Brig., at the P. C. in Fléville:

"Only one officer left in the battalion. Line was ahead of both flanks and compelled to draw back. Now on parallel 85.5. Whitman reported on my left. My officers and men so exhausted they are not effective. Strong resistance—shells—M. G. Prisoners say three regiments in front. A strong counter-attack could not be stopped by us. Request reinforcements. (sgd) Ely."

At 10 hours 45 minutes, the following message was sent to Brigade Headquarters:

"No support on right flank. Both advance battalions almost decimated. Men fought hard. Not a straggler met. Have withdrawn to jump-off road. Slight shelter. Request immediate help. (sgd) Ely."

The Division dossier contains the following record:

"Message No. 131, 11th Oct. 1918—from 164th Brig.— at 11 hours 40 minutes: From Col. Ely at 99.5-84.7, 11 hours 30 minutes. Lost 50 per cent of my command. Boche counter-attacked; filtering in through woods. Unable to get in touch on my right. Line now on Sommerance-St. Juvin Road. Unless I drop back, will probably be cut off."

* * * * *

General Lindsey notified Division Headquarters of his reply to Ely as follows: "Drop back under cover of machine gun fire. Dig in if necessary and hold. Notify Col. Whitman.' Ely said he had. I ordered artillery fire in front."

Major Blanchard received a message at 11 hours 30 minutes from Colonel Ely ordering the withdrawal of troops of the 327th Infantry to a ridge one kilometer south of the Sommerance-St. Juvin Road. Shortly before this time, Colonel Whitman received a message from Colonel Ely stating that the 327th Infantry was withdrawing about one kilometer south of the Sommerance

Road. As the 327th Infantry withdrew to the Sommerance-Fléville Road on practically the same lines from which they had jumped off that morning, Major Hawkins advanced with E Company followed by G Company, both of the 325th Infantry, and took up a position along the ridge on the right flank of the 325th Infantry line, replacing the troops of the 327th Infantry. H Company, 325th Infantry, had been detached from Major Hawkins' Battalion by the Brigade Commander for military police work in the vicinity of Fléville.

About 11 hours, Capt. Lamar Y. McLeod, Operations Officer, was killed, making the third captain lost from the 325th Infantry. Colonel Whitman sent word detailing the serious situation which confronted him and asked that the 1st Battalion, 325th Infantry, in reserve be sent to his assistance. General Lindsey directed Colonel Whitman to hold the ridge at all costs and added that the 327th Infantry would be ordered forward again to the ridge. The companies of the 3rd Battalion on the crest formed a salient, the flanks of which were continually swept by machine gun fire. Companies B and C, 325th Infantry, arrived at 11 hours 30 minutes and were placed below the crest to resist any threatened counter-attack. Companies A and D, 325th Infantry, were sent by General Lindsey to reinforce the 327th Infantry, but Colonel Ely despatched them to Colonel Whitman. Upon their arrival at 325th Infantry Headquarters, both companies were deployed upon the ridge. The entire regiment was now in the breech with the exception of H and K Companies.

At 12 hours, Capt. Louis L. Battey, A Co., was killed while leading his men forward over the bullet-swept Sommerance Road. The regiment had now suffered a loss of four company commanders in a desperate half-day of fighting. Four enemy counter-attacks were made during the day. All the four attacks were bloodily repulsed. Our artillery responded promptly to calls for a barrage. Twice this fire fell upon the ridge and our men withdrew to the south slope, immediately reoccupying the hill as the fire lifted, to follow the retiring enemy. A message sent by Colonel Whitman at 14 hours to Major Pierce, 3rd Bn., illustrates the situation:

"At 2:30 P.M. our artillery fire will stop. After that the ridge must be reoccupied. The troops must advance no further than that. They must dig in for the night. These orders are peremptory. (sgd) Whitman."

At 13 hours, a fifth officer of this regiment was killed, 1st Lt. Farley W. Moody.

327TH INFANTRY RETURNS TO SOMMERANCE RIDGE

At 14 hours, General Lindsey sent the following message to Lieutenant Colonel Burr, commanding the 1st Battalion, 327th Infantry, in Divisional Reserve.

"Report with your command to Col. Ely, who is hereby instructed to counter-attack at once from the woods at 99.5-83.9, straight north and regain the 85.5 ridge, and there dig in and organize for resistance. Col. Whitman will be instructed to advance accordingly. The ridge must be regained, but do not go beyond the ridge to-night."

The 1st Battalion, together with a detail of seventy-five men from the 2nd Battalion, 327th Infantry, went forward under command of Colonel Burr and regained the 85.5 ridge at 18 hours 30 minutes. Here the regiment dug in, organizing the position in depth. At 17 hours 10 minutes, Colonel Whitman sent the following message to the 3rd Battalion, 325th Infantry:

"No troops are to be withdrawn from the ridge without orders from me. The ridge will be held to the last. All company commanders have been notified. (sgd) Whit-man."

Among other messages in the Division dossier, the following are of interest:

No. 137—11th October 1918—From 164th Brig.—13 hours 10 minutes: "Telephone from Whitman at 13 hours 10 said that Boche was counter-attacking him from ridge north of parallel 85 between meridian 98 and 99, but he does not fear for his left flank. Have put all my available artillery on that ridge."

* * * * *

From 164th Brig.—13:15 hours: "My whole brigade is and has been east of the river since H hour. My left flank not far from cross roads 98.2-84.9. It seems that 164th Brig. was the only one to get off at H hour. Report that Division on my right is advancing near parallel 85 is the first I have heard of them. They must have just jumped off. (sgd) Lindsey."

* * * * *

Message No. 140—11 Oct. 1918—Col. Johnston to Gen. Lindsey at 14 hours: "You are authorized to take the Divisional Reserve and retake the crest along the 85.5 parallel. There are supporting troops close in your rear. Having secured the crest, dig in and hold line until further orders."

* * * * *

Col. Johnston to G-3, 1st Corps: "General Liggett was in and is satisfied with the situation. We had the misfortune to be knocked off that ridge, but we are going to take the 85.5 parallel. We are using all that we have on that side (east of the river) and you have those troops just below (78th Division). We would like to have you send one battalion to Fléville. Can you do it? Col. Montgomery said he would take it up with the Chief of Staff and notify us."

In the Division dossier is one memorandum which reveals an estimate of the troops of the 164th Infantry Brigade during a very critical time in the operations of this desperate day. A squadron of the 2nd Cavalry attached to the 1st Army was performing liaison duty in the 5th Corps. A captain from this unit, from a post south of Sommerance, sent the following message to the 1st Brigade, 1st Division, which repeated the message to the 82nd Division. This message reached Division Headquarters at 14 hours 45 minutes:

"Major Blanchard, 327th Inf. with 300 men, holding crest of hill at Sommerance, withdrawing to crest of hill 1 km. south of Sommerance. Morale and confidence of men very good, but officers badly needed by the 327th Inf. Most of companies without officers, who were killed or wounded. Surgeon and bandages requested."

* * * * *

"At 13 hours 40 minutes, from crest of hill 1 km. south of Sommerance. Captain Fraser, 2nd Bn., 325th Inf. has reached this point to support 327th Inf. Fresh troops with splendid morale."

Night found both regiments of the 164th Brigade holding ridge 85.5 between Sommerance and St. Juvin.

Lieutenant Colonel Burr, now commanding the 327th Infantry, received the following message from General Lindsey:

"Congratulate you upon attaining the ridge. Division is greatly pleased but anxious about your defense. Under these circumstances the ridge must not be allowed again to get into the enemy's hands."

The 2nd Battalion of the 325th Infantry was on the right of 327th Infantry, and outposted the brigade line near Sommerance. A patrol from this Battalion got in touch with the 1st Division about a kilometer to the southeast, in the vicinity of the Côte de Maldah. The 1st and 3rd Battalions of the 325th Infantry, partially mingled, extended along Ridge 85.5 for about one kilometer of front on the left of the 327th Infantry. Colonel Whitman's regiment had that day lost five officers killed and twelve officers wounded, among whom was Major Pierce, commanding the 3rd Battalion. Major Pierce refused to be evacuated. Many enlisted men had been killed and more than two hundred wounded men evacuated. The Regimental Surgeon, Major Feaster, had established his advance dressing station where the first casualties occurred and worked with his assistant for twenty hours under continuous fire.

The regiment had taken about one hundred and fifty prisoners and captured twenty machine guns. The Brigade had been tried to the utmost, but had broken through the outpost line of the Kriemhilde-Stellung. From the position gained that day, our troops never receded.

The action of October 11, 1918, banished any thought that the enemy intended an extensive withdrawal. On the contrary, he had evidenced a grim purpose to hold a terrain so admirably adapted for defense. Neither was he content to permit the American line to remain in undisturbed possession of what had been gained. In the four counter-attacks launched against us on October 11, the enemy had shown the utmost prodigality in expending his infantry and selected machine gunners. His assaults had crumbled under our fire, which inflicted heavy losses. As each wave shattered and fell back, substantial numbers of prisoners were left in our hands.

CHAPTER XI

THE MARCQ BRIDGEHEAD

To complete the account of the operations of the 82nd Division on October 11, 1918, there remains only the epic story of the 2nd Battalion, 326th Infantry. This narrative has already described the advance of the 1st and the 3rd Battalions of the 326th Infantry on October 10, 1918, including the occupation of La Besogne and Marcq by the 1st Battalion.

At 14 hours, October 10, the following message was recorded in the Division dossier:

General Duncan to General Cronin: "Hold line of resistance and at the same time press on to the river. Get a bridgehead across."

After message received from Chief of Staff, 1st Corps, General Duncan called General Cronin again adding:

"It will be necessary to advance your line of resistance towards Marcq and drive enemy across the Aire."

At 16 hours 50 minutes, the following telephone message was sent from Division Headquarters to the Commanding Generals 163rd and 164th Brigades:

"Push patrols across Aire River to your north this after noon and to-night. Direct them to investigate and report upon available fords and bridges. Enemy identifications from the north side of the river are desired. Early report on result of these patrols to be made."

The 2nd Battalion, 326th Infantry, less G Company, was in reserve until mid-afternoon, October 10. G Company of this battalion was a combat liaison group between the 1st and 3rd Battalions. About 16 hours, the 2nd Battalion reached Pylône. Here General Cronin met Major Jones, the battalion commander, and directed that the 2nd Battalion effect a passing of lines through the 3rd Battalion; then continue to the town of Marcq, cross the Aire River and occupy the town of St. Juvin and Hill 182, north of the town. Company G rejoined the battalion, which moved through the 3rd Battalion and advanced to the heights, south of Marcq. The 326th Infantry Machine Gun Company was attached to this battalion.

It was dusk when E and G Companies descended from the ridge into the town of Marcq. Major Jones established his P. C. in the edge of the town and directed E and G Companies to proceed north and cross the river. E Company was ordered to use the railroad bridge southwest of St. Juvin and G Company the Marcq-St. Juvin Road bridge. The enemy was now shelling Marcq heavily and this continued throughout the night. No officer or soldier in either company had an opportunity to reconnoiter in daylight the thousand meters of terrain between the town and the river. It was a cloudy night with a bleak wind blowing. G Company (Captain Jeffers) and E Company (1st Lieutenant Huff) felt their way down the road to the marshy lowlands. Here Lieutenant Huff found the railroad and followed it to the left, while Captain Jeffers continued with G Company along the road. Both the railroad bridge and the road bridge were found to be destroyed. Simultaneous with this discovery, G Company at the shattered road bridge received a shower of

Culvert near "bloody angle," Junction St. Juvin-Sommerance Road

Marcq Bridgehead, looking toward St. Juvin

machine-gun bullets from enemy outposts on the north side of the river. The presence of E Company at the railroad bridge was not noted. Captain Jeffers and Lieutenant Huff sent officer patrols along the river bank with orders to discover a ford. The patrols returned after a time and reported that a most careful reconnaissance had been made but that no ford could be found. It was stated that the banks of the river were steep and the water too deep for wading. A soldier with a rifle, 220 rounds of ammunition and 50 pounds of other equipment can not swim a river. The two company commanders held a brief conference and decided to go back to Major Jones in Marcq for further instructions. The Major directed both officers to return and search again, step by step, along the river. Only when certain that no ford existed was the effort to cross to be abandoned. Again both officers and men were sent on this mission. This time also no ford was found.

The Aire deepens and broadens substantially in its run from St. Juvin to Grand-Pré, but there are spots suitable for crossing had the patrols been able to stumble upon them in the blackness of that lowering night. Near the destroyed road bridge the river shallows to a depth of two or three feet of water. This fact escaped our patrols. When this situation had been again reported to Major Jones, the latter telephoned to Colonel McArthur at the regimental P. C. north of Pylône. Colonel McArthur conferred with General Cronin, who directed that determined efforts be made to cross by infiltration. Major Jones instructed the company commanders that patrols should make a reconnaissance along the river from the island southeast of St. Juvin for a kilometer and a half to the west and filter across by any means possible.

As in all previous attempts no ford was found. Captain Jeffers then directed eight successive attempts to cross on the shattered road bridge. It was possible for only one man at a time to scramble along this precarious footing, clinging to sections of the hand-rail. Each of these individual efforts drew concentrated machine-gun fire which killed several of our men and effectively blocked the passage. During the presence of our troops along the river the enemy continued to shoot up Very lights between St. Juvin and the north bank of the river. About midnight the two companies withdrew to the heights south of Marcq.

At this time a conference was held in the battalion P. C. at which Major Jones and the four company commanders of the battalion were present. Following the conference Major Jones telephoned Colonel McArthur that it would be necessary for engineers to construct a bridge before troops could get across the river. Colonel McArthur communicated with General Cronin, who ordered a platoon of engineers to report to Major Jones. This platoon arrived under the personal command of Major Kelly, 307th Engineers, at 2 hours 30 minutes, October 11. General Cronin had informed Colonel McArthur meanwhile that the 2nd Battalion would attack St. Juvin at 5 hours, October 11. The engineers tore down planks from shell-wrecked buildings and strapped the timbers together with their gun slings.

And now came an event of special significance. Through the first half of the night, while the Infantry patrols were endeavoring to cross on the demolished road bridge, the enemy machine guns had chattered out a heavy fire on this point. When the unmistakable noise of the hasty bridge building began, all German machine-gun fire on this area stopped. Only the artillery fire on the general Marcq area continued. The Germans were now ready to receive any Infantry at this crossing.

2ND BATTALION, 326TH INFANTRY, OCTOBER 11, 1918

At 5 hours on October 11, a thick mist made it impossible to see more than a hundred meters away. The battalion moved down the road to the bridge at H hour. All units were in column of twos and in the following order: G Company, one platoon Regimental Machine Gun Company, E Company, one platoon Regimental Machine Gun Company, H Company and F Company.

Company B (1st Lt. Thomas C. Carter, Jr.) and Company C (Captain Wert), both of the 320th Machine Gun Battalion, were disposed in depth on the heights in the vicinity of Marcq and given the mission of supporting the attack with over-head fire.

The enemy was quiet—unusually quiet, and our men made little noise. It was hoped that the mist might curtain the attack until the battalion got at close range. Captain Jeffers led on to the narrow bridge, his company behind him in single file. About half of this first company was over when a terrific burst of machine-gun fire swept the bridge and the straight road lined with men. The men of G Company not yet on the bridge turned to the right and rushed into the water, crossing without great difficulty under cover of the opposite bank which formed a bulwark some three feet in height. The machine gun platoon behind G Company entered the water, followed immediately by Lieutenant Huff and E Company. Captain Jeffers led the men of G Company fifty to one hundred yards on to the open ground just north of the river and east of the road into St. Juvin. G Company was followed by the machine gun platoon attached to it. Lieutenant Huff swung his men to the left, wading down the stream and then crawling up the north bank of the river which offered a natural firing position. Some automatic riflemen were pushed a few yards forward on the left of the St. Juvin Road. The plan of attack as directed by Major Jones prior to H hour called for an enveloping movement against St. Juvin; Company G was to flank out the town from the east while E Company struck from the west. H Company was to support G Company, F Company to support the thrust of E Company. By the time that the machine gun platoon in support of E Company had entered the water and had been followed by half of H Company, it was impracticable to use more men along the river bank on each side of the bridge than were already employed. The two platoons of H Company swung to the right of the bridge along the river, the balance of H Company remained under slight cover beside the road running south of the river to Marcq, while F Company deployed on the first ridge near the railroad track.

By this time the volume of enemy machine-gun fire had grown to barrage intensity. G Company suffered practical annihilation. Lieutenant E. N. Leiboult, G Company, and Lieutenant Tate of the Machine Gun Company were both killed, Lieutenant Ostranger of G Company was wounded or gassed and Lieutenant Walter A. Richards of G Company was three times wounded. Captain Lamar Jeffers was first wounded at the beginning of the action when he received a machine-gun bullet in the leg; he continued to direct the action of his company and some minutes later was shot through the jaw. Captain Jeffers then summoned Lieutenants Huff and Carter of H Company to the river bank where he had been brought back by some of his men. He stated that he was compelled to turn the command over to them and advised that they withdraw the men at once before all were killed. Lieutenant Carter assumed command and the position was maintained for an additional twenty minutes. Our men during this entire period saw few Germans and were compelled to choose as targets the doorways and windows of St. Juvin. Some fire was also directed at the crest of the ridge east and west of the town, along which the enemy appeared to be entrenched.

The Attack Abandoned

A little after 6 hours it was decided to abandon a task so obviously hopeless and for which so heavy a price had already been paid. The men were sent back, a squad at a time, with orders to take wide intervals across the fields to the foot of the ridge south of the river where the men were reorganized and dug in along the ridge. When the withdrawal commenced Lieutenant Frank Carter of H Company was seriously wounded. Three officers of E Company became casualties during this fight: 2nd Lieutenant Stone was wounded, and 1st Lieutenants Lisenby and Rogers were gassed. Of the officers who went down to the river on this day all were casualties except two. The enlisted personnel had suffered about fifty per-cent casualties among the five hundred men who entered the fight. During the night of October 10, 1918, and throughout October 11th until after the withdrawal of the Infantry, two of our machine gun platoons maintained a firing position on the south bank of the river near the burned railroad bridge and about 500 meters west of the road bridge used by the Infantry October 11th. One platoon under Lieutenant Gregorie came from Company C, 320th Machine Gun Battalion and the other under Lieutenant Bell from the 326th Infantry Machine Gun Company. The enemy artillery fire became exceedingly heavy just prior to the withdrawal and during the reorganization south of the river. The artillery continued to pound our line on the heights throughout the day.

The Division dossier shows the following messages received at Division Headquarters regarding this attempted river crossing by the 326th Infantry:

From Adjutant, 163rd Inf. Brig. at 7:20 hours, 11 Oct. 1918. Report from Able 1 (C. O. 326th Inf.): "Major Jones reports three companies on the north bank of the river. Heavy casualties. Meeting severe machine-gun fire. Request immediate barrage on St. Juvin and for 100 yds. on each side of town. Jones has crossed the river. Watkins is within a kilometer of the river and Barrett about 1¾ km. from the river. Our line is out and we have to depend on messages."

* * * * *

From Gen. Cronin, 7:35 hours, 11 Oct. 1918. "Many Germans in St. Juvin. Jones' Battalion very heavy casualties from machine gun fire and guns on the north and northeast of St. Juvin. Request that the artillery shell St. Juvin heavily and hill to the northeast. Liaison with artillery very poor."

* * * * *

From Operations Officer, 157th F. A. Brig., 9:15 hours, 11 Oct. 1918. "One battery of 320th F. A. has been firing on hill northeast of St. Juvin since 7 A.M. and one battalion of the 320th F. A. has been firing since 8:40 hours and the latest reports are that the entire regiment has been firing on that same target since 9 hours."

* * * * *

From C. O., 163rd Inf. Brig., 9:40 hours, 11 Oct., 1918. "Cease firing on St. Juvin. Fire on Côte 182 northeast of St. Juvin. Artillery fire reported falling short. Need fire on 182 and counter battery behind 182. NOTE: Gen. Duncan called artillery and directed them to comply."

* * * * *

By radio from 326th Inf. Hdqrs., 9:53 hours, Oct. 11 to Surgeon, 82nd Div. "Number wounded. Send trucks and ambulances to Pylône. (sgd) Kuhland."

* * * * *

From C. O., 163rd Inf. Brig., 11:06 hours, 11th Oct. 1918. "Our artillery activity has improved in the last 20 minutes. Boche artillery seems to be growing less.

Phosgene gas evident in our area. I have directed C. O., 326th Inf., that he must push forward, if necessary, around the gas.''

* * * * *

From Farrady 1 (C. O., 78th Div.) to Albany 1 (C. O., 82nd Div.), 12:30 hours, 11th Oct. 1918. "One Brigade is marching towards Cornay. Another Brigade is moving north 6 or 7 miles south of the leading brigade."

* * * * *

From Major Wainwright, A. C. of S., G-3, 82nd Div., 13 hours 12 minutes at P. C. of 163rd Inf. Brig.: "Gen. Cronin has been unable to put anybody across the river and he is sending troops to the right flank to cross and filter around the east." Col. Johnston told Major Wainwright to tell General Cronin to use the artillery liaison officer for direct work with the artillery and only report important things for our information. Col. Johnston asked if the front line of 163rd Brig. is exposed to very heavy fire. Major Wainwright replied that it was. Col. Johnston directed the Major to tell Gen. Cronin that if considered advisable, the General can withdraw his line back to the foothill facing the river, maintaining liaison with the right of the Division on his left. "Tell Gen. Cronin that his line facing St. Juvin need not be so heavily held, but can be extended by the right flank."

* * * * *

From Col. Johnston to Adjutant, 163rd Inf. Brig., 14:35 hours. "There is a little change over on the right. The right brigade is going to make a push and dig in along the crest of ridge on 85.5 parallel. You push around your right flank. Tell General Cronin would like him to put one battalion Division reserve in the vicinity of Fléville. You should connect with the left of the 164th Inf. Brig. before dark."

* * * * *

From C. O., 157th F. A. Brig., 15:15 hours, 11 Oct. 1918. "During the last hour and a half had several requests from the infantry to counter-battery hostile artillery in the Bois de Loges about 4 km. north of Marcq. About half hour ago I got the Army Artillery in communication and they are now shelling these woods with No. 9 special gas lachrymose. It is believed that this will have the effect of stopping these hostile artillery batteries from annoying our infantry. (Sgd.) Rhodes."

Evidence that the Divisions on our right and left were also meeting with desperate resistance is found in telephonic messages from our liaison officer at 1st Corps:

"77th Division reports strong resistance on its front. Line just south of River Aire. Patrol crossing river met very heavy machine gun and artillery fire."

* * * * *

"5th Corps meeting machine-gun resistance along present line."

* * * * *

"38th French Corps unable to pass Aire or Aisne owing to machine-gun fire."

* * * * *

Message from Col. Johnston to Col. McArthur, 326th Inf., 20:30 hours, 11 Oct. 1918: "Division Commander does not intend to make direct attack on St. Juvin. Portion of the sector in front of St. Juvin to be lightly held by one battalion and one machine gun company and a couple of 37 mm. guns. Orders given Gen. Cronin still stand, namely: move by the east and north and establish contact with the left flank of 164th Inf. Brig. No serious operations contemplated for to-morrow. Please transmit to Gen. Cronin as we are unable to reach him by 'phone at present. Col. McArthur stated that it is difficult to move troops on account of shell fire. Gen. Cronin had instructed him to use his own judgment as to the time and route in moving his men towards the eastern half of the sector. Col. Johnston answered that the intention was to move by the east and north around St. Juvin avoiding direct contact at that point. Col. Johnston informed Col. McArthur that after careful checking right and left all the way to the rear, it was certain that none of our artillery has been firing upon our troops."

The 1st Battalion, 326th Infantry, had been withdrawn from the outpost line La Besogne to Marcq at about 2:30

One group of graves near Sommerance

Horse lines in Aire Valley during the fight

hours, October 11 and placed in reserve near Pylône. The 3rd Battalion remained throughout the night of October 10-11 in a support position south of Marcq. When the order came to swing some troops to the east across the Aire and hook up with the left flank of the 164th Infantry Brigade, General Cronin designated the 3rd Battalion, 326th Infantry, for this duty. The battalion began this move at about 17 hours, October 11, and forded the river at the island northeast of Martincourt Farm. The battalion was subjected to severe artillery fire, which inflicted a number of casualties.

It was after dark when Major Watkins reported to Colonel Whitman. Company M, 326th Infantry, took over a position on the left flank of the 325th Infantry, and Companies I, K and L were placed in position facing St. Juvin along the little stream which runs from the St. Juvin-Sommerance Road to the Aire River.

CHAPTER XII

CLINGING TO THE SOMMERANCE RIDGE

THE night of October 11-12 was a long night. The enemy artillery was periodically active, and a cold, misty dawn found our men in fox holes along Ridge 85.5. No advance was ordered by the Corps, nor did the enemy make any infantry demonstrations against us during that day. Advantage of this pause was taken to organize the ground in depth. In the 325th Infantry, the 1st Battalion was on Ridge 85.5; the 3rd Battalion in support on the Sommerance Road, and the 2nd Battalion in Brigade reserve. Company K, 325th Infantry (Captain Melton), was relieved from its liaison duty with the 1st Division and rejoined the 3rd Battalion. The 1st Battalion (Lieutenant Simpson) of the 327th Infantry occupied Ridge 85.5 on the right of the 325th Infantry, and was supported in echelon by the 2nd Battalion (Major Blanchard) and 3rd Battalion (Lieutenant Prentiss) respectively. Our front lines on the ridge were continually combed by enemy machine-gun fire and the reverse slope was spattered with shell fire. Our men in the outpost line could not raise their heads from the fox holes without drawing fire. Our artillery continued to play on St. Juvin and Hill 182. Five fires were noted burning in different corners of St. Juvin. Report from the Division Observation Post at 11:15 hours, October 12, stated:

"Martincourt Farm is burning, causing many explosions. German artillery harassing roads just north of Fléville with high explosives. Some shrapnel falling just north of Cornay. St. Juvin still on fire."

On the night of October 11-12, the sector on our right was taken over by the 42nd Division, which relieved the 1st Division. The dossier of the 82nd Division contains the following message from General Lindsey dated 13 hours, October 12:

From Anson 1. "Have sent staff officer to get 42nd Division to occupy Sommerance, to whom it belongs."

Telephone message from General Lindsey's P. C. at 13:45 hours reported that Hill 247, southeasterly from Sommerance, was occupied by the 42nd Division. The message adds that among other *matériel* captured on the previous day were thirty machine guns, two anti-tank guns and much ammunition. At 16 hours 20 minutes, Colonel Whitman received word that the 42nd Division had advanced its left elements to a point just southeast of Sommerance. This released the 2nd Battalion of the 325th Infantry, which moved back in Brigade reserve on the Sommerance-Fléville Road.

At 14 hours, October 12, the 1st Battalion, 326th Infantry, relieved the 2nd Battalion of that regiment north of Marcq, where the 2nd Battalion had been holding its ground since its repulse at the road bridge early in the morning of October 11. The 2nd Battalion, when relieved, moved back to a position in support on the heights just south of Marcq.

328TH INFANTRY RECROSSES AIRE RIVER

The history of these operations left the 328th Infantry on the 10th of October in Division reserve and engaged in caring for wounded, burying the dead, and reorganizing the units that had suffered most heavily. The men were badly in need of food and sleep and both were secured during the day. Late in the evening of October 10, orders were received directing the regiment to assemble at the cross-roads near Pylône. Daylight, October 11, found the regiment assembled at that point. Here the men dug in and remained under cover during the day.

At 15 hours, October 11, orders were received directing the 2nd Battalion, 328th Infantry, to report to General Lindsey at Fléville. On arrival at Fléville, the battalion was placed in Divisional reserve and bivouacked on the ridge just north of Fléville. The battalion remained in this position throughout October 12 and 13. After dark on October 11, the 1st Battalion, 328th Infantry, was moved forward from Pylône to a position in the Bois de Marcq, south of the village of Marcq, and in support of the 326th Infantry. On the morning of October 12, the 328th Infantry was directed to report to General Lindsey at Fléville.

Pursuant to this order, the 3rd Battalion moved at once from Pylône to Fléville, where it bivouacked in the woods just east of the 2nd Battalion of the same regiment. The 1st Battalion was withdrawn from the woods south of Marcq about noon of October 12 and took up a position in the woods some 1500 meters east of Fléville along the east and west road, where it occupied fox holes recently abandoned by the enemy. Regimental P. C. was established at Fléville and the men remained hidden from the observation of enemy airplanes. These positions were subjected to shell fire with little intermission. Enemy airplanes were particularly active during this period and for many days thereafter. This constant observation of our positions which our own air service could not prevent resulted in enemy artillery fire of deadly accuracy.

In anticipation of orders for attack on October 13, the Regimental Commander, 325th Infantry, sent the following message, which reached the Division dossier at 17:55 hours, October 12:

"The regimental commander requests that vigorous artillery action including heavy guns be laid on these machine-gun nests and St. Juvin before advance starts as he believes that it is inevitable that the movement will be checked if these machine-gun nests are not destroyed. Colonel Whitman requests that in case of advance a rolling barrage be furnished."

No attack was ordered, however, for October 13 and our troops continued to dig themselves in more deeply along the 85.5 ridge. The dossier contains a number of messages which indicate the situation during October 13.

From General Rhodes to Chief of Staff, 82nd Division, Oct. 13, 1918, 9:20 hours. "Liaison officer with the left regiment, forward battalion, reports that they are very much worried by snipers and machine guns in St. Juvin and suggests that 500 heavy shells might relieve the situation. Do not like to take it up without request from General Cronin. Suggest that we get in touch with General Cronin and see if he desires it. Col. Johnston, Chief of Staff, called General Cronin and repeated the above and asked if he desired any artillery fire on St. Juvin to reduce machine-gun nests and stop sniping. General Cronin said he thought this fire would be useful. Col. Johnston directed him to take it up with his artillery direct and indicate as correctly as possible where the fire would be most useful."

* * * * *

Message from Bonehead 7 (G-3, 1st Corps) to 82nd Division, 10 hours, 13th October. "Orders to the 78th Division have been rescinded yesterday, and instead of moving to our right, they will move west."

* * * * *

From 164th Inf. Brig. at 11:10 hours, Oct. 13. "Fléville and road to the north is being shelled with high explosives and considerable gas. A few casualties have been caused."

* * * * *

Bonehead 3 (Chief of Staff, 1st Corps), to Albany 3 (Chief of Staff, 82nd Div.), 13:50 hours, 13 October. "Instruct artillery commander that he must use a greater proportion of shrapnel as the supply of high explosives is becoming limited. Arrange for the salvaging of machine-gun strips at once. Supply is rapidly becoming exhausted and the matter is critical. Take care of burying the dead. Bonehead 3 was asked if the Pioneer Companies promised could be given to the Division. Bonehead 3 said he would take it up with G-1."

* * * * *

Albany 3 to Bonehead 3, 14 hours, 13 October. "All American dead will be buried to-day. All German dead will be buried to-morrow. Artillery is using prescribed amount of shrapnel. One company of pioneers has reported. Our G-1 has endeavored by all means to obtain the other three companies promised us, but these have never reported here. We are using our machine-gun troops to salvage the strips and we have 150,000 rounds ready for use."

* * * * *

Telephone message from G-2, 1st Army Corps, 14:45 hours, Oct. 13, 1918. "Corps observer reports heavy circulation (German) east and west of road between Verpel and Beffu."

This brief pause in the attack gave an opportunity for a careful check of battle effectives. The very serious losses which had befallen the 164th Infantry Brigade are shown by the following message sent during the morning by General Lindsey to Division Headquarters:

"The unconfirmed effective strength of the 327th Inf. is at present 12 officers and 332 men. This condition requires consideration."

The following message was sent by Lieutenant Colonel

Burr, commanding the 327th Infantry, at 12:35 hours, October 13:

"In regard to list of effectives submitted by me, all of the medical officers of the regiment inform me that of this number 80 per cent are now totally unfit for duty and the other 20 per cent under different circumstances would be placed on sick report. Cause for this disability is sickness, effects of gas and exhaustion. The 80 per cent indicated as totally unfit for duty, they informed me, would be unable to complete any strenuous maneuver. This is no complaint, but simply a statement of facts submitted for your information, and if the circumstances demand the effort, these men will go over the top and go to the limit of their endurance. The same conditions apply to the officers. (sgd) Burr."

The Division Post of Command had been moved on October 9, 1919, from the cellar in Varennes to la Forge Farm, just south of Montblainville and on the west bank of the Aire. On the 12th of October, General Duncan moved his headquarters forward to the château at Chéhéry, fifteen hundred meters south of Fléville. The headquarters of the 157th Field Artillery Brigade moved into a wing of the same château. General Lindsey's P. C. at this time was established in Fléville, while General Cronin moved from Pylône to Cornay on October 12 with an advance P. C. at Martincourt Farm.

On October 13, by Division order, the 325th Infantry reverted to the 163rd Infantry Brigade and the 328th Infantry passed back into the 164th Infantry Brigade.

Enemy planes were exceedingly active throughout October 13 and moderate enemy artillery fire continued upon our lines.

Enemy Counter-Attack Repulsed

At 16 hours, the enemy laid down a rolling artillery barrage and followed it with an infantry assault. The main force of this blow fell upon the right of the 325th Infantry and left of the 327th Infantry. The barrage rolled over our front line and covered our men with mud, but caused few casualties. Our artillery, in response to calls from the infantry, laid down an effective counter-barrage which fell with great promptness and accuracy. This timely assistance, coupled with the rapid fire of our infantry and machine gunners, smashed the attack before it got at hand's grips with our line. The Germans could be seen running back, and some were observed to throw away their rifles. The enemy suffered many losses in this repulse.

The progress of the counter-attack is shown by messages in the Division dossier:

Message from Austin (Hq., 163rd Inf. Brig.), 16:05 hours, 13 Oct., 1918. "German barrage falling south of St. Juvin on 326th Inf. position. Enemy making counter-attack. General Duncan immediately 'phoned General Rhodes above message, ordering him to put all his guns on position along parallel 86.5 between 98 and 104. 320th F. A. 'phoned that they had been requested to fire on St. Juvin and inquired if they were authorized to do so, it being out of their sector. General Duncan replied 'Yes.'"

* * * * *

Telephone message from Division O. P., 16:10 hours, 13 Oct., 1918. "At 16 hours the Germans started a barrage on the north bank of the river. They are now advancing in a local counter-attack. I can see several hundred men in open formation advancing over ridge between 297.4-285.4 and 298.0-285.5. They seem to be on the ridge advancing south in open formation. It looks as if they were coming over the ridge down to the river valley."

* * * * *

From Lt. Jones, 164th Inf. Brig. Hdqrs, 16:30 hours, 13 October, 1918. "Boche barrage has cut off our front line and Boche coming over. Request planes at once."

* * * * *

Major Wainwright, G-3, 82nd Div., by telephone to

G-3, 1st Corps. "Request aeroplanes at once. Urgent. Rush. Combat planes."

* * * * *

From 163rd Inf. Brig., 16:35 hours, 13 Oct., 1918. "1st Bn., 326th Inf., reports that the enemy has laid a barrage down on his side of the river. No damage done thus far. Our own artillery is coming back well. No signs yet of enemy infantry activity."

* * * * *

Message from 164th Inf. Brig., 16:40 hours, Oct. 13, 1918. "Colonel Whitman reports that German planes are flying low over his front lines and firing machine guns into his lines. He requests aeroplanes from Corps to drive them off. When asked about the progress of the Germans in the counter-attack, Lt. Jones stated that Col. Whitman said the Boche barrage cut off his front line, the barrage falling between the 1st and 2nd lines. He did not know what was happening further than that. Lt. Jones said it took our artillery about two minutes to get to work."

* * * * *

Message to General Lindsey from Col. Johnston, 16:45 hours, 13 Oct., 1918. "Have you anything in the block of woods about 500 meters west of Sommerance?" (Reply) "I have a reserve and 10 machine guns. I have notified people on my left of the counter-attack. Things are going all right." (Col. Johnston.) "If you have troops and machine guns in this bunch of woods, your men on the slope of the hill should be well taken care of."

* * * * *

Report from Division O. P. at 16:55 hours, Oct. 13, 1918. "Boche artillery has weakened. Boche infantry advancing at about 97.4 to 97.6 and 86.4. Our artillery still firing. The Boche seem to be on this side of the hill coming between the St. Georges and St. Juvin Road. Our men seem to be behind little patches of woods along 86.97."

* * * * *

Col. Johnston to Gen. Lindsey, 17 hours, Oct. 13, 1918. "The Division Commander directs you to take charge of the operations on Ridge 85.5 in front of your sector. The Brigade on your left is being directed to comply with your request for troops and is informed that you will command in this operation."

* * * * *

Colonel Johnston to General Cronin: "The Division Commander has directed General Lindsey to take command of troops in this present attack on the other side of the river on Ridge 85.5, and you will comply with his request for troops. This refers only to present attack. General Cronin replied that there was no counter-attack on his left."

* * * * *

From 42nd Div., 17:05 hours, 13 Oct., 1918. "Infantry did not come up in our front following the bombardment now going on. Hostile aeroplanes dropping propaganda."

* * * * *

From Hq., 157th F. A. Brig., 17:15 hours, 13 October, 1918. "3rd Bn. Forward Observer, 319th F. A., reports that the Germans are retreating across the zone on which the 319th F. A. is firing. The 319th F. A. now lifting their fire 500 meters. The German barrage, which was very severe at first, is decreasing considerably. Col. Johnston said that he thought it would be good to shoot shrapnel on the road from St. Juvin to St. Georges. He thought that as the enemy began to fall back on that road short bursts of shrapnel would come in handy. Col. Johnston asked how quickly the artillery got information of the counter-attack and was informed that when Artillery Headquarters called the Artillery Regiment, it was found that our barrage had already been put down 200 meters in front of the infantry. Col. Johnston was informed that this operation was seriously interfering with the intended cutting of enemy wire by artillery and was asked if there would be time in the morning for observing fire. Col. Johnston replied that he thought there would be time."

* * * * *

Message from 164th Inf. Brig., 17:20 hours, Oct. 13, 1918. "Boche barrage stopping and Boche have been driven back in front of the 327th Inf. Positions held by 326th and 325th Inf. and everything is as it was. Our artillery barrage most effective."

* * * * *

Report from Division O. P. 17:25 hours, 13 Oct., 1918. "At 17 hours the Boche started new barrage on Sommerance-St. Juvin Road which at this time has practically stopped. Was able to follow German advance to top of ridge along parallel 85.5. Enemy then lost to sight in the smoke this side of the ridge. Too dark to see now. Only harassing fire by artillery."

* * * * *

From General Rhodes to General Duncan, 17:30 hours, 13 Oct., 1918. "320th F. A. observers report Boche retiring. The counter-preparation has been stopped and we are now pursuing them with shrapnel. On the left the Boche collected in St. Juvin, but did not attack from St. Juvin."

Preparing for Attack of October 14, 1918

Meanwhile plans were going forward throughout October 13 for a coordinated attack along the entire front of the 1st Army. Within the 82nd Division a number of troop movements were ordered, including relief of the 327th Infantry by the 328th Infantry. Colonel Wetherill's regiment had remained in bivouac, concealed along the wooded ridge just north of Fléville. On the afternoon of October 13 the Regimental Commander, Battalion Commanders and Company Commanders of the 1st Battalion made reconnaissance of the terrain north to Sommerance during the heavy shell fire of the German counter-attack. Shortly after dark the battalions drew their iron rations and ammunition and marched by battalions northward. The roads were heavily shelled and a number of casualties were suffered during this advance. Regimental P. C. moved from Fléville to a position near the crossroads about 250 meters south of Sommerance. A little after midnight of October 13-14 the 1st Battalion reached Sommerance and relieved the forward Battalion of the 327th Infantry on the 85.5 ridge.

During the night of October 13 the 2nd Battalion of the 326th Infantry moved from the support position south of Marq through Cornay to Fléville and thence along the Fléville-St. Juvin Road to a ravine about 500 meters south of the St. Juvin-Sommerance Road. Here the Battalion was in support of the 3rd Battalion of the 326th Infantry. Regimental P. C. of the 326th Infantry was established in the gravel quarry several hundred meters north of Fléville. While making a reconnaissance east of Marq, Lt. Thomas C. Carter of Company B, 320th Machine Gun Battalion, was instantly killed. The dossier reveals an interesting discussion of the speed at which the Infantry should advance behind the artillery barrage.

Telephone message from G-3, 77th Division at 17:55 hours, 13 October, 1918, to 82nd Division:

"Stated he would like to arrange for the artillery barrage. Calls attention to the change in the Corps order and to the rate of the barrage in the adjoining Corps (5th Corps), and the instructions from 1st Corps that Divisions will arrange independently the pace of the barrage. He thought it advisable for all Divisions to take the rate adopted by the 5th Corps." (100 meters in 6 minutes.)

Colonel Johnston reminded G-3 of the 77th Division that:

"Divisions on the right are fighting in woods where progress will necessarily be slow. Furthermore, the area in front of the 82nd Division is open and there are dangerous places which we would like to get over quickly."

Colonel Johnston suggested that:

"It would be desirable to arrange a definite zone for the artillery so that there would be no danger of overlapping."

At 20:20 hours, October 13, General Lindsey was asked

by Colonel Johnston at what pace he believed the advance should be made. The General replied:

"Considering the nature of the country in front of me, 100 meters in 3 minutes," and added that he did not care to linger while he was going.

At 21:30 hours, October 13, a message arrived stating that:

"Orders from the Army are that the rate of advance in pending operations will be 100 meters in six minutes."

ORDERS FOR ATTACK OF OCTOBER 14, 1918

The 82nd Division Field Order No. 24 was issued at 22 hours, October 13. Under Par. 1 (Information of the Enemy and Intention of the High Command), it was stated:

"(a) The enemy has been driven north of the line Sommerance-Aire River.
"(b) The 1st Army resumes its attack on 'D' day at 'H' hour. (Secret instructions provided that the attack would be made at 8:30 hours, Oct. 14.) The 5th Corps on our immediate right breaches the hostile lines. The 1st Corps supports the left flank of the attack and pivoting on its left maintains its advance on successive objectives. The 77th Division is charged with taking St. Juvin, attacking from the south and east." The boundaries of the 82nd Division specified were: east—Sommerance, exclusive, Imécourt, inclusive, Sivry-lez-Buzancy, exclusive. West —Marcq, inclusive, St. Juvin, exclusive, Verpel, exclusive, Harricourt, inclusive.

The order provided that the battalion of the 326th Infantry in the front line south of St. Juvin cross the river when relieved by the 77th Division. It was arranged between the brigade commanders of the adjoining brigades of the 77th and 82nd Divisions that the relief of the 1st Battalion, 326th Infantry, in Marcq should be complete before H hour. The 82nd Division Field Order prescribed that, within the Division, the attack should be made by the 328th Infantry on the right, 325th Infantry in the center and the 326th Infantry on the left. The 327th Infantry was placed in reserve in rear of the 328th Infantry. All regiments except the 327th Infantry and the 328th Infantry were to be formed in column of battalions with approximately 500 meters' distance between battalions. The two regiments excepted were so depleted that each regiment consisted of less than one battalion in battle effectives. The rate of advance for the infantry was set for 100 meters in six minutes. The artillery was ordered to cut enemy wire at a number of specified points. In addition to this mission, the artillery was required to use non-persistent gas before H minus 4 hours on ravines and woods. All roads of approach and important crossroads were to be strongly shelled. The artillery preparation for attack was to start at H minus 2 hours. The artillery was further charged with the protection of the left flank from St. Juvin and Hill 182 by the use of high explosive and smoke shells. One battery of the 321st Field Artillery was to be at the disposal of the C. O., 163rd Infantry Brigade, to execute special fires, and one battery of the 320th Field Artillery to perform a like duty for the 164th Infantry Brigade. At H hour a deep barrage was to precede the infantry advance by 300 meters, to be fired from H to H plus 60 minutes on the extreme right and conform to the infantry advance. This barrage was to be taken up again at H plus 1 hour and 30 minutes and continued until the infantry had attained the Corps objective. Smoke shells were to be included in this barrage. One piece of 75 mm. was to accompany each front line battalion and such guns were to report by 6 hours, October 14. E Company of the 1st Gas Regiment was assigned to support the attack of the 164th Brigade with smoke and thermite. A plan was prepared for long range machine-gun fire in support of the advance. The 2nd Battalion, 325th Infantry, and the 319th Machine Gun Battalion were named for the Division reserve and the latter participated in the long range barrages. The axis of liaison was Chéhéry-Fléville-St. Juvin. The plan of Air Service was stated to be without change except that Chéhéry was specified as the dropping ground for weighted messages.

CHAPTER XIII

INTO THE KRIEMHILDE-STELLUNG

OCTOBER 14 proved to be another of the outstanding days in the battle experience of the 82nd Division—a day in which the Division gained much territory, took many prisoners and paid a round price for its important successes. The march of events will be examined first from the messages which reached Division Headquarters where they were recorded in the dossier.

At 5 hours, October 14, 1918, Headquarters of the 163rd Infantry Brigade reported that their "advance P. C. is now in Fléville." At 5:50 hours, October 14, Army Artillery phoned the 157th Field Artillery Brigade Headquarters and asked if they could be of any assistance to our barrage. Our artillery replied that "Army Artillery had already been requested to look after counter-battery fire and that the 82nd Division Artillery was looking after its own end of the work." 8:10 hours, October 14, the Adjutant of the 163rd Infantry Brigade stated that "the 325th and 326th Infantry report everything is all right." 7:30 hours, October 14, the 164th Infantry Brigade "reports that hostile balloons and aeroplanes are in vicinity of 328th Infantry. Request that our planes be sent to their relief. Message communicated to Aero liaison officer."

82nd Division Liaison Officer with 77th Division—8:50 hours, 14 Oct., 1918.

"No changes in position since report at 3 hours this morning. Our artillery has been very active. Considerable enemy artillery within the lines of this Division."

From Capt. Webster, Adjt. 164th Inf. Brig.—8:50 hours, 14 Oct., 1918.

"42nd Div. artillery falling short on the road west of Sommerance, in our brigade area."

Major Wainwright, G-3, to G-3, 42nd Div.

"We have just received report from our forward observers that your artillery is falling short west of Sommerance."

From 164th Inf. Brig.—8:50 hours, 14 Oct., 1918.

"Everything started off all right at H hour. In touch with 42nd Division on our right. (sgd) Tomassello."

From 163rd Inf. Brig.—9:05 hours, 14 Oct., 1918.

"Col. Whitman reports enemy planes have been flying very freely over his lines and are still doing so. They are not being interfered with to any extent either by our planes or anti-aircraft guns." NOTE: Major Wainwright directed Air Service liaison officer to report matter to Air Service.

Telephone message from Division O. P.—9:10 hours, 14 Oct., 1918.

"We have advanced about 1 km. We are now on Hill 230. Some of our men seen there. We are along ridge at 98.0-85.5 and everything is apparently going good. German barrage is behind our men about at the jumping-off position. The Germans are shelling with gas."

Telephone message from 164th Inf. Brig.—9:30 hours, 14 Oct., 1918.

"Prisoners belonging to 45th Reserve Division captured east of St. Juvin by 326th Inf."

Telephone message from Division O. P.—9:45 hours, 14 Oct., 1918.

"Our men along ridge at 98.1-85.5 and are rushing forward at double time. They are going over the ridge. Prisoners coming back and there seems to be a lot of them."

From Capt. Webster, 164th Inf. Brig.—9:50 hours, 14, Oct., 1918.

"328th Inf. reports 166th Inf. came 300 yds. into their sector and 328th Inf. was subjected to double barrage in front of advancing infantry of 42nd Div. 328th Inf. connected up with 166th Inf. and 325th Inf. went forward as per schedule."

9:50 hours, 14 Oct., 1918—By radio to G-3, 1st Corps, G-3, 77th Div., G-3, 42nd Div.

"First objective obtained at 9:10 hours. (sgd) G-3, 82nd Div." NOTE: The 1st objective was an east and west line about 500 meters south of the St. Juvin-St. Georges Road.

From Adjutant, 163rd Inf. Brig., 10:10 hours, 14 Oct., 1918.

"German prisoner states: 'We expect an armistice in a few days.'"

Col. Johnston to Gen. Lindsey, 10:15 hours, 14 Oct., 1918.

"The next plan is to put the 155's on that right switch trench; that is the trench on your front. We will smear it completely and look to you to follow there and flank out the trenches to your left. In other words turn them by your right flank and let the brigade on your left go slow to their wire."

From Col. Johnston, to C. G., 164th Inf. Brig., by radio —11 hours, 14 Oct.

"Will holding of Division reserve on crossroads just west of Sommerance interfere with your plans? (sgd) Johnston."

Aeroplane message dropped at 11 hours.

"At 10:40 hours, infantry showed panels at U7 U9—U9 Q0—R1 Q3—R4 Q4. At 10:45, infantry showed panels at L7 U8—L7 Q0—L8 Q2. These advance troops are being heavily shelled. On crest of hill at R5 U5, many hostile shells falling. Time 10:45. On Hill 182, no shells falling. No panels seen or movement seen. Some gas being used against our troops. Some anti-aircraft fire received over St. Juvin. We drove one enemy plane back which was over our lines. Visibility very poor. (sgd) H. T. Fleeson, 12th Aero Squadron."

Telephone message from 163rd Inf. Brig.—11 hours, 14 Oct., 1918.

"1st Bn. of 325th Inf. captured 2nd Lieutenant belonging to 30th Inf., 15th Bavarian Division. Prisoner came in to lines last night preceding his regiment. The Division has been in rest up north. This confirms presence of 15th Bavarian Division which was first identified by another prisoner captured last night."

From 163rd Inf. Brig.—11:04 hours, 14 Oct., 1918.

"C. O., 326th Inf. reports that his present front line is north and east of St. Juvin."

From 163rd Inf. Brig. at 11:23 hours, 14th Oct., 1918.

"At 11:05 hours Wittenmeyer (Brig. Gen., commanding right brigade, 77th Div.) seems not to have crossed the Aire River. I have just given him information again about fords and foot bridges. 326th Inf. advancing east of St. Juvin. Support battalion moving to cover the left flank. One pounders of 326th Inf. fighting successfully near edge of St. Juvin."

Aeroplane message dropped 11:27 hours, 14 Oct., 1918.

"Friendly troops advancing north of St. Juvin-Sommerance Road at 11:15 hours. Arched over area at 10:45 hours. Few fires visible. (sgd) Pilot Lt. Beaucher, Observer Lt. Patterson."

Memorandum to Capt. Morgan from Capt. Dunlap, 11:30 hours, 14th Oct.

"The Chief of Staff directs that you move message center immediately on receipt of this message from Cornay to Fléville. I am sending this message by the chauffeur of the automobile that will move you. Send couriers notifying brigades that you are on the move."

From Capt. Patton, Division O. P. at 12 hours, 14 October.

"It is certain that American troops were on the Kriemhilde-Stellung line some time ago. The support lines are passing there now and our troops are occupying it in force."

Telephone Message from 163rd Brigade, 12 hours, 14 October.

"One Sergeant, one Corporal, one Private, Company 3, 32nd Regiment, 15th Bavarian Division; also 2 Privates, 1st Machine Gun Company, same Regiment and Division captured by 1st Battalion 325th Infantry on hill east of St. Juvin. The Sergeant has been in America before the war and left America to fight because he loved Germany and hated the Americans."

From General Cronin, 163rd Infantry Brigade, 12 hours, 14 October.

"Request permission for the use of the 2nd Battalion of 325th Infantry now in Division reserve. The 1st Battalion, 326th Infantry, south of the river in front of St. Juvin has not arrived east of the river. Apparently it is held back by the fact that the 77th Division has not crossed north. I want the Division Reserve in case I need it to protect my left flank." NOTE: "General Cronin informed that he might use the Division Reserve in case of absolute necessity."

From 163rd Brigade.

"Major Watkins, 3rd Battalion, 326th Infantry, to C.O. 326th Infantry. Advanced to east edge of St. Juvin. Took

OFFICIAL HISTORY OF 82ND DIVISION   139

50 prisoners, captured many machine guns. Had few casualties. Heavy enemy artillery on me now. Nothing from 77th Division. 'Phone down.''

From General Rhodes, Headquarters 157th F. A. Brigade—12 hours, 14 October.

"The Artillery Liaison Officer with the 328th Infantry reports at 12 hours through commanding officer 320th Field Artillery that an accompanying gun of that Regiment under Lieut. Gunter has in the course of this morning's battle knocked out one machine-gun pill box, and that the gun has been adopted by the Infantry which it accompanies. It is being carried along close to the front lines of our advancing infantry."

From 164th Infantry Brigade at 12 hours, 14 October.
"34 prisoners from the 15th Bavarian Division captured by C Company, 328th Infantry."

From Major Watkins, 326th Infantry, relayed by 163rd Infantry Brigade, 12:35 hours.
"I am at 90.5-85.9. Support lines here. Front line companies 300 yards north. One officer killed and 4 officers wounded. No contact with 77th Division. One platoon 325th Infantry got in on our left; Lieutenant says he is in his right place."

From General Lindsey to Capt. Webster, at 12:18 hours, 14 October.
"Reports from prisoners taken by 328th Infantry indicate our front line at 11:30 hours was within the wire near trenches at 86.7."

From General Lindsey, 12:45 hours, 14 October.
"Reference yours concerning post of reserve Battalion near crossroads west of Sommerance. That will be O. K."

General Cronin to General Duncan, 12:50 hours, 14 October.
"This Brigade is approaching its objective in good form.

General Cronin has no present need for Division Reserve. He will not use it unless pressed and will give notice at once if he should use it."

Telephone report from Lieut. Doll, Aide-de-Camp to General Lindsey, 13:50 hours, 14 October.

"Have been to the nearest hill 230 and observed from there up to the west of St. Georges. The 328th going good as far as I can see. Can not see over second Hill 230, which is on my level. Troops on the right (42nd Division) are going a little slow; on the left they are keeping up very well."

From Adjutant, 163rd Brigade at 13:40 hours.

"Division Reserve has been ordered by General Cronin to position east of St. Juvin in support."

From 163rd Brigade at 13:45 hours, 14 October.

"Last report from Major Watkins states front line is now in the Ravin-aux-Pierres."

Colonel Johnston to Adjutant; 163rd Brigade at 13:55 hours, 14 October.

"Locate the Battalion of the 326th Infantry that is lost (1st Bn.). It becomes the Division Reserve Battalion and will be moved to the crossroads 300 yards west of Sommerance and will be held at the disposal of the Division Commander only."

From Adjutant, 163rd Inf. Brig., 13:12 hours, 14 October.

"General Wittenmeyer reports that 77th Division has not yet crossed Aire River. 326th Inf. reports that there are numbers of enemy planes flying over front lines. This fact probably accounts for a good deal of the accurate artillery fire which the enemy has been directing on the 326th Inf."

13:25 hours, 14 October.

"Captain Morgan reports that Division Message center

is now at Fléville and will be ready for business at 13:30 hours."

Adjutant, 163rd Inf. Brig. reports at 14:55 hours, 14 Oct., that:

"Headquarters, 326th Inf. is at 99.2-82.8. Headquarters, 325th Inf. at 98.7-85.1. Headquarters, 163rd Inf. Brig. Fléville."

Adjutant, 164th Inf. Brig. reports at 14:50 hours, 14 October.

"Headquarters 328th Infantry at 99.6-84.55; 327th Inf. at 99.7-83.3; headquarters 164th Infantry Brigade, also the headquarters of 319th Machine Gun Bn., 320th Machine Gun Bn. and 321st Machine Gun Bn. all in Fléville."

The messages in the Division dossier for the remainder of October 14 will be discussed later in this chapter. Meanwhile, it is desirable to follow more closely the progress of the attacking regiments of this Division.

328TH INFANTRY ON OCTOBER 14, 1918

The 328th Infantry, pursuant to Field Orders No. 24, occupied about a kilometer of front on the right flank of the 82nd Division. The 1st Battalion constituted the assaulting unit. At 2 hours, October 14, it had relieved the 327th Infantry on a line about 500 meters north of the Sommerance-St. Juvin Road, with the right flank of the attack a little west of a north and south line through Sommerance. C Company was on the right and D Company on the left, with A and B Companies in support of C and D Companies respectively. The 328th Machine Gun Company (1st Lieutenant De Saussure) was attached to the 1st Battalion, together with the 37 mm. and trench mortar platoons of the Headquarters Company. The 2nd and 3rd Battalions were in support along the St. Juvin-Sommerance Road. A platoon of C Company, 321st Machine Gun Battalion, was attached to the support and the other platoons of that company cooperated with the combat liaison unit between the 328th and 325th Infantry. Early in the morning a detachment of two non-commissioned officers and two privates were sent from M Company as runners to the 166th Infantry. One non-commissioned officer was wounded and one private killed while effecting this liaison.

Just prior to H hour, Regimental P. C. was moved up to a hole on the south side of the St. Juvin-Sommerance Road. At 8:30 our artillery laid down a strong creeping barrage, and a moment later a portion of the barrage of the 42nd Division fell upon our right flank and elements of the 166th Infantry came from south of Sommerance, overlapping our line for two hundred meters west of Sommerance.

As our infantry arose from the fox holes and started to attack, it was met with very heavy artillery and machine-gun fire and considerable gas was laid down in the vicinity of Sommerance. The machine-gun fire was particularly severe, and we suffered many casualties before our troops had advanced one hundred meters. 1st Lt. J. W. Hatton, leading the front platoon of C Company, was instantly killed while taking a rifle shot at an enemy machine-gun nest. Lieutenants Folsom and Coombs of D Company were both severely wounded. Four sergeants in D Company went down before this fire. Both C and D Companies advanced slowly, working around and silencing machine-gun nests which they found scattered in the little patches of woods or hidden by small folds of the ground. The leading companies pushed through the wire which marked the main line of the Kriemhilde-Stellung position about 500 meters southwest from St. Georges. B and A Companies followed in support with two platoons of H Company detailed as moppers-up covering the rear.

When D Company had crossed the St. Juvin-St. Georges Road, B Company went forward and filled in a gap between the 328th and 325th Infantry. At this point Lieutenant Royal of B Company was severely wounded, but continued to direct his platoon. 1st Lt. Y. Lyons Joel, who commanded the two "mopping up" platoons of H Company, was severely wounded by shrapnel and died later in a base hospital. The 166th Infantry had failed to make similar progress on our right, and as a result the right flank of the 328th Infantry became exposed to enfilade fire from the east.

Shortly after the jump-off, Major Boyle moved his P. C. forward with the attack, accompanied by Lieutenant De Saussure of the Machine Gun Company, who had been previously wounded but refused to be evacuated. But a short distance had been covered when Lieutenant De Saussure was instantly killed by a shell fragment. Regimental P. C. at this time moved to a cellar in the western part of Sommerance, from which point it was in wire communication with Battalion and Brigade P. C.'s.

At about 11 hours, the 2nd Battalion moved forward in support, following the 1st Battalion at 500 meters. G and H Companies were leading with E and F Companies in support. The 3rd Battalion followed the 2nd at the same distance. The enemy laid down a heavy barrage across the line of the advancing battalions. At 13 hours, the 2nd Battalion executed a passing of the lines of the 1st Battalion and G Company, with a platoon of H Company worked three or four hundred meters north of the St. Juvin-Sommerance Road. The 166th Infantry was a kilometer southeast of this point and the fire received from the vicinity of St. Georges, as well as from the front, made further progress impracticable. In consequence, the regimental front line was established just south of the St. Juvin-St. Georges Road. This line was held by the companies of the 2nd Battalion, plus A Company, while C Company's line was refused to establish combat liaison with the left of the 42nd Division. B and D Companies were withdrawn in support. The regiment was extended to the utmost in an effort to cling to the advancing 325th Infantry on its left and maintain contact with the 166th Infantry, which had been definitely checked on the right.

The 1st and 2nd Battalion P. C.'s were consolidated in a single shell hole in rear of the line, and while this move was being accomplished Lt. Robert F. Mitchell of the 328th Machine Gun Company was killed. The strength of both the 1st and 2nd Battalions had been greatly reduced by casualties and the two units were combined under Major Boyle as an operating Battalion, although all the companies retained their identity. The 3rd Battalion, now reduced to ninety men, dug in on a position a kilometer north of the St. Juvin-Sommerance Road. During October 14 the 327th Infantry, in support, took up a position along the Sommerance-St. Juvin Road.

325TH INFANTRY ON OCTOBER 14, 1918

The 325th Infantry, because of its advanced position on the crest of the ridge 85.5, was already on the first objective assigned by the Corps and, in accordance with the time schedule prescribed, did not attack until 10 hours. The 1st Battalion, 325th Infantry (Captain Castle), led the assault, supported by the Stokes Mortars and 37 mm. platoons. The 325th Machine Gun Company (Captain Williams) sent six guns to the 1st Battalion and four to the 3rd Battalion which supported the attack at a distance of about 1200 meters. The 2nd Battalion was held in

Division Reserve. The assault Battalion, following closely behind an excellent barrage, advanced for one and one-half kilometers, reaching the St. Juvin-St. Georges Road and the crest immediately north of the road. The 3rd Battalion also advanced and later the 2nd Battalion moved forward in line of combat groups as if on drill. Some of the messages received by Colonel Whitman during the morning indicate the progress of events.

"10:30. 1st Battalion started over the top as per schedule. No information received from front line at this time, but rear waves and support Battalion can be seen from this position. About 40 prisoners have passed through our hands. CASTLE."

"10:59. Reports show line advancing as per schedule. Prisoners are seen coming over the hill in large groups. Support Battalion is now passing my P. C. I will move forward at once with my personnel except adjutant and establish new P. C. Everything looks roseate. CASTLE."

"12:03. Have established new P. C. at 98.6-85.8 in ravine. Front line is being held up. Meeting stiff resistance from ridge north of St. Juvin-St. Georges Road. 3rd Battalion should be pushed forward to our first objective and make preparation to resist counter-attack. CASTLE."

"12:45. C. O. 3rd Battalion. Report position of your companies. Castle is meeting resistance from ridge north of St. Juvin-St. Georges Road. Send forward to see if he needs support and put one company in if necessary. WHITMAN."

"C. O. 325th Infantry, 13:20. Co. L extends right of leading Battalion of 326th which is halted on St. Juvin-St. Georges Road. Co. L is on the road from 98.1-98.4. Co. K from 98.4-99 on parallel 86.2. Co. M is 300 yards behind L's right. Co. I is 200 yards behind K's right. Have pushed one platoon Co. L out 150 yards to cover the

1st Battalion left. The leading Battalion of 326th Infantry say they are ordered to hold this road. They are digging in on it. Our Regiment can not go on without putting left flank in air. PIERCE."

"14 hours. To C. O. 3rd Battalion. Disregard distance of 1200 meters from 1st Battalion. Take up position on ridge in rear of Castle. Dig in and hold to the last if attacked. Get in touch with 328th Infantry on your right at once. WHITMAN."

"From C. O. 3rd Bn. 326th Inf. to C. O. 325th Inf. 16:00. Occupy road to your left and am under heavy M. G. fire from St. Juvin, flank wholly unprotected. Will let you know of any change. WATKINS."

From Major Hawkins after a reconnaissance:

"1. Our 1st Battalion has passed beyond observation over ridge through parallel 86.8.

"2. Our 3rd Battalion has 2 companies on line of road from about 98.3-86.3 to about 98.9-86.6, and 2 companies in support on reverse slope about 400 meters southeast.

"3. The 326th Infantry front line Battalion has prolonged Major Pierce's line on the road leaving left of our 1st Battalion unprotected.

"4. This Battalion will move east of St. Juvin as directed after reconnaissance. HAWKINS."

"14:30 to C. O. 1st Bn. Good work. Hold what you have. The 326th has been ordered to push forward to cover your left, and the 328th to cover your right. Do not go too far ahead of your flanks. Pierce will support you. Give me exact position of your lines. Do you need ammunition and if so at what point? WHITMAN."

"15:45. To C. O. 325th. No change in dispositions since I wrote except that company B 320th M. G. Bn. is placing guns in new support. Support Battalion 328th is on my immediate right. Everything standing still. I surmise advance waits on St. Juvin although A and D both wanted artillery on final objective a while ago. Boche plane flying straight back and forth along our line, I think marking it for fire. None of our planes in sight. PIERCE."

"15:50. To C. O. 1st Bn. The 326th has been ordered to push forward to protect your left. Artillery has been called for 500 yards north of your position. Is 328th as far advanced as you on your right? Am sending ammunition to your P. C. Hold what you have until your flanks are covered. Fine work. WHITMAN."

"15:07. D Co. reports short of both kinds ammunition. Suggests details from reserve battalion be sent in sufficient numbers to carry 7000 rounds both rifle and Chauchat ammunition to each company. Enemy planes have been driven off by our planes, but not until they had done serious damage. D Co. reports heavy losses. B Co. is now in front line. Request C. O., 3rd Bn., be instructed to place two companies in support of my front line on the St. Juvin-St. Georges Road at once. I have instructed my companies to dig in for the night. Request artillery fire heavy barrage for ten minutes at intervals of 50 minutes and harassing fire between times during entire night. 326th Inf. stopped on St. Juvin-St. Georges Road and say they have instructions to go no further. Our flanks are exposed. Our front line extends from 98.2-86.5 to 99.2-86.9 (sgd) Castle."

An excellent statement of the general condition of all our troops at the close of operations on October 14 is found in the following summary by Colonel Whitman, taken from the history of the 325th Infantry:

"Nightfall found us well north of St. Juvin-St. Georges Road and dug in, utilizing shell holes for the combat groups. Men were tired and wet and cold. Casualties very heavy.

"Two Stokes Mortars and 2 Pounders were placed near the St. Juvin-St. Georges Road and were used against the Ravin aux Pierres and woods north thereof. Stokes fired 300 rounds. Pounders fired 850 rounds.

"Rations and water were brought up at night but it was a difficult matter to get them distributed to the men. Details were sent to the crossroads for food but it was a slow process under shell fire. Many men had lost their raincoats and overcoats. A cold persistent rain reduced their spirits—the shell holes were deep in mud and water. It was a time that called for the best stuff in every officer and man.

"Our positions had undoubtedly been thoroughly studied by enemy planes during the day. Our front battalion was conspicuous on the ridge north of the main road; its flanks were unsupported. The position was an exposed one, facing a very strong position of the Boche.

"During the day the following officers were casualties:

KILLED

1st Lt. William P. Spratt
1st Lt. Norman A. Garrett
2nd Lt. George W. Huston

WOUNDED

Major Thomas L. Pierce
1st Lt. J. H. Thompson
2nd Lt. Everett Shepherd

"This made the third day on which Major Pierce had been wounded. The very serious nature of the wound received this day compelled his evacuation."

326TH INFANTRY ON OCTOBER 14, 1918

The 326th Infantry attacked at 8:30 hours, advancing on the left of the Divisional sector on a front of about 600 meters, extending east from St. Juvin, exclusive. The 3rd Battalion (Major Watkins) was the assault unit, with Companies K and M leading on the right and left respectively. Companies I and L were in support. Two platoons of Company K were maneuvered to protect the left flank against fire coming from St. Juvin. This platoon entered the eastern outskirts of the village, destroyed several machine-gun nests, captured fifteen machine guns, one cannon and about seventy-five prisoners. This successful exploit enabled the Regiment to move forward past St. Juvin to its objective.

The advance of this battalion was supported by A Company, 320th M. G. Bn. (Captain Shivers). Of the many gallant deeds which were performed by all ranks during this attack we must credit here that of Lt. Wm. C. Acheson, commanding the 3rd Platoon of this machine-gun company. The platoon was operating with the right flank of the battalion. At 9:30 hours the machine gunners captured and sent to the rear thirty-six prisoners. As the advance continued, more and more pressure fell upon the battalion's right flank. All but a few men in this platoon were killed or wounded by 10:30 hours. At this time, all the men at one gun had been killed or wounded. Lieutenant Acheson at once took charge of this gun himself and continued firing without assistance until he also was killed.

The advance continued to the St. Juvin-St. Georges Road, where it was held up awaiting the arrival of supporting troops on the right and left. A position was organized with Companies K, L and M on the road and Company I perpendicular to the road, facing St. Juvin. The 2nd Battalion in support followed the assaulting battalion, taking a position in the ravine across the St. Juvin-Fléville Road, just north of its junction with the road to Sommerance. Here it remained until about 16 hours, at which time it moved forward to protect the left flank of the 3rd Battalion along the St. Juvin-St. Georges Road. The 1st Battalion, 326th Infantry, was not released from its position north of Marcq and west of the river until a little after 13 hours, October 14, when it was relieved by elements of the 77th Division.

The plan of attack had contemplated the relief of this battalion during the night of October 13-14, and following such relief the battalion was to be used as a reserve in the operations east of the river. As has already been indicated in the messages of the dossier, considerable anxiety was felt because of the non-appearance of the battalion, until the cause for the delay was made known. The 1st Battalion forded the Aire River on the afternoon of the 14th in small groups because of the intense artillery fire. While en route, orders reached this unit directing it to take station at Sommerance in Division reserve.

The 326th Infantry Regimental P. C. was moved to a ravine south of the St. Juvin-Sommerance Road at a point 99.3-83.3 and on the morning of the 15th moved to the ravine at the junction of the St. Juvin-Fléville-Sommerance Roads, known throughout the division as the "Culvert" or the "Bloody Angle."

A message from the 1st Battalion, 320th F. A., to the 157th Field Artillery Brigade at 16:35 hours indicates the final enemy reaction for the day against the center of our line:

"German counter-attack on 325th Inf. approximately between meridians 98 and 99. I have laid down barrage at 87.2 between meridians 98 and 99. The 325th front line extends from 86.6 to 86.9. Tell 319th F. A. to give some firing along line 87.5 between meridians 98 and 99."

NOTE: Artillery Headquarters reports that 238th Field Artillery (French) and 320th Field Artillery (American) are executing barrage now (16:30 hours), also that it is a heavy counter-attack.

This enemy effort was shortly dissipated by this fire.

CHAPTER XIV

THE TAKING OF ST. JUVIN

No little confusion has resulted from the contradictory reports concerning the capture of the town of St. Juvin. There could be no better illustration of the "Fog of War" which often envelops local details of large operations. Sometimes the confusion is created by the failure of observers to interpret correctly events watched from a distance. In other cases subordinates report that a certain course of action is being undertaken, and the successive transmission of this information results in the confident assertion at a Division or Corps Headquarters that the effort has succeeded; or, the effort succeeds for the moment and is later reversed by the enemy. These are but some of the causes which, in the heat of battle, give rise to controversy which may be sincerely maintained by both parties for a lifetime.

The 82nd Division does not consider that it is a matter of paramount importance whether the 82nd Division or the 77th Division captured St. Juvin and Hill 182, north of St. Juvin. Both Divisions can agree that the town was captured by the 1st Corps, and it is doubtlessly equally true that St. Juvin fell because of the joint sacrifices of these two Divisions.

The admiration that the 82nd Division entertains for the achievements of the 77th Division will forever prevent any acrimonious sting in a discussion of this question—a question which, at the most, will be of interest only to the two

Divisions involved. Nevertheless, those charged with the duty of presenting an accurate record of the battle history of the 82nd Division are impelled by a sense of obligation toward those of our Division who fell in and around St. Juvin to present here the findings of our painstaking investigation. We have no disposition to press the official letter from General Pershing which appears in an Annex of this history, in which the Commander-in-Chief, months after the Armistice, congratulates the Division upon the capture of St. Juvin. Nor again does the 82nd Division desire to over-emphasize the fact that the town of St. Juvin became untenable for any substantial force of the enemy after the left of our assaulting line had swept through the eastern outskirts of St. Juvin during the forenoon of October 14. It is true that no one doubts the military maxim that in modern warfare, small towns fall when enveloped, or that the possession of commanding points outside of towns inevitably requires the evacuation of such centers. It is therefore unfortunate that a practice has persisted by which military successes have been measured in terms of unimportant villages rather than by reference to terrain features, which were the governing factors. The physical presence of a few soldiers in a cluster of ruined buildings has often received an emphasis quite unmerited.

It is proposed, however, to discuss briefly the capture of St. Juvin entirely from the angle of physical presence within the town. It is also proposed to discuss here the taking of Hill 182—that formidable hump covering about a square kilometer of ground, rising to a plateau crest a little north of St. Juvin. The town itself is located on the southern slope of this hill. The St. Juvin-Grand-Pré Road marks the southern boundary of St. Juvin and runs in a general northwesterly direction parallel to the Aire River. At St. Juvin, the river and road are separated by low, level ground, about 500 meters in width.

Orders from Higher Authority

The Field Order of the 1st Corps assigned to the 77th Division the mission of taking St. Juvin. The plan called for an attack from the south and east. The sector of the 82nd Division was bounded on the west by St. Juvin, but the town was specifically excluded from the Divisional sector. This entirely sensible plan for a coordinated advance by the two divisions first broke down when the 77th Division failed on the night of October 13-14 to relieve the 1st Battalion of the 326th Infantry, which was holding the lines south of the river and squarely facing St. Juvin. Consequently, the 77th Division did not attack north across the river at 8 hours 30 minutes on October 14. In fact, the 1st Battalion of the 326th Infantry, as previously said, was not relieved until after 13 hours (1 o'clock in the afternoon) on the 14th day of October, 1918. As a consequence, the 82nd Division fought its way forward through the daylight hours of October 14 with a left flank more perilously exposed with each hundred meters of ground gained. Heavy casualties were inflicted by the fire which came from St. Juvin and more especially from the crest of Hill 182. The machine guns which operated from the eastern edge of St. Juvin were for the most part silenced by the two platoons of K Company, 326th Infantry, already mentioned, which swept through the eastern outskirts in a successful raid. Fire from the northern part of the town continued throughout the day. Our units which pushed past St. Juvin were particularly harassed from Hill 182. Word was anxiously awaited at Division Headquarters stating that the 77th Division was crossing the river and had cleaned up this menace to our line.

The 82nd Division dossier records a question by Colonel

Johnston, Chief of Staff, 82nd Division, to General Cronin, commanding the left brigade of the 82nd Division, asking if the General believed it would be better to take St. Juvin. The General replied that he believed he could take it. Colonel Johnston directed that the brigade wait for further instructions on this point. The dossier also shows a conversation between the same two officers an hour later, at 14:35 hours. Colonel Johnston said he had been talking to the 1st Corps about St. Juvin and that the Corps had told him that if the 77th Division did not hurry and take St. Juvin, the 82nd Division would have to take it. Colonel Johnston requested the General to prepare plans for occupying the town, but to await orders before making the attack.

At 15:20 hours, the 82nd Division Observation Post on the high ground back at Marcq reported that no one had been seen entering St. Juvin from the west, and that their observation covered the entire town of St. Juvin and Champigneulle.

At 15:30 hours, October 14, a message reached Division Headquarters from Pilot Lieutenant Paradise and Observer Lieutenant Wright, 12th Aero Squadron, stating that a half-hour previously they had machine-gunned enemy troops in trench on Hill 182.

At 16 hours 10 minutes, a telephone message from the 82nd Division O. P. reported that troops could be seen advancing north along the edge of the woods located east of Martincourt Farm. This was the first evidence seen by observers of an advance by troops of the 77th Division along the west bank of the Aire River. At 18 hours the liaison officer with the 77th Division telephoned 82nd Division Headquarters that the 154th Brigade (77th Division) reports that two battalions of the brigade got across the river at 16 hours and that one battalion of the 306th Infantry was crossing behind them between meridians 98 and 99 and moving forward. The message continues as follows:

"In addition to two battalions, the Brigade reserve is in the process of crossing the bridge at Fléville and will march north together with Brigade Headquarters. A report will be made when they are entirely across. Another battalion of the 305th Inf. is crossing the bridge about 1 kilo north of Fléville. An officer of Brigade Headquarters is with that battalion. Col. Smedberg is going to take these two battalions of the 305th Inf. and Brigade reserve and march them north. That makes four battalions, and one more will soon be there."

This message was immediately followed by a message from 77th Division Headquarters that Hill 182 was occupied at 18 hours by the 77th Division.

The final report from the 77th Division Headquarters of the day's activities was sent to the 82nd Division at 21:15 hours October 14th.

"77th Division line extends from—east boundary

97.1-86.4
96.8-86.3
95.9-85.5
94.3-85.5
93.9-86.7
93.0-86.11

From the right Brigade, 77th Division, at 19:30 hours.— "80 to 90 prisoners have been taken from St. Juvin by the 306th Inf. As yet they have not been brought into the Division and identifications are not known at this time."

From the right Brigade, 77th Division, at 20:15 hours.— "We have H Co., 305th Inf., on hill north of St. Juvin. Two battalions of the 305th Inf. are in support east of St. Juvin. We have perfect liaison with the 325th Inf. The C. O. of the 305th Inf. now with C. O. of 325th Inf. at

98.6-84.9. H Co., 305th Inf., arrived at Hill 182 shortly after 5 hours.''

The sequence of these messages from Headquarters of the 77th Division would indicate that some time after 16 hours, October 14, the units of the 77th Division occupied St. Juvin, and that after 18 hours the plateau on Hill 182 was occupied in force.

What Transpired on the Front

But during these hours events were taking place on the left flank of the 82nd Division, which have since been substantiated in detail by officers from the 82nd Division who have gone over the ground step by step with the officers who led the left flank units of the 82nd Division on the 14th of October, 1918. During the afternoon the 3rd Battalion of the 326th Infantry, in line just northeast of St. Juvin, was receiving a very harassing fire from machine guns located in the northern edge of St. Juvin and just south of the plateau crest of Hill 182. It became a matter of immediate necessity to silence this fire and occupy the terrain. Lt. Andrew K. Benjamin, Co. A, 320th M. G. Bn., with the 1st Platoon of that company, was supporting the 326th Infantry from a point just east of St. Juvin. At about 15:30 hours, Benjamin led his platoon, plus a small infantry detachment, into St. Juvin and attacked the German machine gunners established in the northern half of St. Juvin. He speedily captured three German officers and twenty German machine gunners and drove out some other small enemy detachments found in the northern part of the town. Lieutenant Benjamin then set up his guns in the north edge of the town, where he had complete observation on the plateau of Hill 182. Prisoners were sent under a guard back to the St. Juvin-

Fléville Road. Before entering the town Lieutenant Benjamin was in a position from which all of the terrain between St. Juvin and the Aire River was under his observation, and he had closely watched this territory in order to discover either the approach of supporting troops on his left or an enemy attempt to envelop our flank from the west. When Lieutenant Benjamin's men returned to the Hill after turning over the prisoners they informed him that they had seen troops of the 77th Division advancing in open formation just south of St. Juvin. They also informed him that a body of the enemy hidden in the south edge of the town along the Grand-Pré Road had given themselves up to the 77th Division. Lieutenant Benjamin remained in position and at the alert throughout the night. No troops from the 77th Division were seen or heard in the northern part of the town, nor were any Americans apparent at any time on the plateau crest of Hill 182.

At this point it is necessary to interrupt the discussion of events on Hill 182 in order to follow the march of events throughout the Division on the night of October 14 and the morning of the 15th. Attention is here invited, however, to the discussion of the taking of Hill 182, on the morning of October 15, which will follow in sequence a little later in this narrative.

The Machine Gun Battalions of the Division rendered the utmost assistance during the period October 15th to November 1st, 1918, by firing overhead barrages and cross fires which searched the ravines and gullies utilized by the enemy. These firing schedules were carefully prepared by Major Moore, the Division Machine Gun officer, assisted by Captain Louis Marchand of the French Mission attached to the 82nd Division.

CHAPTER XV

THE ST. GEORGES' ROAD AND HILL 182

82ND DIVISION FIELD ORDERS No. 25 issued at 21 hours, October 14, directed a continuation of the attack at 7:30 hours, October 15, 1918. The order stated that "the Kriemhilde-Stellung has been breached by the 82nd Div." It provided that troops be formed for attack at 6 hours, 15th October, jumping off at 7 hours 30 minutes and continuing without halt to the Corps objective. Artillery preparation was to continue throughout the night, using quantities of non-persistent gas until H minus 4 hours. A barrage was prescribed 300 meters in front of the jumping-off line at 7 hours 25 minutes to move forward at the rate of 100 meters in 6 minutes at 7:30 hours. One paragraph of the order contains the following:

"Attention is invited to the advisability of covering the advance with scouts separated by wide intervals. In the attack supports and reserves will be kept well echeloned in depth and will advance in lines of small columns. It must be impressed upon all that the wide front the Division is called upon to cover, necessitates considerable intervals between combat groups. Thickening of front lines where resistance is encountered by feeding in supports and reserves must be avoided. Full use will be made of all auxiliary infantry weapons and the forward guns of the field artillery."

The Posts of Command in the Division were specified:

82nd Div. Headquarters...No change.
163rd Brig...............98.4-84.9, from 10 hours.
164th Brig...............Sommerance, from 10 hours.
157th F. A. Brig.........No change.

The order of regiments on the Division front was unchanged. The 328th Infantry still occupied the right flank, with the 325th Infantry in the center and the 326th Infantry on the left. The 327th Infantry continued in support behind the right flank of the Division.

The orders which reached the 328th Infantry during the night of October 14-15 were further supplemented with the direction that the regiment would attack as soon as the 42nd Division came up abreast of the leading battalion of the 328th Infantry. Captain Weaver of C Company, 328th Infantry, went over to the Captain of the left company of the 166th Infantry and informed him of the contents of the order received. Captain Weaver was told that the 42nd Division would advance at H hour.

SERIOUS ENEMY ATTACK, OCTOBER 15, 1918

At about 7 hours the enemy made a very determined infantry counter-attack along our entire Divisional front, preceding the assault with a particularly vicious barrage of artillery and machine-gun fire.

Visibility was very poor on the morning of the 15th and our men had practically no warning of the approaching enemy infantry. The German barrage held our men on the exposed ridge, flattened in fox holes, and a swarm of the gray-uniformed enemy was on top of our outposts before the combat groups a little in the rear could grasp the full significance of the peril. A desperate fight of an individual character followed at hand-to-hand range in all three regiments. Full force of the blow fell upon the left flank units of the 328th Infantry and the right flank of the 325th Infantry. Some of our combat groups were forced back a couple of hundred yards on to the St. Juvin-St. Georges Road. The support groups on the road, however, at once advanced to engage the enemy while the men in the 328th Infantry, a short distance to the right of the point of impact, stood up in their fox holes and opened rapid fire with their rifles and Chauchots. Furthermore, troops were pushed forward on the right of our line from which point they could shoot enfilade volleys down the German infantry lines.

The spirit of resistance which our men everywhere evinced shattered the enemy assault and inflicted very heavy losses. In about fifteen minutes the German survivors were running back, pursued by American fire. During this encounter both sides lost in captured about an equal number of prisoners—perhaps thirty or forty. There was little inclination to surrender shown by either side. At 7:25 hours our own bombardment fell as previously scheduled and hastened the enemy retirement.

328TH INFANTRY ON OCTOBER 15, 1918

The 166th Infantry did not advance at H hour and the 328th Infantry was in consequence unable to advance except for a short distance. The left flank of the regiment, however, endeavored to stretch forward in liaison with the 325th Infantry. At 8 hours, German skirmishers were discovered on the right flank of the 328th Infantry, and in front of the 166th Infantry. Lieutenant Day with a strong patrol was sent to attack these enemy elements and succeeded in capturing prisoners and compelling the retirement of German elements encountered.

Throughout the day the enemy poured a terrific shell

and machine-gun fire upon our lines while enemy planes flew at low altitudes and machine-gunned our infantry.

Lieutenant McArthur, 328th Inf., moved his 37 mm. Platoon into the front line and fired point-blank at machine-gun nests and other targets. The 328th Machine Gun Company (Captain Jones) occupied the woods on the right flank of the regiment and did effective work. An artillery observer occupied a shell hole near the forward Battalion P. C. and numerous targets were given to the accompanying 75 mm. guns. Telephone wires were continually cut by enemy shelling, but the men from the Signal Platoon worked steadily under enemy observation repairing the breaks. It rained intermittently throughout the day and at night a steady downpour set in.

325TH INFANTRY ON OCTOBER 15, 1918

In the 325th Infantry, arrangement of troops on the morning of October 15 was the same as on the previous day except that the 325th Machine Gun Company was scheduled to join the 2nd Battalion of the 325th Infantry in Division reserve. C Company, 320th M. G. Bn., was assigned to the assaulting battalion of the regiment.

The counter-attack against the 325th Infantry fell with especial force against Companies B and D which temporarily retired to the St. Juvin-St. Georges Road. Captain Castle, commanding the 1st Battalion, telephoned at once to Colonel Whitman and the support Battalion was immediately thrown forward to stiffen the line. Prompt action by Captain Taylor with A and C Companies on the right flank broke up the Boche line in front of the Regiment and the enemy retired leaving seven machine guns and nine prisoners. Shortly after H hour the 325th Infantry advanced to the crest north of the road but could go no farther. Heavy machine-gun fire from the front and flanks held our men at this point. The Division now ran out into a salient between St. Juvin and St. Georges, and it was apparent that no substantial progress would be possible until the Divisions on our right and left were able to get forward in turn. During the afternoon our attack was again pushed in the center, and elements of the 325th Infantry reached the Ravin aux Pierres. Twenty machine guns and a number of prisoners were taken. This ravine was destined to be a very formidable obstacle and the scene of much hard fighting before it became the permanent possession of this Division. The ravine was very deep, with a fairly perpendicular drop on the southern side. It was filled with a dense growth, and the northeast end of the ravine ran up into a strong enemy position northwest of St. Georges. As a result enemy machine gunners could easily filter into this open end and gain a position on the flank of our forward elements without coming under observation. Deep dugouts in the south wall of the ravine gave the enemy security from our fire, but were not so happily placed for protection from the north when we occupied the position. It was from this ravine that the enemy counter-attack emerged on the morning of the 15th, and to this shelter that it returned after the repulse. On the afternoon of the 15th our men who reached this point were exposed to a fire of such intensity that the survivors withdrew to the crest north of the St. Georges Road and dug in for the night. Our men were now at the point of exhaustion from lack of sleep and constant exposure to cold and rain.

The 1st Battalion, 325th Infantry, reported 7 officers and 125 men as fighting effectives, while the 3rd Battalion of that regiment made a return of 3 officers and 175 men.

326TH INFANTRY ON OCTOBER 15, 1918

In the 326th Infantry Colonel McArthur had planned to make the assault on the morning of the 15th with the 1st Battalion which was to move from its position in reserve near Sommerance and, passing through the 3rd Battalion in the front line, continue in a northerly direction to the high ground east of Champigneulle, keeping in liaison with the 325th Infantry on the right. The 1st Battalion was delayed in making the considerable movement required, and Major Watkins, knowing that the attack must go off at H hour, did not wait for relief but initiated the attack with the 3rd Battalion. The advance here, also, was made in the face of very intense fire. The Battalion succeeded, however, in getting forward until its right flank was within a short distance of the Ravin aux Pierres. The left flank of the Battalion was on the northeast slope of Hill 182. At this point the 1st Battalion, with Companies A and D in assault and B and C in support, passed through the 3rd Battalion and continued the attack. It was found possible to make only a slight advance, but a considerable number of prisoners were captured. Both flanks of the Battalion were receiving fire and Captain Knowles gave orders to dig in and hold.

THE AFFAIR ON HILL 182

The order of events now moves farther to the west, where a very extraordinary affair raged for a half-day on the top of Hill 182 and left that strategic point in the possession of the 82nd Division. The 82nd Division regards the exploit on Hill 182 during the forenoon of the 15th as one of the striking episodes in the war and a brilliant example of success won against great odds by a small American unit. The whole business smacks of modern knight errantry. Capt. Frank M. Williams, commanding the 325th Machine Gun Company, had been directed to take his company to Hill 182 and from there to support by machine-gun fire the advance of the Division's left flank. At about 6 hours Captain Williams sent runners to his company, then supporting the line of the 325th Infantry, directing his lieutenant to move the company on to Hill 182. Captain Williams started alone for the hill intending to reconnoiter machine-gun positions before the arrival of his men. The previous experience of this officer is sufficiently unusual to deserve mention. For several years he was a Deputy Sheriff in both Wyoming and Montana, and during that time had won some twenty individual gun fights against cattle outlaws. He once won the bronco riding championship at the big Cheyenne open tournament. Later he had joined Buffalo Bill's "Wild West" show where he gave exhibitions in riding untamed horses and was pronounced by Colonel Cody the greatest bronco breaker the Colonel had ever seen. Captain Williams walked through the eastern part of St. Juvin and saw no American or German troops. On the eastern slope of the hill, near the north edge of the town, he found a lieutenant with a platoon from the 77th Division occupying a piece of trench. The lieutenant informed him that the platoon had become separated from other troops of the 77th Division and did not know where they were now located. He had therefore placed himself on the flanks of the 326th Infantry. He arrived there during the night and had no information of the enemy. Captain Williams advised him to send a runner to find his battalion commander. Captain Williams then strolled on to the top of Hill 182. The mist was so heavy that he found it impossible to see more than approximately a hundred yards to the front. Shortly after his arrival a heavy barrage fell on the Hill during which he took shelter at the north edge of the town where he found men of Lieutenant Benjamin's platoon. The Lieutenant had left the hill a few moments previously for a conference with his Battalion Commander. When the barrage lifted Captain Williams walked back on to the crest of the Hill. Here he observed a group of five German soldiers walking toward him at about a hundred yards' distance with an American prisoner. Captain Williams walked over to the group empty-handed and when within a few yards made a lightning reach for the pistol on his belt and in the fight that followed killed four Germans and took the fifth prisoner. As the fifth German raised his arm in surrender, Captain Williams caught sight of a long enemy skirmish line coming over the northern end of the plateau attacking directly toward St. Juvin. The enemy party numbered roundly about 200 men. Using a dead German's rifle, Captain Williams shot one of the enemy who marched a few paces in advance of the attacking skirmish line. The German line took cover and Captain Williams jumped down the bank on to the sunken road near the cemetery on the western slope of the hill and ran back under cover toward St. Juvin. He crossed through the northern part of the town to the eastern slope where he met his machine-gun company at the bottom of the hill. Captain Williams, shouting "Follow me!" ran back on to the hill, his leading gun close behind him. This gun opened fire on the German line which was then advancing at close range. The other guns almost immediately joined. In the fight which followed the entire German party were killed, wounded or driven from the hill and about half of our company were casualties. A column of several hundred of the enemy was observed in the vicinity of the railroad yards just west of Hill 182. Our machine gunners turned their attention to this force and scattered it with heavy losses. This German attack was part of the assault made against our entire front and to which reference has already been made. The lieutenant and the platoon of the 77th Division met by Captain Williams on the east slope of Hill 182 were not present during this fight. When the enemy counter-attacked the lieutenant retired with his platoon and passed through Captain Williams' company as it came up the east side of St. Juvin. By noon on October 15 when activities had ceased in the vicinity of Hill 182 Captain Williams personally went back through the town until he reached the St. Juvin-Grand-Pré Road in the vicinity of which he found a Captain from the 77th Division who stated that he was in command of the right Battalion of the 77th Division. Captain Williams reported to this officer and stated that his own company was within this officer's sector and badly in need of reinforcements on Hill 182, where it had without assistance beaten off a very strong counter-attack. Captain Williams also asked the Battalion Commander if he had any instructions to give him. Captain Williams was informed that the Battalion Commander could not make any dispositions until he had reported the situation to higher authority. Captain Williams returned to his company and remained alone on Hill 182 throughout the afternoon and night until 2 hours on the morning of October 16. At this time about two platoons from the 77th Division came to the Hill and dug in near the line occupied by the men from the 82nd Division. Two hours later these platoons of the 77th Division were relieved by units from the 78th Division.

Some messages in the Division dossier for October 15 are given herewith:

"From Gen. Cronin at 8 hours, Oct. 15, 1918. Pushing our counter-attack on the right of the 325th, and Colonel

Whitman has asked for artillery support. He does not think he will need the Division Reserve. Thinks he can handle the situation with some artillery support."

"From Gen. Cronin at 8:45 hours, Oct. 15. Just received message from Whitman that his right flank has been forced back to the position of his left. That flank is unprotected." Colonel Johnston inquired if he could push a battalion in direction of the left flank moving under the nose of the Hill near St. Juvin and attack the enemy in the flank.

"From Adjutant 163rd Inf. Brigade 8:55 hours, Oct. 15. Message from Major Watkins at 8:49 hours. Off in good shape. Men in fine spirits. Some machine-gun opposition. I can handle that. Have taken 30 odd prisoners. Need some litter bearers."

"From Adjutant 163rd Inf. Brig., 9 hours, 15 Oct. 326th Infantry advancing in good shape. 325th have advanced to parallel 87 and are holding their own but not advancing."

"From Adjutant 163rd Inf. Brigade at 9 hours. 325th holding well. Will advance in a few minutes behind new artillery barrage. Major Watkins wants 14 ambulances."

"Message from Adjutant 164th Inf. Brigade, 10:10 hours, 15 Oct. 1918. Captain Tomasello, Operations Officer 328th Infantry, reports 42nd Division can not advance on account of heavy machine-gun fire. Suggest that they fall back and call for barrage. Combat liaison will sit tight and cover flank. The balance of Regiment will go ahead. Doing all business by runners."

"From 163rd Inf. Brigade at 10:40 hours, 15 Oct. Am sending 2 officers and 32 men in as prisoners. They were taken this morning northeast of St. Juvin by 326th Infantry at about 8:30 hours. Also report that prisoners and guard marching down road to Division Headquarters have been fired on by 77th Division on our left. Please take this up and have it stopped."

"Colonel Johnston to Chief of Staff 42nd Division, 10:45 hours, 15 Oct. Your elements on your left are held up in front of the wire. This is holding back the entire advance. If agreeable, we will take St. Georges for you. If not, we wish you would consider the possibility of moving your troops by the left flank and using the eastern slope of Hill 230 to flank out St. Georges from the west. Our troops can turn the right flank back along the heights and allow you to use the slopes. The Brigadiers are in direct communication with one another and it would be agreeable to us for them to mutually arrange this plan of attack with the understanding that the western limit of your artillery fire will remain unchanged."

"Optimist 3 (Chief of Staff 42nd Division) replied: This seems a good plan and we are willing to try it. Will notify our left Brigade if you will notify your right and direct them to proceed with this maneuver."

* * * * *

Colonel Johnston telephoned the substance of this message to the Adjutant of the 164th Infantry Brigade.

"From Headquarters 157th Field Artillery Brigade, at 10:30, October 15, 1918. 320th Field Artillery reports at 10:30 hours heavy artillery shells passing over B Battery of that Regiment. Shells are falling in our lines. Rotating bands have fallen at 00.46. Have called up Corps Artillery, also 42nd Division and reported same to them, as we believe it is from this Division, their batteries being directly in rear of the battery reporting this fire."

"Report of examination of a detachment of 25 prisoners, at 10:40, 15 Oct. The prisoners including one lieutenant were captured this morning about 1 kilometer northeast of St. Juvin, just south of road leading from St. Juvin to St. Georges. Prisoners had received orders to carry out a counter-attack against our troops, but before well under way were encountered by our forces and captured. Prisoners stated that our effective machine-gun fire which came from all sides kept Germans from advancing and attack broke down. Most of prisoners belong to 1st Battalion of 210th Regiment, 45th Reserve Division, which had been kept in reserve until this morning. When questioned as to the enemy defenses in the rear and the positions which were to be occupied in case of retreat, prisoners stated that no prepared positions existed to their knowledge. In all cases their orders had been to hold their positions at all costs."

"From 166th Infantry (83rd Brigade, 42nd Division), at 10:30 hours, 15 Oct. Do not need any special assistance in getting through wire if we can get to it. Are held up by machine-gun fire and not by obstacles. General Lenahan advises that artillery preparation is now in progress on St. Georges and Landres-St. Georges and on the road between the two towns. The fire will be lifted to the 3rd objective at 11:15 hours when Infantry will renew attack."

"Liaison Officer with 42nd Division reports at 11:30 hours, 15 October, 1918, that Tank Commander with 42nd Division started with 25 tanks. He arrived at our lines with 16 tanks. Went into action with ten tanks with the advance element. He went across the ravine northwest 199 Woods about center of the sector. He went across the wire and across trenches receiving very heavy fire. Infantry unable to keep up with him. He was forced to retire with only 7 tanks. His personnel and machinery are seriously damaged. He says that he can do nothing more in this vicinity and tanks are now withdrawn from this line."

"From Capt. Webster, 164th Infantry Brigade, 12:20 hours, 15 Oct. Prisoners captured by 328th patrol at 9:30 hours at 00.2-86.9 say that they belong to the 31st Regiment, 15th Bavarian Division. Were in reserve and came in line at 6 hours this morning. Report that they were given notification yesterday officially by a Division Commander that armistice was hourly awaited."

"From 77th Division, 12:40 hours, 15 Oct. 154th Brigade has two companies on the road 400 yards west of St. Juvin. Will proceed on St. Juvin-Grand-Pré Road and mop up between it and the river."

"Reports received by Capt. Dunlap at 12:42 hours from the adjutants of both infantry brigades indicated following fighting strength in those two organizations:

    163rd Inf. Brig.......98 Officers, 2815 Men
    164th Inf. Brig.......43 Officers, 1068 Men

"15 Oct. 1918 at 14:15 hours. Maj. Hawkins reports 326th Inf. and 306th Inf. support lines were mixed up but have been reorganized by the officers. Roads in vicinity of St. Juvin passable but very muddy."

"15 Oct. 1918 at 14:25 hours. From Lieut. Mitchell, Liaison Officer with 77th Division. Just received message from Col. Smedburg, 77th Division, stating that he knows disposition of 77th Division troops on our left, and that he can have the line straightened out very soon."

"15 Oct. 1918, at 15 hours. 163rd Inf. Brig. reports that 326th Inf. is held up in its advance on account of inability of 325th Inf. to advance. 325th Inf. has been reorganizing. Barrage is being requested and they are now advancing. 326th suffered from machine-gun fire at 97.0-87.0. Artillery is hammering on this point. Artillery fire on Champigneulle would be very acceptable."

Col. Johnston called on the artillery to fire for 25 minutes on Champigneulle and trenches along southwestern edge of town.

"15 Oct. 1918 at 15:10 hours. From Capt. Webster. The P. C. of advance Bn. of 166th Inf. now in Sommerance reports that after advancing this morning they had to withdraw. Are now waiting for advance of 165th Inf. on their right. Nothing to report on 164th Brig. front."

"15 Oct. 1918 at 15:45 hours. Pigeon message to Albany-7 from Hdqrs. 328th Inf. at 15 hours. Message received 15:40 hours. Place Sommerance. We are under heavy fire from large caliber guns. Have planes spot these guns and put our heavies to work on them. Have this this done at once. (Signed) TOMASELLO."

"15 Oct. 1918 at 16:15 hours. From Maj. Wainwright at P. C. of Gen. Cronin at 16 hours. Report received that 325th Inf. has advanced through enemy position and was at that time at Ravin aux Pierres, 326th Inf. on the left. Asked by Col. Johnston if the men will stay in the ravine, Maj. Wainwright replied, 'They are attacking now. Request that the outfit on the right be pushed up to join them.' "

"15 Oct. 1918 at 16:20 hours. To 164th Inf. Brig. From Col. Johnston. Brigade on your left pushing out of the Ravin aux Pierres. Join them."

"15 Oct. 1918, at 16:20 hours. Telephone message from Lieut. Carlisle, Liaison Officer with 42nd Division. G-3 of 42nd Division says that there will be no further advance this afternoon. Another advance to-morrow morning. Orders will come over later."

"15 Oct. 1918, at 16:20 hours. Army Artillery reports that the army observer states heavy massing of artillery and infantry at F-5383, just behind woods Bois Bantheville. Army artillery has two guns reaching it. 157th F. A. has reported this to air service for bombing work."

"15 Oct. 1918 at 16:30 hours. Anson-1 to Albany-1. Maj. Boyle, 328th Inf. at 15:30 hours advised that 325th Inf. is preparing to advance. 328th can not advance until 166th Inf. advances. 166th Inf. is waiting on 165th Inf., who are 1000 meters behind. Maj. Boyle has asked for artillery preparation so he can advance when 166th moves up."

"15 Oct. 1918 at 16:15 hours. 157th F. A. Brig. reports that Air Service notified them of heavy massing of artillery and infantry north of Bantheville Woods, at F-5383. Only two army guns can reach them."

"15 Oct. 1918, at 19 hours. Col. Johnston with G-3, 1st Corps. G-3 inquired as to possibility of using troops of 82nd Division for taking Champigneulle. Col. Johnston replied that it was perfectly possible to take Champigneulle but that such action would extend the front of the Division, inasmuch as no other troops are moving up on either flank. In other words, the Division now holds from about 86.2 northwest to about parallel 87, thence swings southwest to the north slope of Côte 182 and must face the Boche on this entire line. The right brigade has only about 1000 men and the left brigade about 2000. We are perfectly capable of attacking and advancing in any direction on a front proportionate to our strength, but this extension of the front would require more and more men which, of course, must be supplied from the rear echelons. The people on our right are not moving at all, and the hill north of St. Georges is of course exceedingly important, as it sweeps the plateau on which we are located. The P. C. of our right brigade is at the same place as the P. C. of the front line battalion of the Division on our right. It does not seem that the taking of Champigneulle would relieve this situation to any extent. G-3 said he would inform the Division what would be required.''

"15 Oct. 1918 at 19:30 hours. Received wireless message from 328th Inf. Holding our first line against heavy artillery fire and machine-gun fire. Repulsed counter-attack on left flank this morning. Our troops exhausted. Can not continue advance."

"15 Oct. 1918 at 20:30 hours. Telephone message from Intelligence Officer of 325th Inf. Our positions to-night are the same as this morning. The strength of the 2nd Bn. is about 800 men. Two bns. went forward this afternoon at H hour and found in the ravine German machine-gun nests. Only one company (K Co.) was able to penetrate through the ravine and this company went up the forward slope. 7 prisoners of the 45th Res. Division and 10 machine guns were captured. The latter were turned against the enemy and fired into them, inflicting heavy losses. This company was driven back to this side of the ravine by direct fire above them. A few men of K Co. could not get back and stuck to their positions and were shot down fighting. Stated that the regt. was in liaison on right and left. Stated there was less air activity to-day than yesterday. Prisoners who had been used as litter bearers are now being sent back to hdqrs. Believe the Germans are heavily entrenched in the ravine and immediately north of the ravine."

"15 Oct. 1918, 20 hours. Report of examination of two prisoners of the 1st Bn. of the 31st Regt., 15th Bavarian Division. Prisoners were captured this morning at 8 hours in the course of an enemy counter-attack about 700 yds. south of St. Georges. The prisoners were put in line with their bn. during the night, reinforcing the 30th Res. Regt., which holds the sector from St. Georges to a point approximately 1 klm. west. Prisoners stated their orders were to advance and take the position held by our troops on Hill 206, 1 klm. south of St. Georges. It appears that our machine-gun fire was so effective that the 7th Co., already reduced in strength when going into the line, is now almost annihilated. Stated that their average strength of companies within the 2nd Bn. was as low as 30 to 40 men, the regt. having suffered greatly in recent operations up north. They had not received replacements. Prisoners stated that the regt. arrived in Buzancy on the night of Oct. 12th. The following night they marched south and remained in the vicinity of Imécourt until placed in line. They stated that Brig. Hdqrs. was at Verpel, and Regt. Hqrs. was located in a mill southwest of Imécourt, at 99.4-10.3. Further stated having seen elements of a Prussian division in this vicinity but were unable to give identification. Our artillery fire yesterday and to-day caused heavy casualties in their bn. The positions which they occupied immediately south of St. Georges gave little protection. In the absence of trenches they were compelled to occupy ditches in the form of squares. They stated that their company commander several days ago read Germany's reply to President Wilson's message and added that an armistice might be expected to follow any day."

CHAPTER XVI

DEEPENING THE SALIENT

ANOTHER dreary wet night followed, marked by heavy shell fire throughout the Divisional Area. At 23 hours, October 15, Field Orders No. 27 were issued from Divisional Headquarters. This order stated that the 1st Army Corps would attack at 6 hours, October 16, 1918. It further specified that the 42nd Division would attack on the right of the 82nd Division. The mission assigned the 82nd Division was to support the attack of the 78th Division by protecting that unit's right flank. The Corp objectives included Champigneulle and Beffu et le Morthomme. The 2nd Battalion, 325th Inf., was placed at the disposal of the Commanding General, 163rd Brigade, for the purpose of capturing Champigneulle. The 164th Brigade was directed to conform to the advance of the 163rd Brigade. The Bois des Loges would be gassed with nonpersistent gases throughout the night until 5 hours, October 16. A special paragraph in the Field Order warned all Commanders against the practice of placing machine guns in the first wave of assaulting battalions. The machine guns must accompany second waves and supports.

327TH INFANTRY RELIEVES 328TH INFANTRY

During the night of October 15-16 the 327th Infantry, consolidated into one battalion under Lieutenant Colonel

Burr, relieved the 328th Infantry on the right flank of the Division front. At 6 hours the 327th Infantry advanced by infiltration about two or three hundred meters. The 42nd Division made no advance whatever, and the 327th Infantry was compelled to dig in with its right flank faced squarely east for a depth of one kilometer back to the 42nd Division. This effort created a still more serious salient and the right flank of the 82nd Division was exposed to strong enfilade fire from the east, in addition to the normal resistance from the north. During the day the enemy attempted to penetrate between the strong points of our line, creeping close enough on one occasion to use hand grenades against one of our groups. The enemy artillery continued to harass our troops throughout the day. A detachment from the 328th Infantry in support was ordered forward and used to reinforce the refused right flank.

The physical condition of our men was at its lowest ebb on this day, as messages from many units testified.

Lieutenant Colonel Burr, commanding the 327th Infantry, sent the following message to Brigadier General Lindsey at 10 hours 50 minutes, October 16:

"I again call to your attention the physical condition of the men of my command. I strongly recommend their relief to-night. To men in their condition, the weather conditions of last night were very trying. They will be in no condition to-morrow morning for any strenuous operation."

The 328th Infantry at this time was reduced by all causes to one or two officers and from twenty to forty men in each infantry company. The 328th Infantry Machine Gun Company on October 16, 1918, consisted of twenty-seven men and no officers.

325TH INFANTRY ON OCTOBER 16, 1918

The attack of the 325th Infantry in the center of the Division sector was made by the 3rd Battalion which passed through the line of the 1st Battalion and in spite of severe machine-gun resistance pushed K and L Companies into the Ravin aux Pierres. This advance of our Infantry was supported by a machine gun barrage fired by B Company, 320th Machine Gun Battalion. The right flank of the 325th Infantry could not advance and remained just south of the ravine in liaison with the 327th Infantry.

The following message was received by Colonel Whitman from the 3rd Battalion, 325th Inf., at 9:20 hours:

"Left and center of front line in Ravin aux Pierres at 98.0-86.8 to about 98.5-87.0. The right of our line is just south of the ravine held up by M. G. from right flank. Troops on our right reported not advancing. Our second line is just north of road from St. Juvin to St. Georges. Our 3rd line is 500 meters further to rear.
"MELTON."

Later in the day a heavy fire from the east portion of the Ravin aux Pierres aided by enemy artillery fire from the north drove our men out of the ravine. This was the second day on which we had obtained a foothold in this important position. On each day the survivors of the assault had been compelled to evacuate the ravine to avoid annihilation.

During the afternoon the following message was sent by Lieutenant Colonel Campbell, 325th Inf., to General Cronin:

"16th Oct., to Austin-1. Came out through vicious barrage. All over now. M. G. fire coming over, not bad.

Varnado killed. Estimate less than 250 in both Battalions remaining fit for duty. Counter-attack by enemy would be bad. Lines as stated by phone. I am not a calamity howler, but the officers and men are all in. Jones in good position as reserve but, of course, no shelter from elements. Will get Melton and Castle together and organize. Will move Jones back slightly and put Melton in support with his Battalion—less than 100. Castle with 1st Battalion and Cozine to hold line of road and have advanced parties in shell holes in front 200 yards. I am starting this now, execution of same to be made in dark. CAMPBELL."

The report concerning the death of Captain Varnado proved later to be incorrect, but forms the background for one of the most amazing incidents in the history of the Division.

During the withdrawal of the 325th Infantry from the ravine a large caliber, high explosive shell burst within a short distance of this officer. The force of the explosion tossed him in the air and dropped him in a limp heap on the ground. One of his non-commissioned officers ran to his assistance and satisfied himself that his Company Commander was dead. For five days Captain Varnado lay unconscious in this ravine. During this period a cold rain fell almost constantly and the ravine was heavily shelled with gas and high explosives. At intervals a machine-gun barrage was poured into this area. At the end of five days, on October 21, the ravine was again taken by our troops and Captain Varnado was found unconscious but still faintly breathing. There were no wounds upon his body. After a long period in the hospital he recovered full possession of his strength and senses and returned to the United States with his regiment after the War was over.

In addition to the serious physical condition of the troops there had been a grave deterioration in the condition of all weapons during the many days of exposure to rain and mud. The Chauchat rifles had nearly all ceased to function.

During October 16 our men were continuously exposed to the observation and harassing fire of enemy aeroplanes which flew low over our lines with little interference from the American Air Service.

The effective strength of the 325th Infantry the night following was reported as follows:

    1st Battalion.......... 5 Officers, 175 Men
    2nd Battalion..........17 Officers, 361 Men
    3rd Battalion.......... 3 Officers, 120 Men

When the 2nd Battalion, 325th Infantry, was assigned to a special mission by the Divisional Field Order, the 2nd Battalion of the 326th Infantry was transferred to the command of Colonel Whitman and during the night of October 16 this unit relieved the 1st Battalion, 325th Infantry, in the front line.

326th Infantry on October 16, 1918

Meanwhile, the 326th Infantry on the left of the Division had attacked at H hour, October 16, with the 1st Battalion in the position of honor, supported by Company D, 320th Machine Gun Battalion. Elements of Company D crossed the Agron River and reached the railway cut at Champigneulle extending along the line at 96.2-86.65 to 96.5-86.8. Company C had passed through Company A and reached a position on the hill north of the Ravin aux Pierres along the line 97.5-86.9 to 97.8-87.1. A platoon of Company D covered the interval between C and D Companies. These points marked the line of farthest advance reached by the 326th Infantry in its operations. Intense artillery and machine-gun fire and

OFFICIAL HISTORY OF 82ND DIVISION

the isolated nature of the positions forced these Companies to withdraw under cover of darkness on the night of October 16. Consequently, night found the front Battalions of the Division on the St. Juvin-St. Georges Road with outposts covering the ridge north of the Road.

The following are some of the messages contained in the Divisional dossier for October 16, 1918:

From General Cronin to Divisional Headquarters, 7 hours 35 minutes, 16th Oct., 1918.

"Everything started off on time. Extreme left Battalion had to be somewhat re-arranged to avoid shell fire. This was accomplished before starting. Everything going good."

From C. O. 327th Inf. Gen. Lindsey, 8 hours 5 minutes, 16th Oct., 1918.

"325th Inf. advancing; 166th Inf. is not. Am advancing and keep in touch by 'phone. Advancing under heavy machine-gun fire."

From 157th F. A. Brigade, 8 hours 48 minutes, 16th Oct., 1918.

"321st F. A. Reports that the Infantry line has been temporarily checked by large machine-gun nests 98.6-87.3. There are both trenches and woods at that point. Fire is coming from these woods and trenches from machine guns and infantry requested fire of one battalion for 15 minutes just as fast as it could be put into them. Infantry was told that this would exhaust our ammunition supply but that two rounds per gun per minute would be fired.

"8 hours 50 minutes. In addition machine-gun nest located 98.3-87.5. One battalion of 320 F. A. directed to open fire on this nest with two rounds per gun per minute for 15 minutes. In the coordinates there is a telegraph pole at the base of which it is reported there are ten hostile machine guns."

From Lt. Mitchell, liaison officer, with 78th Division, 9 hours 20 minutes, 16th Oct., 1918.

"78th Division reports that it has relieved 77th Division. Reports that the attack as ordered went off in good shape, but have not heard as yet whether any advance has been made."

From Chief of Staff 42nd Division to Chief of Staff 82nd Division, 9 hours 20 minutes, 16th Oct., 1918.

"We were all set for 6 o'clock this morning and received orders from the army not to attack. The fighting has been very severe on our right. Only able to gain one kilometer yesterday. Think the understanding is that we are to advance with you." Col. Johnston asked how they can say they are waiting to advance with us when our line is facing east and northeast to join with them. "This ties down our right flank. We are now attacking on the left. Still think it advisable for you to maneuver by the left flank and take St. Georges and hill north of it. Col. Johnston was informed that 42nd Division is strictly forbidden to use any artillery or make any attack."

From 78th Division, 9 hours 45 minutes, 16th Oct., 1918.

"We are moving all right on our right flank. On the left Boche is still in Grand-Pré and Chevières. Prisoners taken at night during course of relief.

"Col. Johnston. 'Are you going to continue to go on the right?'

"Answer. 'Yes, we are pushing hard and will stick with you.'

"Extract from examination of 23 prisoners belonging to 45th Reserve Division. Prisoners were captured northeast of St. Juvin in and near Ravin aux Pierres, state that their units have suffered heavy losses in the fighting of the last few days. Strength of companies does not exceed 40 men each. Enemy has no organized defensive position in the rear. The Agron River can be forded at and above Champigneulle by horse-drawn vehicles but owing to its great distance and higher banks crossing further south can only be effected by means of a bridge. The average width of the river is about 6 to 7 meters. Some replacements have been received in the last few days but in small numbers only. Prisoners state that they have been told to hold their positions. Companies holding advanced positions are invariably commanded by non-commissioned officers. This policy meets with considerable criticism on the part of enlisted men. None of the prisoners know when their organizations are to be relieved. The 45th Reserve Division prior to its arrival in this sector was engaged in the Champagne in recent fighting. They state that their units have suffered heavily from our artillery fire. Several men were very outspoken in their condemnation of the present German Government.

"An examination of additional prisoners from this Division brought out the statement that the 45th Reserve Division had participated in the counter-attack by the enemy arranged October 15th. A prisoner from the 212th Reserve Regiment stated that his regiment had received 300 replacements two days prior to the attack. Prisoner from 210th Reserve Regiment stated his regiment had received 120 replacements, asserted that the 47th Scharfschützen Abteilung (machine gun unit) was holding a position in rear of their regiments east of Champigneulle."

Colonel Johnson to G-3 1st Corps, 11 hours 20 minutes, 16th Oct., 1918.

"How about using the 42nd Artillery on machine-gun nest? We are getting a great deal of direct fire from southwest of St. Georges 00.87 on the road to St. Juvin from St. Georges. Some artillery fire on that point will help."

"G-3 replied that he would have it done."

11 hours 45 minutes, Col. Johnston talking with Adjutant 325th Infantry.

"Asked if regiment was using its field artillery.
"Adjutant replied he thought so.
"Colonel Johnston told him to push those guns and Stokes Mortars out in front and find them (the enemy). Asked if anything was known about the Division on our left. Was told that troops of 78th Div. were still on Hill 182."

From Gen. Lindsey to Col. Johnston, 11 hours 25 minutes, 16 Oct., 1918.

"C. O. of advanced lines in support of 166th Inf. has just called. He was informed that the location of the right flank of my advanced Battalion is on the St. Georges-St. Juvin Road about 00.1-87.1 with Company of 166th further in rear and in liaison with left flank. My advanced line seems to be stuck out in a V shape. Have arranged with 166th to echelon forward on the left flank further to the left of St. Georges and in succession to the east taking the enemy line on the flank so as to ease in the 166th and 165th Inf. I believe that similar action by 325th echeloning forward by the right flank to the ridge west of St. Georges will enable concentrated fire to be brought on the strong Hill in vicinity of Hill 230 at 00.4-88.3 and on Côte 253."

From Gen. Lindsey.

"Reports his troops in a V shape formation apex of the V being at 00.1-87.1. His left wing extends southwest parallel to the St. Juvin-St. Georges Road and his right wing running due south parallel to 00. He says that the greatest enemy activity is coming from woods on Côte 230 at approximately 00.5-88.0 to 88.6."

Col. Johnston to Gen. Cronin, 12 hours, 16 Oct., 1918.

"Have you any information about the people on your left?"

"They are on the east and northeast slopes of Hill 182."

"Are they moving forward?"

"They are on Contour 180 on northern and eastern slopes."

"What help are you getting from the artillery this morning?"

"Knowles was forced to fall back, due to shortage of artillery and re-organize in the ravine."

"Are you using the 326th Inf. to help the 325th Inf.?"

"They are fighting together."

"Do you feel it necessary to push the 326th down in that ravine?"

"No. They won't go down in the hollow but will keep up on the high ground, east of the Agron River."

Col. Johnston to Bonehead 3 (Chief of Staff, 1st Corps), 12 hours 10 minutes, 16th Oct., 1918.

"We have just gotten a report from our left that the Division on our left is sticking along 180 Contour on Côte 182. Our line about an hour ago was in the ravine fighting up the slopes and we were having a severe fight at 98.7-87.4."

Col. Johnston to Gen. Lindsey, 12 hours 18 minutes, 16 Oct., 1918.

"It is reported that you have troops east of the 00. meridian."

General replied he had some at 00.1.

Col. Johnston directed him to move his troops west of the 00. meridian as they were within the artillery boundary of the 42nd Division, which was preparing to shoot there now.

At 12 hours 22 minutes Col. Johnston called 42nd Division and asked them to stop their artillery fire west of St. Georges reporting back immediately.

Gen. Duncan to Chief of Staff 1st Corps, 12 hours 45 minutes, 16 Oct., 1918.

"I have just been up to the front and talked with the Regimental and Brigade Commanders and looked over the situation. Because of physical fatigue, I don't believe these men can go forward any more. I think we have got to hold on to what we have got. The 325th Inf. got into that ravine and took 12 machine guns in front of them. The Hun counter-attacked and we lost about 40 men in hand to hand fighting. The Huns are putting up tremendous resistance and our men have come to the limit of their endurance and I don't believe that they are in physical condition to go any further. We have got to stabilize on present line, because we haven't men enough to go on. This is the 10th day of our attack and the whole front is covered by machine-gun fire from Hill 230 and then to the left. The men of this Division have behaved splendidly and have lost heavily. There are not fifty men to a Company and these are practically at the end of their strength. The spirit is fine but to-day they are at the end of their physical endurance."

From 163 Brigade, 12 hours 55 minutes, 16 Oct., 1918.

"Very heavy artillery and machine-gun fire prevents advance of our left. Our artillery seems to have no effect in reducing his fire. Same condition exists on our right. Infiltration across Ravin aux Pierres is possible to some extent but so far without enough power to advance line. Liaison good with left Division. Losses considerable. Almost all my outfit tired and worn out."

To Gen. Lindsey from Col. Johnston, 13 hours 10 minutes, 16 Oct., 1918.

"Albany 1 is very much concerned about your contact with the right 163rd Brigade. He feels that perhaps you have got too far to the east and wishes to re-establish contact."

Gen. Lindsey replied that two hours ago he gave an order to that effect and had no doubt that it had been complied with.

To Col. Johnston by radio from Liaison Officer with 42nd Division, 13 hours 30 minutes, 16 Oct., 1918.

"42nd Division not advancing until further orders."

To Col. Schley from Col. Johnston, 13 hours 40 minutes, 16 Oct., 1918.

"Are your engineer Companies where they can be readily assembled?"
"No, I don't think so. They are at their own work."
"What would be the most convenient place for concentration of the forward Battalion?"
"Fléville."
"Assemble that Battalion at Fléville as promptly as possible and notify this Headquarters when they are there."

Gen. Cronin to Col. Johnston, 14 hours, 16 Oct., 1918.

"We could not stand in the Ravine on account of gas, but we are on the south slope and in liaison with our right and left and we can stick."

"Albany 1 directs you to dig in for the day."

Message from Gen. Cronin, 14 hours 10 minutes, 16 Oct., 1918.

"Boche plane has just been flying over us registering presumably for its artillery. Characteristic feature of last two days has been the freedom with which Boche planes have been flying over our front lines. I believe this accounts for enemy's very effective artillery fire and the inability of our batteries to be effective in counter battery work."

Gen. Duncan immediately ordered Air Service to go out and do something irrespective of weather conditions.

From 157th Field Artillery Headquarters, 14 hours 55 minutes, 16th Oct., 1918.

"A hostile plane was brought down by the machine gun fire of Battery A, 320th F. A., at 14.25 hours just northeast of Sommerance."

From Gen. Lindsey, 15 hours 3 minutes, 16th Oct., 1918.

"Left flank of 327th pushed forward and joined right flank of 325th. Both had to drop back to the St. Georges-St. Juvin on account of machine gun fire and consolidated with my right at cemetery and left at 99.3-86.6."

From Captain Tomasello, 15 hours 40 minuetes, 16 Oct., 1918.

"There is a big enemy gun working on the south and west of Sommerance at the present time. This gun has been in action for the past 3 days. This fact has been reported numerous times. Request that Air Service locate this Battery and report to Army artillery for counter battery."

Memorandum by Captain Dunlap, 15 hours 55 minutes, 16 Oct., 1918.

"General Cronin requests that 15 Chauchat rifles together with carriers and ammunition be supplied to his Brigade to-night."

From Division O. P. at 16 hours, 16 Oct., 1918.

"Enemy shelling Champigneulle with shrapnel. A number of men standing on the road on the eastern edge of the town. Visibility very poor. Road running northeast from St. Juvin being shelled. Friendly troops seen on the south edge of Bois des Loges. Boche shelling railroad yards west of St. Juvin. Ravine east of Champigneulle is filled with smoke and haze. Visibility so poor that enemy cannot see our troops. Bois des Loges is full of Boche."

By radio from Liaison Officer with 42nd Division, 16 hours 35 minutes, 16th Oct., 1918.

"Both flanks of 42nd Division advancing slowly."

Advance notice by telephone of 1st Corps Order, 16 hours 45 minutes, 16th Oct., 1918.

"The Corps Commander directs that arrangements be made within the Division for the utilization of not to exceed one Battalion in each Regiment in line for the day's work. The support and reserve battalion should be utilized only in case of great emergency and returned to their positions when the emergency ceases. Support battalion to be used in front line on succeeding days. Send front line battalion to reserve. This will enable the Army commander to count upon constant use of Division for one month or more. The Corps Commander desires that this arrangement be put into effect in the 82nd Division at once."

Message from Chief of Air Service, 16 hours 50 minutes, 16 Oct., 1918.

"I would like to have flares displayed from now till dark, or a white rocket to be fired about every 3 minutes; or gasoline burned on the ground."

CHAPTER XVII

CHAMPIGNEULLE AND EXTENSION OF LEFT FLANK

The remaining messages in the Divisional dossier for October 16, 1918, are concerned with a confusing situation which arose on our left flank with the 78th Division. Our Divisional Headquarters was informed that troops from the 78th Division had entered the Bois des Loges and penetrated to the northern edge of the woods. It was further claimed that the 309th Infantry (78th Div.), on our immediate left, had entered the town of Champigneulle. Both General Duncan and Colonel Johnston doubted that the Bois des Loges had been penetrated to its northern edge. Nevertheless, it was at once agreed that if such proved to be the fact the left flank of the 82nd Division would be pushed forward to connect with such advance. Our liaison detachment reported meanwhile that the right of the 78th Division had not advanced.

General Cronin, however, was directed to push elements directly north toward Champigneulle with a reservation that if Champigneulle proved to be strongly held by the enemy, General Cronin would not commit himself to a serious attack. These directions were dictated by the consideration that if Champigneulle was found strongly held, it was positive evidence that the enemy had not been expelled from the Bois des Loges.

Possession of the Bois des Loges by either side, entirely controlled Champigneulle and the Agron Valley.

Division Field Order No. 28 issued at 22 hours, Oct. 16, 1918, contained the following brief directions for the contemplated operation on the following day:

a. "The 163rd Brigade will support and protect the right flank of the 78th Division by advancing its left to the ridge due east of Champigneulle.
b. "164th Brigade will hold present front.
c. "Artillery support, no change in plan.
d. "Machine gun, no change.

Paragraph one stated that the attack would be continued at 6 hours 30 minutes, October 17.

At "H" hour, a detachment from Major Hawkins's Battalion endeavored to advance from Hill 182 and met at once with intense enemy fire from Champigneulle. This checked for the time any further advance by our left flank in accordance with instructions already given to General Cronin.

Later in the morning, however, a determined effort was made by the 2nd Battalion, 325th Infantry (Major Hawkins) to advance north from Hill 182 up the Agron Valley. This attack advanced for about 500 meters when it was halted with heavy losses by concentrated machine gun and artillery fire.

As the right flank of the 78th Division did not advance during the day the 82nd Division remained stabilized. This was in compliance with the Corps Order which defined the mission of the 82nd Division to be the support of the right flank of the 78th Division.

The orders which Major Hawkins received from General Cronin prior to the attack just described were as follows:

From Austin-1, to: C. O. 2nd Battalion, 325th Inf. 16th Oct.

"You will advance with your battalion and establish a line from Champigneulle exclusive to points 97.3-87.4

South East to 98.0-86.3 connecting on your right with first battalion 326th Inf. The principal left position will be in the Hollow 97.3-87.3 and other positions in the Ravine will be taken along the Western slopes between the mouth of the Ravine South East to the end of your line.

"You will advance one company at a time at long distances keeping pace with the 78th Division on our left. Your movement is designed to protect right flank of the 78th from the east side of the valley of the Agron. You will not advance to your Northern limit unless protected from counter attack from Champigneulle either because Champigneulle is in American hands or the ground prevents counter attack from that direction."

By command Gen. Cronin.

The following are a few of the messages contained in the Division dossier for October 17:

From Lt. Hare, 163 Brigade, at 13 hours 30 minutes.

"The Battalion commander of the right battalion of the 78th Division reported to the 163rd Brigade that Hill 182 forms a salient on the front as the 78th Division has fallen back to the St. Juvin-Grande-Pré Road.

"15 hours 15 minutes Oct. 17th, from Lt. Fravier, 317th Heavy Artillery (French). Reports that at 15 hours Oct. 16th the P. C. of the 317th French Heavy Artillery was blown up by an explosion of a German ammunition dump. The P. C. was at 97.7-78.6. There was also an explosion of a German ammunition dump at about 10:45 hours this morning. Delayed fuses were found by the French officers in dug out near by, indicating that the dumps had been exploded by this means. In a great many dumps in La Chêne Tondu, delayed action fuses were found. In a dug out on the Chêne Tondu a small thermometer was found which was so designed as to explode a mine when the mercury reached a particular height. If a fire had been built in the dug out the mercury would have risen and the explosion followed."

From 310th Infantry at 15 hours 35 minutes.

"Germans are massed across the road between Champigneulle and Bois des Loges. 78th and 82nd Artillery to be notified."

From 78th Division 15 hours 40 minutes 17th Oct.

"Germans are massed across the road at point 96.65-87.80 between Champigneulle and Bois des Loges. Artillery requested at 95.4-87.7 to 95.9-87.7."

"16 hours 17 minutes from Chief of Staff, 78th Division. Artillery fire scattered the Huns."

From Col. Montgomery G-3 1st Corps to Maj. Wainwright, 16 hours 15 minutes, 17th Oct.

"The following boundaries between 82nd and 78th Division will be established at 5 hours, 18th Oct.
Châtel Chéhéry to 78th
Marcq to 82nd
Champigneulle to 82nd
Résille Farm to 78th
78th Division is charged with carrying out the relief made necessary by this change of boundary.
H hour is 6:30 hours."

20 hours 45 minutes 17 Oct. Col. Johnston-Col. Herron, 78th Div.

"Col. Herron reports 78th Div. holds the entire Southern edge of Bois des Loges. Their troops have penetrated and to-night intend to mop the entire woods to the Northern edge and there leave light holding detachments, withdraw the main body in the main body of the woods preparatory to an attack in a westerly direction. It seems they have never been able to secure Grand-Pré, still heavy fighting in that town and strong forces North of it. The French were driven out of Talma this morning by a heavy counter-attack.

"Col. Johnston asked in what way the 82nd Div. can best support their flank and whether he considered it sufficient if we remain in contact and move forward if their right does. Col. Herron replied 'yes, entirely so.' Asked if they expected to stabilize their right flank to-morrow, Col. Herron replied that as far as he could see now it will probably remain in place, depending on events in the

West. Col. Johnston asked how he could best assist them with fire, and was told to fire on Champigneulle and to the south and west slopes of the Agron River. Col. Johnston said he was asking particularly about this to make certain to avoid complications like yesterday afternoon when 2 of the 78th Division interior battalions advanced much further than their troops on the extreme right flank with whom we were in liaison. Col. Herron answered he understood that perfectly and that it would be entirely satisfactory if we maintain contact with their right flank."

During the 17th of October the regiments of the Division carried on considerable patrolling in the face of direct machine gun fire. Other than this there were no offensive activities.

The orders issued by General Duncan for a schedule of relief throughout the regiments bore immediate results. In consequence of this order the following Field Order was issued by General Lindsey in the 164th Infantry Brigade:

"Howsoever great the necessity, the indications are that there will be no immediate relief. All officers must, therefore, exert themselves to the utmost toward reorganizing their commands. Conditions are never so bad but what they can be hopefully improved by rejuvenated effort.

"The basis of relief schedule will be as follows:

"The 327th Inf., the 328th Inf. and a combination of 300 men and proper proportion of officers taken from both regiments, forming three commands for the advance, support and reserve. Reliefs will be effected late in the afternoon before dark, if possible, every day without further orders; reserve to support, support to advance, advance to reserve in the usual rotating manner. The 328th Inf. will occupy the advance this afternoon, the combination the support and the 327th Inf. to the reserve. The C. O. 328th Inf. will designate an officer to command the combination. The strength of the three commands will be kept about equal. Both regimental commanders will remain at Sommerance and by frequent consultation effectively prosecute the above plan.

"Fruitful results will accrue from energetic efforts towards securing places in reserve where men returning from the front can be dried out, warmed up, fed up, slept up and re-clothed and re-equipped.

"Salvaging parties will be immediately organized by troops in reserve to gather up arms and equipment and establish a dump. Other parties must be set to work cleaning and assorting arms and equipment, other parties to cleaning out places where fires can be built and straw beds made. Billets should be carefully classified and numbered to facilitate occupation after dark. The C. O. 328th Inf. is charged with the duty of immediately beginning work along the lines set forth. The greatest mistake that can be made is to let officers and men remain idle expecting relief. As soon as such a sort of resting place is started, improvement in the morale of the men will be immediately noticed.

"An inspection of the reserve lines shows that the men were not properly caring for their rifles, automatic rifles and machine guns. This condition was much improved in a brief hour by attention being called to the matter.

"C. O. 321 M. G. Bn. will assign his companies and arrange for their relief and rest according to the general plan above."

82nd Division Field Order No. 29 was published at 20 hours, October 17, 1918, and provided for a continuation of the offensive at 6 hours 30 minutes on October 18, 1918. The mission assigned the 82nd Division was again that of supporting and protecting the right flank of the 78th Division.

While the east boundary of our zone of action was unchanged the west boundary prescribed the change indicated by the message from the 1st Corps received during the afternoon of October 17. The Commanding General of the 163rd Brigade was directed to relieve, with one battalion and one machine gun company, the 309th Infantry in the area between the present left boundary of the 82nd Division and the new boundary marked by a line drawn through Marcq (inclusive) -Champigneulle (inclusive -Résille Farm (exclusive).

The Commanding Officer of the Battalion from the 82nd Division making this relief was directed to report upon receipt of this order to the Commanding Officer, 309th Inf., at the latter's P. C. at the east entrance of St. Juvin on the St. Juvin-Fléville Road, and arrange necessary details. The order required that relief be completed by 5 hours, October 18.

A change was also made in the boundary between the two Infantry Brigades of the 82nd Division. This change resulted in extending the front of the 164th Infantry Brigade about one kilometer further to the west. The Commanding General of this Brigade was directed to make the necessary disposition in the new area assigned him before 5 hours, October 18.

In compliance with the change of boundary between the Brigades, G Company, 328th Infantry (Captain Danforth), moved to the west and covered the additional front necessary to connect with the 163rd Brigade, which had also swung a similar distance to the left, where the 2nd Battalion, 326th Infantry, shifted over, relieving the 1st Battalion, 326th Infantry.

The relief of the 309th Infantry, 78th Division, was accomplished by the 2nd Battalion, 325th Infantry, within the time set by Division Orders. It is interesting, however, to read the report on this relief submitted by Lieutenant Mitchell, Liaison Officer, with the 78th Division.

"On night of October 17th, I was called by 'phone and told to report to Division Headquarters and about half an hour later, I reported to Col. Wainwright.

"The Corps orders of that day had caused a change in our west boundary, necessitating the relief of troops of the 309th Infantry, 78th Division, in their present sector and placing our troops in positions as held by the 309th Infantry in the space referred to.

"My mission was for the purpose of reconnoitering the positions we were to hold and to find out from the C. G. 163rd Brigade which Regiment was to supply the Battalion that it would take to make the relief. I first went to Brigade Headquarters and had to wait for their order to be made before going to Regimental P. C.'s of the 325th and 326th Infantry. With an officer of Brigade Headquarters I arrived at 326th P. C.'s at about 1:30 A.M. I explained to the Regimental C. O. the purpose of my mission and he in reading the Brigade order found it so complicated in its wording that it was hard for them to understand for some time just what was to be done. It took some time to decide and I finally said that the question most important now was to locate just the Battalion that was to go into this position I was to locate, and so the Battalion Commander could be making his arrangements as it was then getting late. The Battalion was then located in the Brigade order and the C. O. 326th gave orders for Major Hawkins to report to him at once. After the Major had read his orders and had studied the positions we were to occupy, Major Hawkins and myself then left to go where his troops were in camp, where he gave instructions to his Adjutant to have the Companies moving so as to reach St. Juvin fifteen minutes apart; first company to arrive at about 3:45 A.M. With three of his regimental runners we started out to locate 309th P. C. We were unable to locate it, so we decided to go to front lines and get some Company Commander to direct us to it and doing so we ran across Battalion headquarters, it being really the place we wanted. We made our mission known to the Battalion Commander of the 309th Infantry and he had no instructions about being relieved. He had just finished making a relief of another Battalion. He phoned his regimental C. O. and the latter had received no instructions but told the Battalion Commander to go ahead since we had the change in boundary and he gave instructions where to take the Battalion after it was relieved. We then arranged for runners to go down the road, each runner to meet a certain company, the runners taking these companies to positions as occupied by the companies being relieved.

"First troops arrived at about 4:00 o'clock. Between

4:00 and 5:00 o'clock two companies of Infantry and one Machine Gun Company were relieving the Battalion of 309. The other two companies were said to be in the town at 5:00 o'clock, but in some way the runners lost them and I think it must have been 6:00 to possibly 7:00 o'clock before the relief was complete.

"Having the place located and most of the Battalion relieved, I asked Major Hawkins if I could do anything else to help him in the relief. He told me that he would not need me any longer, so I left to go to the P. C. of 309th Infantry, being directed by runner. I talked to Col. Morgan and explained that the boundary had been changed by Corps; that this necessitated our putting in a Battalion to cover the additional ground it gave us. He stated that he had never been informed about a relief or change of boundary and I took my map and gave them the new boundary line as I had gotten it from my Division Headquarters. I also told him in the order I had noticed that the 78th Division was to attack at 6:30 A.M. and our Division was to support the attack. I thought it strange that he did not know of his Division attacking at this hour, as I had seen the Corps order myself. I left at 6:10, came back by Brigade Headquarters, dropped a note to Major Parker telling him the relief was well on its way when I left and also stopped by our Division Headquarters and dropped a note to Col. Wainwright telling him the relief was well on its way, and was back at my station at 78th Division Headquarters at 8:00 A.M.

"I talked to the Chief of Staff of the 78th Division later in the day and told him that the C. O. 309th did not know the 78th Division was to attack. I was informed that the right Brigade had been ordered not to attack but would hold, covering their front with strong patrols."

The 2nd Battalion, 325th Infantry, was still under the orders of the Commanding Officer of the 326th Infantry. The elements of this Battalion were disposed as follows:

Company G (Lieutenant Bettes) in position at 96.0-86.5. This Company maintained liaison with the 309th Infantry in the edge of the Bois des Loges by means of one platoon in the woods on the right flank of that battalion.

Company H (Lieutenant Martin) held Hill 182 at 97.0-86.2.

Company E (Captain Fraser) held the east slope of the Hill and the St. Georges Road leaving from St. Juvin.

Company F (Captain Fournoy) was in support on the St. Georges Road in St. Juvin.

Following are a few messages from the Divisional dossier for October 18, 1918:

From Lt. Carlisle, Liaison Officer with the 42nd Division, at 8 hours 30 minutes, 18th Oct. 1918.

"The 42nd Division will not advance to-day. The 83rd Brigade are sending out patrols. The patrols which were sent out last night have returned. Report that they could get no further. No information obtained."

From 163rd Brigade 10 hours, 18 Oct., 1918.

"Enemy planes flying low under 1000 foot level.

"Col. Johnston replied that he got in direct touch with the pursuit service some time ago and was informed that they were taking the air at once."

Col. Johnston to Wide-wing, 13 hours 45 minutes, 18 Oct., 1918.

"We have just received a message from the front line that Boche planes are still flying very low over our support lines and directing the artillery fire.

"Wide-wing replied that the Air service Liaison Officer was at Divisional Headquarters for the purpose of taking care of such matters.

"Col. Johnston replied that this Liaison Officer states that he is merely representing the Observation end of the Service and reports to the Corps, who in turn report somewhere else.

"Col. Johnston asked if there was any objection to the Commanding General of the 82nd Division reporting direct to them.

"No definite reply was elicited."

Major Lee (G-2), from Sommerance.

"Reports that at 13:45 hours two enemy planes were

over the front line battalion directing Boche artillery fire and causing us heavy losses. They had been over our lines since 8 hours this morning. Two of our planes showed up early this morning, stayed for about half hour and have not been seen since.

"Reports quite a few Boche seen above the Ravin aux Pierres and some enemy seen in the ravine to the northeast."

From Major Lee, G-2, 328th Infantry Headquarters, 16 hours 40 minutes, 18th Oct., 1918.

"Regimental Adjutant wants me to report to you that a German plane fell in flames in the area of Mr. Boyle's Battalion. It was a Fokker and the pilot escaped in a parachute. Pilot is now at 328th Infantry Headquarters. He says he was operating a plane pursuing an American bombing plane. He was brought down by American planes that came up and took him by surprise. He said also that another German plane was brought down in front of the Division on our right."

Later Message from Major Lee.

"I have been out to the lines and have found two planes there. One of them is at 99.5-86.2. That one landed out of control and is in fair condition with one blade of the propeller broken and the landing gear smashed up. There are no papers nor marks of identification. Out of that plane was taken one pilot, who is badly injured and is being evacuated to-night. This plane was a single-seater. The other plane crashed in flames at about 99.9-86.2. This was the plane from which the pilot landed with a parachute. The parachute fell further to the west."

Message dropped from aeroplane, 19 hours 10 minutes, 18 Oct., 1918.

"Artillery of enemy growing more active after 16:45 hours. Darkness setting in now. The air was full of hostile machines. From 15:30 hours to 16:30 hours there were 30 Boche pursuit planes over our sector. There was one formation of 14 planes and three formations of 5 each. They were pursuit planes painted a bright red all over."

No Field Orders were issued by the Division until the night of October 20. Our troops continued to hold their line and carried on the usual aggressive patrolling. The 78th on our left continued to struggle with the extraordinary difficulties presented by the Bois des Loges. Two battalion messages indicated the situation.

From Lieutenant Mitchell, Liaison Officer with 78th Division, 19th Oct., 1918.

"At 9:30 hours 309th Infantry reports troops in grove in Bois des Loges. Are being troubled by machine-gun fire from hostile aeroplanes.

"At 11:15 309th Infantry. Things going well, casualties high. Liaison with 326th Infantry on the right and 310th Infantry on the left. One pounder crew gassed."

From 163rd Infantry Brigade, 14 hours 30 minutes, 19th Oct., 1918.

"Major Hawkins just had a runner from the 309th Infantry stating their location as about 100 yards inside the edge of the woods. They are reorganizing and feel confident to hold. Enemy near. Fire from machine guns and snipers heavy."

An indication of the growing desperation of our enemy at this time is found in the following propaganda addressed to German troops and intercepted by our wireless on October 19, 1918.

"At its reconstruction, the economic life of Germany must find the world open; no measures should withhold from us raw materials and bar to us markets. We are ready to support any government striving for a peace on such a basis. Arrangement and rebuilding of our national life are the issues on the program of the Christian national workers' movement.

"You fighters at the front, our hopes on the successful issue of an uncompromising peace depend upon your heroic spirit. We remember your noble deeds on the battlefield. We thank you for having spared our motherland the woes of devastation. At this fateful hour it is more urgent than ever to hold up the live wall which you have built for the past four years in order that the enemy may not trespass the holy ground of our fatherland. You will not, at this last hour, allow the dreadful horrors of war to visit our country and homes.

"You at home, for years you have borne the greatest privations and sacrifices for our sacred cause. More than ever, it is now necessary to do our duty and with redoubled strength, to stand up for the achievements of an honorable peace.

"THE COMMITTEE OF THE GERMAN WORKINGMEN'S CONGRESS."

On October 19 Colonel Ely rejoined the 327th Infantry and on October 20th, 1918, Colonel McArthur, commanding the 326th Infantry, was evacuated to a rest hospital. Lieutenant-Colonel Burr was transferred to command the 326th Infantry. On October 20 the 2nd Battalion, 325th Inf., was returned to its own regiment and the 2nd Battalion, 326th Inf., in turn passed out of the command of Colonel Whitman. Reliefs were arranged within the regiments and the usual patrolling continued. Our front lines, however, did not advance.

A few messages follow from the Division dossier.

From Chief of Staff 78th Division to Chief of Staff 82nd Division, 2 hours, 20th Oct., 1918.

"We are pulling back our line. We will hold the general line, St. Juvin-Grand-Pré Road. This change will be made before daybreak."

From Major Hawkins, 2nd Bn., 325th Inf., 17 hours, 20 Oct., 1918.

"Colonel Morgan commanding the 309th Infantry has been fully informed of the position of the 2nd Battalion, 325th Inf., since the first morning we moved next his right flank. Company G, 325th Infantry, has maintained actual contact with the right of the 309th line in the Bois de Loges since 10 hours, 18th Oct., 1918. Colonel Morgan has expressed himself in the presence of Colonel McArthur and Major Hawkins as satisfied with the liaison and out-post protection afforded his right flank by this Division. Colonel Morgan has been asked by the Battalion Commander if he wished one or more companies of this Battalion to reinforce Company G on his immediate flank, but stated that he thought it unnecessary."

Ravin aux Pierres Taken for the Last Time

82nd Division Field Order No. 30 issued at 21 hours, October 20, 1918, stated that the 1st Army Corps would continue to improve its position for a general advance by local operations on October 21. The order further provided:

"The 82nd Division will develop the enemy's main line of resistance by pushing out strong exploitation detachments on its front and will seize and hold any advantageous ground from which the enemy may be driven or may withdraw. Infantry Brigade Commanders are charged with carrying out local operations on their own fronts as prescribed but will not involve themselves in a serious operation or bring on a general attack."

As a result of this order a strong patrol from the 164th Infantry Brigade pushed up to the woods at about 99.0-87.1, while troops from the 163rd Brigade seized the slope north of the Ravin aux Pierres. This third attempt to secure this formidable ravine proved to be a final and successful effort. The enemy never afterwards succeeded in retaking this ground.

A report to Division Commander from Brigadier General Cronin gives the story of this operation.

"The operation of this Brigade to-day resulted in establishing its front line north of the Ravin aux Pierres on the line 97.5-86.8 to 98.4-87.15. This line is held by both regiments; 60 men of the 326th Infantry on the left, and the 1st Battalion 325th Infantry (something less than 200 men), on the right; the whole under command of Captain Castle, 325th Infantry. At dark two machine guns were to be carried across the ravine to the vicinity of the infantry line, the rest of the company, six guns, to be just south of the ravine. The whole constitutes to-night the first line of the 325th Infantry. The line is in contact with the 164th Brigade on its right, who joined us this afternoon. The 2nd line, 325th Infantry, is along the St. Juvin-St. Georges Road, and is the same as last night's first line. Last night's 2nd line has disappeared, as I passed it through the first line to-day to make the front line to-night. The 3rd line last night remains the 3rd line to-night and is on the slopes on a general line 97.7-85.7 to 98.4-85.5. One platoon is detached to-night from the 3rd line to occupy the right end of the vacated 2nd line, with orders to keep out small liaison patrols between the right flanks of both the 2nd and 3rd lines.

"The line of the 326th Infantry remains the same as last night, except the 60 men of the 2nd line sent forward along the east side of the valley, whose meridian is 97.3, with orders to infiltrate into the ravine from the west.

"Little enemy infantry was noticed, but exposure brought on heavy artillery and machine-gun fire, but not to the same extent as yesterday. The Commanding Officers of both regiments, and Machine-Gun Battalion, carried out very carefully my instructions given from time to time during the day. Progress was made by persistent infiltration aided by Machine Gun and occasional artillery.

"While the line is well advanced, and forms a salient, it has been carefully prepared for resistance during the night."

Another very human account of this small operation is contained in a report made by Lieutenant Ulmer of Company A, 325th Inf., one of the units involved:

"The company had one Officer and 40 men left of an original strength of 4 officers and 220 men. These 40 men were practically dead from exhaustion and sickness.

When the company reached its objective, there were but 11 men left; the others having succumbed to fatigue. The spirit was willing but the flesh was weak. After reaching the high ground north of Ravin aux Pierres the Battalion commander was notified and the rest of the Battalion brought up. A new line was consolidated and wired, and nothing further of interest occurred, except the system of regular two-day reliefs.''

This exploitation operation was protected by machine-gun fire and artillery fire of twelve guns, commencing at 5:30 on the north slope of the ravine. This fire was raised at 6 hours and continued until 7. Both flanks of the Company were covered by patrols.

The situation as reported at 4 P.M., by Lieutenant-Colonel Campbell is shown by his message to Colonel Whitman:

"Oct. 21st.

"I gave D Company back to Castle at his request. 'Phones all out, please try to get them in. Everything lovely so far. Pretty heavy shelling. Will stick around for an hour or so and mosey back. Castle is driving this thing in good style. M. G. positions being reconnoitered and I think everything O. K. if 326th will look out for left.''

CHAPTER XVIII

A THIN LINE'S POINT OF HONOR

AFTER October 21, 1918, our front lines did not advance. In the week that followed until November 1, 1918, the American army was devoting its energy to a preparation for the final drive which was to determine effective enemy resistance in front of the American army. A tremendous concentration of artillery of all calibers took place on a depth of many kilometers behind our front line. Great quantities of ammunition were carried up and dumped in forward locations. Partially rested American Divisions poured into the back areas ready to relieve the exhausted remnants of the Divisions which had borne the brunt of furious continued fighting in the past days and weeks since the great offensive began. During this period of preparation the front-line Divisions continued to exist in cold mud and water-soaked fox holes, always subjected to harrassing artillery and machine-gun fire. The support and the reserve lines were subjected to the same degree of artillery fire as was suffered by the first line. The reliefs also were accomplished under very trying and dangerous conditions.

The dossier of the 82nd Division contains many references to the conditions under which our men existed. It indicates that a number of advances were contemplated if the neighboring divisions succeeded in getting forward. The salient in which the 82nd Division was placed made it prohibitive to advance until adjoining units succeeded in getting fully abreast of our position in the Ravin aux Pierres. Attacks were ordered for both October 22 and October 23 in both the 42nd Division and the 78th Division but on neither day did either Division succeed in coming abreast of our most advanced elements. Consequently the 82nd Division remained in place.

Extracts from the Division dossier:

"From Alto 1 (326th Infantry) at 10 hours 30 minutes, 22nd Oct., 1918. 7 Boche planes over our front lines."

C. O. 327th Inf. to C. G. 164th Inf. Brigade, 11:10 hours, 22nd Oct., 1918.

"My surgeon just now reported that at least 90 per cent of men suffering from diarrhœa and exhaustion. He expresses the opinion that great majority unable physically to endure an advance much less make attack. All other information confirms this. In my opinion grave consequences would follow any use made of this regiment as now contemplated and believe entire Brigade equally out of condition. I feel that these facts should be clearly made known."

From Lieutenant Mitchell, Liaison Officer with 78th Division, 11:45 hours, 22nd Oct., 1918.

"Patrols from 310th Infantry during the night encountered very strong machine-gun fire from enemy at the south edge of Bois des Loges."

Air message: "Dropped propaganda in the region of Verpel. 2000 copies of President Wilson's and Germany's messages. Dropped candy and cigars to Americans."

From C. G. 164th Infantry Brigade to C. O. 327th Infantry, 12 hours, 22nd Oct., 1918.

"Referring to report of your surgeon this morning on physical condition of your men, the Division Commander informed me during a visit this morning that the Division will probably remain in the line for quite a while yet. It is therefore imperative that every attempt be made to build up the physical condition of the officers and men. Many things can yet be done in addition to those originating at Brigade Headquarters to improve the officers and men. Officers and men should be evacuated only when absolutely necessary. Your report will, of course, be forwarded to Division Headquarters."

From 164th Brigade at 12:30 hours, 22nd Oct., 1918.

"Recommend that Private Alfred R. Simpson, Company D, 321st Machine-Gun Battalion be decorated for extraordinary valiant conduct in manning and operating alone a hostile machine gun and successfully covering a withdrawal of a portion of his command. This at a time when he constituted the only fighting element between his organization and the enemy. Immediate and all intermediate Commanders approve."

From Lieutenant-Colonel Wainwright at 163rd Brigade Headquarters, 14 hours, 22nd Oct., 1918.

"Engineer companies in reserve have an effective strength of about 125 men. Recommend that 2 companies be placed at disposal of General Cronin for dugouts or else that one company from this Battalion be used together with a company now working on roads."

General Duncan directed Lieutenant-Colonel Wainwright to carry out his recommendations.

From 164th Infantry Brigade by request of Colonel Johnston, 14 hours, 22nd Oct., 1918.

"Recommend that 2nd Lieutenant Francis H. Mason be decorated for unusual bravery in refusing to be evacuated though wounded while in command of patrol on dangerous mission and subject to heavy machine-gun fire. This on battlefield in front of Sommerance, October 21, 1918. All immediate and intermediate Commanders have approved."

From Division O. P. at 14:50 hours, 22nd Oct., 1918.

"At 13:30 hours Boche shelling railroad west of St. Juvin.

"At 13:35 hours Boche shelling Marcq and the ridge.

"At 14:20 hours heavy shelling on St. Juvin which still continues. Heavy barrage to the left of the 78th Division."

From Captain Patton at Division O. P. at 16:30 hours, 22nd Oct., 1918.

"3 German planes flying very low shooting at the ground where engineers were at work on barb wire on top of the ridge ¾ of a kilometer southwest of Marcq. They were run off by American planes."

Colonel Johnston to Captain Webster, 164th Brigade, 16:55 hours, 22nd Oct., 1918.

"General Duncan has approved recommendation of General Cronin that the relief be effected every other night instead of each night as at present. This for the information of General Lindsey and applies to him also if he so desires."

From 325th Infantry, 11:20 hours, 23rd Oct., 1918.

"9 enemy planes over our lines at 11:15 hours. 6 planes were painted red. One of our men in St. Juvin found a can of apricots marked 'For the Belgian Relief.' This evidently has been left by Germans on their retreat."

From Lieutenant Mitchell with 78th Division, 14:30 hours, 23rd Oct., 1918.

"Airplane reports 78th Division troops on the ridge north of Farm de Talma and have taken Grand-Pré. Troops are now north of Grand-Pré at 92.0-87.0, approximately."

Colonel Johnston to 163rd and 164th Brigades, 15 hours, 23rd Oct., 1918.

"Report from hospital indicates that patients, sick and wounded, bring practically no equipment with them.

Please have this checked up right away and see that all equipment goes back with the patients, so they can be re-equipped when they come out. We are getting short of equipment and a lot is disappearing."

"7 hours, 24 Oct., 1918. 325th Inf. and 326th Inf., both report heavy gas (phosgene) shelling."

Lieutenant-Colonel Wainwright to Brigade Commanders at 16:30 hours, 24th Oct., 1918.

"Instructions for to-day as per Field Order No. 33 will apply for to-morrow. No order will be issued to-night."

From Lieutenant Mitchell with 78th Division, 20:10 hours, 24th Oct., 1918.

"Memo. from General Craig, Chief of Staff, 1st Corp, to C. G. 78th Division states that the Division has used entirely too much ammunition for their preparation for attack in proportion to successes gained. This complaint comes from Army Headquarters."

TRANSLATION OF EXTRACTS OF LETTERS FOUND ON DEAD GERMANS GATHERED BY A PRISONER BELONGING TO THE 30TH BAV. RES. REGT., 15TH BAV. RES. DIV., CAPTURED WEST OF ST. GEORGES, OCTOBER 23, 1918. LETTERS WERE DATED OCTOBER 23 AND WERE WRITTEN BY NON-COMMISSIONED OFFICERS OF THE 30TH BAV. RES. REGT.

"I will write you a few more lines to-day—this time from the position which we now occupy. Following my return from K—— I immediately rejoined my organization and was placed in charge of two companies. Now, however, an officer is here who has been placed in command. The word 'Position' (Stellung) is really not the proper expression for same and the line we occupy might be more appropriately named a 'Squatting Place' (Sitzung). During the entire day we are compelled, on account of enemy fire, to remain in holes we ourselves have dug, protected only by shelter halves, waiting for nightfall when we at least can move around a bit. If the occupation of our line became known to the enemy artillery there would be nothing left to do, owing to the absence of dugouts, but to pack up one's belongings and pull out. Last night the Americans drove us out with their fire so that, for better or for worse, we had to dig in in a new position.

"According to rumors we are to be relieved within the next few days."

Extract from letter by a Corporal belonging to the 12th Company of the 30th Bav. Regt., dated October 23rd:

"Of the 40 men and 4 officers who manned our position when we went into line, but 4 men remain. I have been placed in command, there being no officers left."

Translation of German document issued at Headquarters of the 5th Army. The document was among the letters extracts of which are given above:

"GERMAN SOLDIERS!
"BEWARE!

"The word 'Armistice' passes through trenches and camps.

"EVENTS HAVE NOT YET REACHED THIS STAGE!

"The word is taken by some as a certainty and by others even as the long-hoped-for peace. This fellow or the other fellow believes that matters no longer depend on him and relaxes his watchfulness, courage, endurance, and distrust of the enemy.

"EVENTS HAVE NOT YET REACHED THIS STAGE!

"An armistice has not yet been concluded.

"THE WAR IS STILL ON JUST AS IT ALWAYS HAS BEEN!

"At this very moment you must be watchful, staunchly persevering! At this very moment you are on the enemy's soil, the rampart of the Fatherland.

"At this grave hour the Fatherland sees in you its salvation and its hope.
"Headquarters of the 5th Army."

From C. O. 3rd Battalion, 325th Inf., 7 hours, 25th Oct., 1918.

"Patrol along left front last night fired on as it crossed trail 97.5-86.8. Enemy machine gun dominated ridge in front of our position. Seem to be located on northern slope of ravine. Enemy patrol of about 30 ran into one of our positions and was driven off. We had one man slightly wounded by grenade. Boche were seen to drag two wounded away with them. This happened about 4 hours."

From Division O. P. on the right at 16:20 hours, 25th Oct., 1918.

"2 of our planes driven back across our lines by machine gun fire coming from the northeast edge of Bois des Loges, also from the trenches southeast of Champigneulle."

Colonel Montgomery, G-3 1st Corps to Colonel Johnston, 11:15 hours, 26th Oct., 1918.

"All movements and reliefs directed by Field Order No. 86 are suspended for 24 hours."

Colonel Montgomery to Colonel Johnston, 11:40 hours, 26th Oct., 1918.

"You will replace the 77th Division and take their present camp. Furnish the same garrison for the occupation of the security position and continue the work they are now engaged on."

Colonel Johnston. "In other words we take that letter you wrote the 77th and follow it."

Colonel Montgomery. "Yes. The 77th are in Camp Bouzon and the Chêne Tondu."

From Division O. P. on the left at 15:40 hours, 26th Oct., 1918.

"7 Boche planes over our front lines but driven back by our anti-aircraft fire."

To C. G. 163rd Brigade from C. O. 325th Inf., 26th Oct., 1918.

"The C. O. 1st Battalion reported at 16:10 hours 2 planes firing with Machine Guns on his position along St. Juvin-St. Georges road. These planes were clearly marked with U. S. insignia and were numbered 2 and 17. At 16:15 hours similar report was received from C. O. 3rd Battalion that same 2 planes fired on his front line in position north of Ravin aux Pierres. From observation point near Regimental P. C. these planes were seen firing tracer bullets. The planes were later seen retiring in a southerly direction. Request prompt investigation and proper action."

From 164th Brigade by courier, 9:35 hours, 27th Oct., 1918.

"Telephone shot out. In front of our left flank Boche were heard driving stakes and stringing wire through the night. This was about 300 yards in advance of 99.75-86.30. Artillery scattered fire over entire front during night. Sommerance shelled and gassed all night. Heavy shelling and sneezing gas from 4:20 hours to 5:30 hours this morning."

To C. G. 82nd Division from St. Disier, Oct. 28, 1918.

"1800 replacements are on route for your Division. They should arrive at Auzeville at 1 o'clock Oct. 28th. At present they are in two trains, one train has 1500 men and the other 300 men."

From Lieutenant Mitchell with 78th Division, 11 hours, 28th Oct., 1918.

"Berlin announces the resignation of Ludendorff which has been accepted by the Kaiser."

From Division O. P. on the left at 9:05 hours, 29th Oct., 1918.

"Shelling in the valley south of St. Juvin. Aeroplane fight in air, about five machines engaged. Visibility poor."

Messages dropped from aeroplane 10:50 hours, 29th Oct., 1918. To G-2 82nd Division.

Time of departure 9:10 hours, time of return 10:40 hours, mission reconnaissance.

"Covered St. Georges-Grand-Pré. Pilot Lieutenant Smith, Observer Lieutenant Wright, Squadron 12, altitude 1000 meters. Boche patrol of nine planes over Verpel at 9:50 and another patrol of five planes over Verpel at 10:20. One Allied plane probably hit by anti-aircraft artillery. Seen to crash just west of Champigneulle at 10 o'clock. Dropped 2000 sheets of propaganda just north of Bois des Loges over Beffu et Morthomme at 10:15."

From 78th Division 15:20 hours, 29th Oct., 1918, to 1st Corps.

"A Boche plane fell about 100 yards in front of 78th's front line just north of Marcq."

From Captain Dunlap at Fléville at 19:40 hours, 29th Oct., 1918.

"First truck of replacements arrived in Fléville 17:50 hours and last truck of replacements arrived at 18:35. Hospital replacements arrived at 19 hours; all now on way to organizations."

NOTE. Between 5000 and 6000 replacements from several replacement divisions were sent to the 82nd Division during the last week of October, 1918. These men were placed in camps around the Headquarters of our rear echelon south of Clermont. Many of these soldiers were recent recruits from the United States and had not received more than two or three weeks' training. Fortunately the Division was relieved before it became necessary to attack with this untrained material.

From Lieutenant Mitchell with 78th Division, 10 hours, 30th Oct., 1918.

"Streamer message taken from enemy aeroplane that fell to-day in front of our lines contained names of American and French aviators captured or killed. Contained names of eleven French aviators and two American aviators. Stated that information as to eighteen German aviators would be appreciated."

The following message from Lieutenant Stynes was in the streamer container:

"Can you store my baggage in University Club, Paris? 1000 francs I loaned mess in the Farmers Loan and Trust Company. All very well with me. Morriss was killed in action."

At 11 hours, October 30, 1918, Division Field Order No. 34 announced the long-delayed relief.

"The 82nd Division less the 157th Artillery Brigade and Ammunition Train will be relieved in its present sector by the 77th and 80th on the night of the 30th-31st October.

"The outpost screen of the 82nd Division consisting of the 2nd Battalion, 326th Infantry; 3rd Battalion, 325th Infantry and the 328th Infantry (less detachment combined with the 327th Infantry) will remain in place and will be relieved at 24 hours on 'D' minus one day by Commanding Generals 77th and 80th Divisions."

The part of the Division relieved on the night of the 30-31st October, 1918, was directed to move back a short distance to the Corps line of resistance. This force consisted of one regiment, 163rd Infantry Brigade, one battalion, 307th Engineers, the 319th Machine Gun Battalion and Company C, 320th Machine Gun Battalion. The remaining elements were directed to assemble in the vicinity of Apremont and Champ Mahaut.

The outpost screen was not required by orders of the Corps or Army but was furnished in compliance with orders of the Division Commander in his final Field Order, October 30th.

"It will be considered a point of honor to the front line battalions of the 82nd Division left in the sector to prevent the entrance of hostile patrols, thus keeping from the enemy the fact that fresh troops are being assembled in the rear."

It therefore stands to the credit of these troops that for twenty-four hours before the attack by the new Division on November 1, 1918, our men securely held nearly five kilometers of front and prevented the enemy from learning that a great drive was impending.

The outpost screen was relieved before daylight, November 1, 1918. As the troops moved south through Fléville and Cornay they heard the roar of the tremendous barrage striking north of the Kremhilde-Stellung and those ridges where so much blood had been given to win a foothold. The Division was conscious that its efforts during the October battles had helped drive the enemy into open country where fresh Divisions of fellow-Americans could more easily complete the task.

CASUALTIES IN MEUSE-ARGONNE OFFENSIVE

	Officers	Enlisted Personnel
Killed in action or died of wounds	37	865
Known Prisoners	7	178
Missing	0	25
Wounded, including "Gassed"	171	4726
Total	215	5794

CHAPTER XIX

AFTER THE FIGHTING

(Contributed by Lieut. Colonel George E. Roosevelt.)

THE night of October 31-November 1, the 82nd Division, on being relieved by the 80th Division, moved back in the Argonne Forest, with Division Headquarters at Champ Mahaut, and the following day, November 2nd, the Division continued south, Headquarters moving to Florent. After remaining there one day, the Division began a movement to the Vaucouleurs area. The motor transport moved by Les Islettes, Clermont, Fleury, St. Dizier, Commercy and Void. The infantry proceeded by bus. The animal-drawn transportation started on November 4 under the Commander of Trains, and reached Vaucouleurs after staging four times—at Autrecourt, Chaumont-sur-Aire, Kœurs-la-Grande and Neuville. Beginning November 10, the Division again moved, this time by marching, to the Bourmont area, each brigade making the march in three days. The stay at Bourmont was as short as at Vaucouleurs, for on November 16, the Division was again on the march, this time for the Tenth Training Area, with Division Headquarters at Prauthoy. The march was made with three stages, and by the 19th of November, the Division, less artillery and ammunition train, was billeted in the towns around Prauthoy, where it was to remain for the winter. The Prauthoy area had been used in the previous spring by various American organizations; notably, the 32nd and 79th Divisions, but was by no means a completely equipped and thoroughly organized area in which to pass a comfortable winter. In addition, almost immediately upon arrival, the Training Section at General Headquarters directed that maneuvers of all kinds be commenced with great vigor. These maneuvers were immediately commenced; and it was attempted to put into practice all the lessons learned in the recent fighting. Particular attention was given to correcting deficiencies that had been noticed, and obtaining the benefit of co-operation of all means at the disposal of the troops. Some of the problems were simple problems in liaison, with only the commanders and methods of communication actually present. In other problems, all the troops were out, and attention was concentrated on the proper tactical employment, and maximum co-operation, of all arms. The improvement was very rapid, and most satisfactory. There were many difficulties to contend with—the troops were tired by their long marches; they were very scattered, and large numbers of replacements were arriving to fill up the gaps caused by death, wounds and sickness, and the inevitable wear and tear of war. In addition, many changes occurred in the officer personnel, and for a considerable time the artillery brigade and ammunition train, which had moved forward with the 80th Division in the 1st of November attack, were completely lost. No one at Division Headquarters, at Fifth Corps Headquarters (the Division now being part of the Fifth Corps), or anywhere else, seemed able to discover the location of these units. Lieutenant-Colonel Wainwright left the Division Staff almost immediately after the withdrawal of the Division from the line; and Major Lansing Lee and Lt. Col. Troop Miller left a little later. Their places were taken by Lt. Col. (then Major) George E. Roosevelt, Maj. James C. McMannaway, and Lt. Col. James P. Barney, respectively. In the 163rd Infantry Brigade, General Cronin was replaced by General Bradley, and Colonel Preston and Colonel Miller took command of the 327th and 326th Infantries, respectively. Lt. Col. B. Moore was replaced as

Division Machine Gun Officer by Maj. I. C. Holloway, who had commanded the 321st Machine Gun Battalion during the fighting.

The maneuver program involved battalion, regimental and brigade maneuvers, and called for a Division maneuver to be managed by Corps Headquarters, at least once a month. The weather, which had previously been cold and wet, became colder, so that the wet turned to snow. Many of the men were required to eat out of doors, as no proper housing facilities were provided. The Division maneuver showed the great difficulties of conducting such operations under the existing conditions. Distant organizations were required to bivouac for two nights, and so many cases of colds and pneumonia developed, that the Corps Commander, Maj. Gen. Charles P. Summerall, terminated the maneuvers, and most fortunately, the experiment was not repeated.

During December, the artillery brigade finally rejoined the Division, and immediately commenced to replace the horses of the 319th F. A. regiment with tractors. At the time the regiment was originally organized, it was designated as tractor-drawn, and recruited and trained on that basis. During its operations in France, it was supplied with horses; but after the armistice it again made a valiant effort to turn horsemen into mechanics and chauffeurs. Immediately, artillery officers were detailed permanently with infantry organizations, in order that there should be the most thorough mutual understanding and co-operations between the two arms, and the extremely satisfactory results obtained in maneuvers, thoroughly justified this policy.

It was during December that after considerable effort, a number of buildings were secured, to be used as messhalls, and the untiring efforts of all did a great deal towards improving the conditions under which the Division was required to work. A Division show was organized under Captain Dunlap of Headquarters Troop, and also the Division horse-show, the first in the A. E. F., was held, and was so successful, that horse-shows of a similar nature were ordered throughout the A. E. F. The work of Captain Dunlap, Captain Holbert, the Division Remount Officer; the enthusiasm and inspiration furnished by Col. Gordon Johnston, the Division Chief of Staff; and the backing of General Duncan, the Division Commander, were all of prime importance in successfully carrying out the horse-show in spite of the conditions of weather that prevailed.

The month of January saw the further alleviation of the pressure by the reduction of the training program from GHQ; and by this time, the Division personnel was practically completed; the transportation was in excellent shape, both horse and motor; and the organization running very smoothly and satisfactorily. During this period, the First Army held conferences on recent operations for the Division and Brigade commanders; the Corps held conferences for the officers, including many of the battalion commanders; and the Division included schemes along this line from which a great deal of benefit was derived. Once a week the brigade and regimental commanders met the Division Staff officers for the transaction of routine business, and in order to listen to the stories of various officers and men who could throw light on particularly interesting features of the operations of the Division. It was partly as a result of these conferences and stories that Lt. Col. (then Major) G. Edward Buxton, Jr., was detailed to prepare a complete and accurate Division History. In order to verify many important details, sufficient transportation was provided so that he could take parties of officers up to the scene of the Division fighting in the Meuse-Argonne offensive and go over with them disputed and important points, verifying on the actual ground the details of exactly what occurred. It was also provided that brigade commanders should hold conferences with their battalion commanders at which either the Chief of Staff, or the Assistant Chief of Staff, G-3, should be present; and in that way, Division Headquarters was able to keep closely in touch with the thoughts of the men of the Division.

In February, General Summerall, the Corps Commander, visited the Division and, in a whirlwind tour, reviewed all the organizations. This trip required an entire day, and General Summerall's opinion was expressed in an official communication contained in the supplementary material in this volume. In this month, the Division held its second horse-show, even more successful than the first, and as an additional feature, General Summerall reviewed the Division, brigade and regimental officers mounted, in a very impressive ceremony. During this ceremony, and to the entire surprise of the Division officers present, General Summerall called out Sergeant York, who was carrying the Division flag, and in an impressive speech, commended him for his wonderful fight which was to later gain him the Medal of Honor. The following week, the Corps horse-show was held, and was won by the 82nd Division. Too much credit cannot be given to Captain Holbert for the condition of the horses and transportation; and to Captain Patton, of the 325th Infantry, who had charge of the Division hangar and the care and discipline of the men; and to Captain Dunlap, who worked untiringly while the transportation from all the different units was billeted in Prauthoy. The band representing the 82nd Division also won the competition for bands in the Corps.

Shortly after this, the Commander-in-Chief reviewed the Division. The field on which the review was held, large enough to have accommodated an entire Corps, was covered with snow, and presented a most impressive appearance. In order to consolidate the Division, it was necessary to borrow 50 trucks, and to utilize all the trucks in the Division trains. All the distant units had to commence moving at daylight; whether they marched or were transported. When the Commander-in-Chief arrived on the field, the Division was completely formed, with the winners in the Division horse-show in the rear, representing the transport. Every company was personally inspected by the reviewing party, and immediately afterwards, the Division passed in review. A communication from the Commander-in-Chief to the Division Commander immediately after this review, is printed in the supplementary material.

It was shortly after this that intimation was received that the Division would return home, and excitement of course became intense. The intimation took the form of orders to turn in property, and during the last part of February, trucks, tractors, guns, escort wagons, machine guns and other property, were turned in at the railhead at Vaux, or were transported to other places designated. On February 26th, the move to Bordeaux commenced, and on March 2nd Division Headquarters was opened at Castres, on the Garonne River, near Bordeaux. The journey by train was two days and two nights for those who were on time, and somewhat longer for others. There were but two trains per day and the movement covered more than one week. In addition, as the Division moved without animals or transportation, and the trains were of the strategic, and not the tactical, type, containing no flatcars; there was a general feeling that war-time conditions were coming to an end, and that the journey home had really begun. The area near Bordeaux in which the Division was billeted had never been used for a complete combat Division before, and inadequate telephone service and insufficient transportation were the principal difficulties with which we contended. On the other hand, in the Bordeaux area, troops were required to drill but two hours a day, and to occupy their spare time many devices were employed. Major Cunningham was appointed athletic and welfare officer; a baseball league was organized; shows were organized in the Division, and additional shows secured from Bordeaux and booked throughout the area; movies were provided, and leaves on a liberal scale to the nearby leave areas were arranged. Practically every man entitled to leave was able to get away.

Of special interest in this connection is the leave train to Italy which was finally secured and which I believe was the only leave train sent by the A. E. F. to Italy. Eleven hundred men were sent on this train, which was in charge of Major (then Captain) Danforth of the 328th Infantry, and the men kept up the excellent record that they had made with the Division in combat. During the stay in this area the schools which had been started in Prauthoy were developed still further under the general supervision of Chaplain Tyler, the senior Chaplain of the Division, and more than 8000 men were attending the schools regularly. While in the Prauthoy area, some of the units had held memorial services for their members who had been killed in action or died in France. In the Bordeaux area all the remaining units held such services, and on most occasions, the Division Commander was present, and made an address. Reviews were held frequently in order to encourage the snappiness and soldierly appearance of all units and at one such review General Lindsey was presented with the Distinguished Service Medal, and on another, Sergeant York received his Medal of Honor. During this entire period every effort was made to impress upon the men of the Division that they must now prepare to return to civil life, and that the preparation was fully as important and difficult as their previous training had been to prepare them for military life. The following memorandum, which was one of a number, indicates in a general way how this was carried on:

HQ. 82D DIV., AMERICAN E. F., FRANCE

17 March, 1919.

G. S. MEMORANDUM No. 14.

Although the training of the Division at the present time is very different from the training required in anticipation of operations, it is no less important and fully as difficult. Within a short time all but a few members of the Division will return to civil life and they should be as well fitted to take up civil pursuits as the present conditions permit. The qualities acquired during the period of military training should make all members of this command more useful citizens than they would otherwise be, and the knowledge of foreign countries and customs, submission to discipline, individual initiative, pride of organization and self-sacrifice for a cause, are just as necessary after discharge from the army as they have been in the A. E. F. No effort should be neglected to continue the development of these qualities.

The conditions in the United States will be found very different from those which prevailed at the time the Division left, and the great economic readjustment caused by the termination of the war is now in process of changing the conditions and customs with which most of us are familiar. Every help will be given to the members of this Division to insure their fitting into the peace-time system at home in the most advantageous manner possible. But it must be impressed on all that the future of the individual in civil life will depend, primarily, on his own qualities, character and initiative, and that any assistance that can be rendered is supplementary.

Members of the command should realize that, because of their experience as members of the A. E. F. and because of the part they took in the operations during this war, they have the opportunity and the obligation to become leaders in the life of the nation at home and they will be expected to assume that position. This is an opportunity and an obligation of the greatest importance, for the future of the United States now lies in the hands of the members of the A. E. F. if they are properly prepared to grasp the existing situation. In solving the problems that will be presented, the spirit of subordination and of co-operation so essential in military life will become equally essential after the return to civil life. All soldiers must now realize that discipline is an essential requisite to military success. They should realize likewise that true discipline is the basis of team play. Team play, rather than individual or factional struggles, will lead to the true solution of the difficulties ahead. The splendid record made in the past should be a spur to even greater accomplishments in the future, and the pride in having done one thing well should be the incentive for doing the next thing well; and the mutual confidence acquired to working together in a military organization should form the basis of a mutual confidence in working together when released from military life.

G. S. Memorandum No. 12 directs that one hour per day be used in the instruction of members of the command in many important subjects. In addition to those subjects, instruction will be given in the principles outlined above.

BY COMMAND OF BRIGADIER GENERAL LINDSEY:

GEORGE E. ROOSEVELT, Lieutenant Colonel, Chief of Staff.

In April the orders for the shipment home finally arrived, and the first units of the Division marched to the embarkation camp on April 20. All units sailed from Base Section No. 2, at Bordeaux, and were landed in New York. At New York the Division was split between Camps Upton, Dix and Mills, and demobilized as rapidly as the demobilization machinery could work. The unfortunate organization to return last was the 326th Infantry, which was quarantined at Pauillac, and did not start for home until well on in May; but by June 1 practically every member of the Division who did not desire further service in the army had returned to civil life, and the Division as a military organization had passed into history.

SUPPLEMENTARY MATERIAL
RELATING TO THE
HISTORY OF THE 82ND DIVISION, A. E. F.

I
LIFE OF GENERAL DUNCAN

Major General George B. Duncan assumed command of the 82nd Division October 4, 1918, just before the Division entered its great offensive in the Meuse-Argonne operations.

General Duncan was graduated from the Military Academy in 1886 and after graduation was assigned to the 9th Infantry, and served with that regiment for six years in Arizona. His duties during this time involved the charge of the Apache tribes, the Hualpi and the Yava-Supi Indians whose homes were near the Grand Canyon of the Colorado, in addition to his regular work with his regiment.

From 1892-4 he served upon the personal staff of Maj. Gen. John M. Scofield in command of the Army. He was relieved from this duty early in 1894 to join, as 1st Lieutenant, the 4th Infantry to which he had been promoted the previous year for duty as regimental adjutant. He continued in this capacity until the Spanish-American War. He was then given a Volunteer commission of Captain, Adjutant General's Department, and saw field service as Adjutant of a brigade in front of Santiago, Cuba, and later as Adjutant of a division of the first troops landing in Porto Rico. He joined his regiment, the 4th Infantry, in time to proceed with it to the Philippines in January, 1899. He was promoted Captain in March, 1899.

He served three years in the Philippines as Adjutant of a brigade and in command of his company, and took an active part in the field operations of the Army, notably in the Province of Cabiti. After three years' service in the Philippines, he returned with his regiment to the States for a period of fifteen months. He returned to the Philippine Islands in June, 1903, where he continued on duty for six years, during the first part at the Headquarters of the Department of Luzon, as Acting Chief Quartermaster of that Department. He was given a temporary commission of Major of Philippine Scouts in February, 1905, and organized the noted Third Battalion of that organization. In 1908 he was placed in charge of all Philippine Scouts, on the staff of the Division Commander, and continued on this duty until July, 1909, when, on account of illness he was returned to the States.

He was promoted to Major of Infantry and assigned to the 2nd Infantry upon his return and served with that organization for two years. In 1911 he took a special course at the Army Service Schools, Fort Leavenworth, which was followed by the course at the Army War College at Washington, from which he was graduated in 1912. He was transferred to the 9th Infantry and served with that organization in Garrison and upon the Mexican border until April, 1914, when he was detailed upon the General Staff of the Army and assigned to the War Department branch of that Staff.

He continued upon this duty until our entry into the present war, except for a period of five months' service with the 17th Infantry on the border in 1915, when he was promoted Lieutenant-Colonel of that regiment in September of that year. He was promoted a Colonel of Infantry, September 18, 1916. In June, 1917, he was relieved from the General Staff at his own request and assigned the command of the 26th Infantry, one of the regiments of the 1st Division about to leave for France.

He took command of the 26th Infantry as it was embarking at New York with the 1st Division, A. E. F., the first troops to go to France after our entry into the war against Germany; and held command of the regiment till September 1, 1917. He was promoted Brigadier General, August 5, 1917, and participated in the French offensive at Verdun, August 16-19, 1917, with the 94th French Infantry, an attacking regiment. He was awarded the Croix de Guerre for his part in this battle.

General Duncan was assigned to command the 1st Brigade, 1st Division, September 1, 1917, and had part in its front-line training in the battle sector east of Nancy, November, 1917. This Brigade, under General Duncan's command, held the battle-sector near Toul in January, February and March, 1918, and this was the first battle-sector command exercised by an American general officer in France. He went with the 1st Division to Picardy in April, 1918, and his men were the first troops of the 1st Division to take part in the battle north of Montdidier.

OFFICIAL HISTORY OF 82ND DIVISION   225

Promotion to Major General came on April 12, 1918, and the following month he was assigned to the command of the 77th Division, the first of the National Army divisions to reach France. After he had trained the division with the British, it was transferred to the Baccarat sector in June, 1918, and thence to the Vesle for offensive action in July, 1918. General Duncan commanded the 77th in action on the Vesle till August 19, 1918.

He was assigned to the command of the 82nd Division on October 4, 1918. After the armistice General Duncan received the Distinguished Service Medal and was made a Companion of the Order of the Bath.

II

THE ARTILLERY OF THE 82ND DIVISION

CONTRIBUTED BY

CAPTAIN J. G. PENNYPACKER, F. A. A., A. C. OF S., G-3

The graduates of the First Officers' Training Camp at Fort McPherson, Georgia, reported to the Commanding General of the newly-formed 82nd Division at Camp Gordon, Georgia, on August 29, 1917. The artillery officers were members of the 1st, 2nd and 3rd Batteries of the 7th Provisional Training Regiment and formed the commissioned personnel of the three artillery regiments of the 82nd Division—the 319th, 320th and 321st. According to the new Tables of Organization of August, 1917, the Field Artillery Brigade of a Division was to be composed of five separate organizations: three Regiments, one of which was to be equipped with a six-inch howitzer and two with three-inch guns, a Trench Mortar Battery, and a Brigade Headquarters. Brig. Gen. Charles D. Menoher had been designated by the War Department as the Commanding General of the 157th Field Artillery Brigade, but at the time of the organization of the Brigade General Menoher was in France, nor did he ever assume command of the Brigade. Colonel E. D'A. Pearce, the commanding officer of the 319th Field Artillery, acted as Brigade Commander until Brig. Gen. Charles D. Rhodes was assigned in February, 1918, with the exception of the period from August 29, 1917, to September 9, 1917, when Brig. Gen. Brady was in command.

The first enlisted men reported on September 5, a small training nucleus, composed of non-commissioned officers and privates in the Regular Army. The bulk of the personnel, from the states of Georgia, Alabama and Tennessee were received during the next few weeks. In November, however, practically all these men were transferred to other camps and in place of them men were received from Texas, Oklahoma, Iowa, Minnesota and all of the states east of the Mississippi River, Camps Upton, Devens, Meade and Lee furnishing the majority of the recruits.

The training of the artillery was seriously hampered by lack of equipment. In September one battery of three-inch guns was received which was shared for training purposes by all three regiments of the Brigade. Gun squads had the use of the guns for instruction purposes for a total of about ten hours during the period of approximately two months before going to the range for target practice. A large part of the training, however, was accomplished with wooden guns, the *matériel* of the Brigade consisting of these crudely made structures fashioned from the trunks of small trees, tin cans, spools, gas pipes and any available material which could be made to represent the sight, the quadrant, the breech block, traversing and elevating mechanism and other important parts of the real gun. It required constant endeavor and almost infinite patience on the part of the officers and men to overcome handicaps and to develop accuracy and speed in the gun squads. In the instruction of the specialists of the batteries and of the various headquarters serious obstacles were also encountered, there being an absolute lack of fire control and signal equipment. With tedious labor signal flags, telephones, buzzers, battery commanders' telescopes, plane tables, etc., were manufactured within the organizations. In this way training in the problems of communication and preparation of firing data were successfully carried on.

In the fall of 1917 land suitable for an artillery range was leased by the government at Blackjack Mountain, about one mile from Marietta, Cobb County, Georgia, and twenty-two miles northwest of Camp Gordon. Another battery of three-inch field pieces having been assigned to the 157th Field Artillery Brigade, two batteries were available for target practice. Firing was begun early in December and was continued from that time until the departure of the Brigade in May. This opportunity for some real firing was not only a valuable experience in itself but lent added interest to the entire training period. The visits to Marietta were always looked forward to with pleasure by the officers and men on account of the realities of the training on the range and the especially hospitable spirit of the people of Marietta.

During this training period both the 319th and 321st were designated as motorized regiments. Many men were transferred out of these organizations who were unsuited for handling trucks and tractors, their places being filled by men who had had experience in civil life with gas engines. Motor trucks and tractors not being available, it was necessary in instructing men to be mechanics and chauffeurs to resort to the use of drawings and paper illustrations of the workings of the gas engine. In the spring several trucks were assigned and the training was greatly expedited. The 321st, however, never was motorized and the 319th was horse-drawn throughout the entire period of preliminary training and of fighting, partial motor equipment being received only after the armistice. This necessitated the reorganization of these regiments when horses were received after arrival in France, and it became necessary to organize stable details, veterinary details and all other institutions necessary for the care of the artillery horses and the training of the men in their care and handling.

On May 8th the Brigade began entraining for Camp Mills, Garden City, Long Island, and on May 19 set sail from New York. Brigade Headquarters and the 320th Field Artillery sailed on the British transport *City of Exeter*, the 319th on the *Lapland* and the 321st on the *Arctic*. These ships formed part of a convoy of twelve vessels protected by the U. S. S. *Montana* and the converted cruiser *St. Louis*. The voyage was uneventful. Landing at Liverpool on May 31 the Brigade entrained for Winchester, spent two days at the Winnal Downs Rest Camp and crossed the Channel from Southampton to Le Havre. Here the regiments again entrained for La Courtine, where they arrived on June 5, 6, 7 and 8.

At La Courtine the Brigade drew its full equipment of *matériel* and transportation, and underwent a thorough two months' course of training, culminating in a Brigade firing problem worked out in its most minute details. The armament of the 320th and 321st Regiments consisted of 75 mm. guns, and the 319th received 155 mm. howitzers. It was here that the Brigade had its first opportunity to fire and become otherwise familiar with these weapons. An equally important feature of the work at La Courtine was the developing and training of enlisted and commissioned specialists in telephone and radio work, operations, material and Intelligence, as well as balloon and aeroplane observers.

From La Courtine the Brigade moved by train on August 5-10,

to the area behind Château Thierry to form part of the reserve of the First Army in the operations along the Vesle. On account of the favorable progress of the campaign, however, the Brigade was not needed in this sector and moved by train to Toul. It was in the little villages in this vicinity, about August 15, that the German bombing planes, on their nightly visits to Toul, gave the different units of the Brigade their first experience under fire.

On the night of August 18-19 the Brigade started the march to the Marbache sector where, on August 22, it completed the relief of the 2nd Brigade of the Second Division. The 1st Battalion, 319th Field Artillery, and the 1st Battalion, 321st Field Artillery, had previously been detached from the Brigade, and attached to the 89th Division. It was a forward gun of Battery A, 319th Field Artillery, at Manonville, that fired the first shot of the Brigade at the front, at 3.10 p.m., August 20. These units rejoined the Brigade just before the St. Mihiel offensive.

The Marbache sector had well constructed dugouts and battery positions and an intricate system of telephone communication, the result of four years of French occupation. The sector being purely a defensive one, the infantry was organized in great depth, which necessitated, of course, equally deep formation of the artillery. Accordingly, each battery was divided into platoons, one posted well forward to defend the outpost position with barrage fire, and one platoon placed in a rear position for the final defense of the infantry line of resistance. A very elaborate system of defensive barrages and counter-preparation fire was planned. The plan of defense provided, moreover, that in case of a general assault the forward platoons would at once fall back to prepared positions. Except for a limited amount of registration, practically no fire was permitted, however, until September 12. The first official shot fired at the front by the 75 mm. Regiments was fired August 22, on Norroy, by Battery F, 320th Field Artillery, as a reward for the excellent work of its gun squads in competition at La Courtine.

Notice of the St. Mihiel offensive was received in ample time to construct forward gun positions for practically the entire Brigade. Much assistance was rendered by the infantry. The batteries were moved up one and two nights before the attack, every precaution being observed to maintain secrecy. In the matter of O.P.'s the Brigade was fortunate, there being in this sector two of the best on the whole front—Mousson Hill and Ste. Géneviève. O.P.'s were also established on the forward slope of Xon Hill, which is directly in front of Mousson and marks the extreme front of the infantry lines. Trench mortar emplacements were dug just behind the town of Les Ménils. It was intended to wipe out a quadrangular section of woods, Bois de la Voivrotte, by means of trench mortar fire. This woods was a strongly held advance position in the Boche line, infested with machine guns and mortar emplacements and provided with deep dugouts. This attack was unsuccessful. The Germans must have learned of the plan, for while the projectiles were being fused the Boche put down a heavy fire of 77's and 150's. Lieutenant Blackman, in charge, fired the ammunition that was fused and then marched his men back to their dugouts in the rear of the hill without losing a man.

The artillery preparation started at H minus 4 hours (1 hour, September 12). The mission assigned to the Brigade was purely that of counter-battery work. A large amount of gas—No. 5 and No. 20 (phosgene and mustard)—was furnished for this purpose. Certain French heavy artillery of the sector was assigned to the Brigade for assistance. After frequent consultations with the Corps Artillery Commander, sixteen German batteries were assigned to this Brigade for counter-battery work. In addition to this other German positions were given. In all a total of thirty-five German battery positions were definitely located before our sector. A large amount of Corps and Army artillery was placed in the sector, but most of it was assigned to assist the Divisions on our left. The French had in the sector a splendid S.R.O.T. (*Service Renseignement Observation Terrestrial*—Terrestrial Information Observation Service) section, some of its personnel having been in this sector for four years. Shortly after the attack started, at 5 A.M., the S.R.O.T. service evidenced its uncanny accuracy. The telephone at Brigade Headquarters would ring and S.R.O.T. would state that an enemy battery, giving exact co-ordinates, was in action. This target would be assigned to one of the batteries or battalions of the Brigade and in ten minutes S.R.O.T. would report "Battery silenced." In addition to counter-battery work considerable harassing and interdiction fire was undertaken, and one battalion each of 75's and 155's was assigned to fugitive target work. Boche troops on the roads were fired upon, and one avion which had made a forced landing was destroyed by fire from Battery C, 321st Field Artillery.

On September 13, about noon, the Division was ordered to take prisoners for identification on our front. A hastily planned operation was worked up for a raid into Bois Fréhaut by the 327th Infantry. This included a smoke screen, box barrage and severe interdiction fire by the 155's. A total of about 10,000 rounds of ammunition was fired by the 75's, and 1500 by the 155's.

The 328th Infantry advanced to Norroy at dusk on September 13th while our Brigade was supporting the raid above mentioned, but the Brigade assisted this regiment by counter-battery work throughout the day and night of September 14th. The Brigade supported the advance of the 328th Inf. to Vandières on September 15th.

The result of the St. Mihiel operation, as far as the Brigade was concerned, was the establishment of a confidence, born of performance, that was of inestimable value in the more difficult operations that were soon to follow. Over 50,000 rounds of 75 mm. ammunition and 13,000 rounds of 155 mm. ammunition were fired during this period.

On September 20 the 82nd Division was relieved by the 69th (French) Division, and the Artillery Brigade was assembled in the vicinity of Marbache. On September 22 the long overland march to the Argonne was begun, in a rainstorm and a sea of mud. As with all the troop movements in preparations for the Argonne drive, all marching was at night. The days of the 23rd, 24th and 25th were spent near Lagny, Boncourt and Pierrefitte, respectively, and Beauzee was reached on the morning of the 26th, when the far-off roar of masses of artillery gave notice that the big attack was on. From Beauzee the march was continued in the daytime to Futeau, a little town in the Argonne Forest about twelve kilometers from the front. Here the entire Brigade was in bivouac until October 5, in constant readiness to enter the line. The long night marches had been especially hard on the horses, and a number had been lost. This period at Futeau was utilized for the conditioning of horses and as much training of the personnel as was possible under the circumstances.

On the afternoon of the 5th of October the Brigade was ordered to bivouacs north of Les Islettes, and on the morning of the 6th, to move again to just south of the former front line, near Pierre Croisée. Brigade Headquarters left Futeau at 8 hours, October 6, the Brigade Commander with the Adjutant and Operations Officer proceeding to Varennes by auto. At Varennes information was received from the First Corps, under which command the 82nd Division had passed, that the Division was to hold itself in readiness to relieve either the 1st, 28th or 77th

OFFICIAL HISTORY OF 82ND DIVISION   231

Divisions, or to go into line between any of these. Further instructions were to send liaison officers to the artillery brigades of each of these Divisions to become familiar with the sectors. This information was sent back to the regiments of the Brigade which, between noon and 14 hours, had reached their various bivouacs. The 82nd Division and the 157th Field Artillery Brigade established P.C.'s in the town of Varennes. At 13 hours orders were received from the Division that it was to attack the next morning at 5 hours. The regiments were at once ordered to send forward reconnaissance parties that battery positions might be selected during the few remaining hours of daylight.

On the morning of Oct. 6th, Col. Pearce of the 319th F.A. sent forward his Operations Officer, Bn., and Battery Commanders to select battery positions. He, himself, accompanied by his telephone officer went forward to Baulny, established Regimental Headquarters and perfected plans for liaison throughout the regiment and with the infantry units."

From 1 hour, Nov. 2nd and throughout the 2nd some of the most important work done by the 319th F.A. was on request of the infantry to clean out machine gun nests that were delayin their advance.

The road leading over what had been "No Man's Land" for four years was well-nigh impassable, and the conditions of congestion and darkness and rain which did so much to impede the Infantry's advance to their position, were even a greater obstacle to the forward movement of the artillery. The 320th, which led the column, resumed the march at 14 hours. Colonel Williams, with his Operations Officer, Captain Dighton, went forward to Varennes, where prospective positions were outlined by the Brigade Commander. Returning along the column the Colonel picked up in his machine the Battalion and Battery Commanders, with whom he drove along the Baulny-Fléville Road to l'Espérance Ferme. A reconnaissance which, due to approaching darkness, was necessarily hasty, was then made of the ravine eastward to the eastern edge of Montrebeau Woods. Heavy shelling of the ravine and woods by enemy batteries also added to the difficulty. However, positions for all the batteries were selected. The Regiment was placed approximately in line in the eastern edge of the woods, with fields of fire to the northwest. The route was carefully marked. The column came up in good order, the last gun going into position at 1 hour, October 7.

The 321st, however, experienced greater difficulties. Colonel Deems and four officers arrived at Brigade Headquarters about 16 hours 30, and were assigned an area near l'Esperance Farm, of which a hurried reconnaissance was made before dark. Battalion areas were assigned and officers posted at Montblainville, Baulny and l'Espérance to guide the Regiment into position. The Post of Command was selected at Chaudron Farm, where the P.C. of the 320th Field Artillery was also established. Meanwhile the Regiment, under the command of Major Mehard, marched from the Four-aux-Moines at 15 hours 30. Orders were to proceed via Pierre Croisée. At 17 hours 30, just as the column was crossing the almost impassable road across the original trench system in the Argonne, the following order, unsigned, but in the handwriting of Major D. M. Beere, Adjutant, 157th Field Artillery Brigade, was delivered to Major Mehard by an officer of the 319th Field Artillery:

"The 321st Field Artillery will march north from Pierre Croisée via Abri du Crochet (99.3-72.6)—Montblainville—main army road to Baulny—l'Espérance into position. Do not clear woods into open until dark."

Leaving these instructions with the officer at the head of the column Major Mehard at once proceeded to a reconnaissance of the route. At Abri du Crochet instructions were left with an M.P. on duty to direct the column north. Proceeding north, however, Major Mehard discovered that the road was impracticable for field artillery on account of heavy mud and that practically all the road north of P 91-36 (one kilometer northwest of Abri du Crochet) was under artillery and long range machine-gun fire. He was further informed by infantry officers that a portion of the road to Montblainville was not within our lines. Returning at once to Abri du Crochet he left instructions with the M.P. there to direct the Regiment to the Abri du Crochet-Varennes Road. He then went by motor-cycle to l'Espérance via Montblainville, to obtain information and reconnoiter his battalion position. By the time the column reached Abri du Crochet the M.P. who had received instructions to divert the column toward Varennes had been relieved and had failed to transmit these orders to his successor, who was the one first ordered by Major Mehard to direct the column north. The column, accordingly, marched north. Shortly before reaching the crossroads two kilometers northwest of Abri du Crochet the conditions of the road became so bad and the hostile fire increased to such an extent that the column was halted by

Captain Kemker and 1st Lieutenant Lindsey, who were in the lead. Information obtained from an infantry officer close by was that the road to Montblainville was not entirely within our lines and that it was practically impassible. On the basis of this the column was counter-marched after considerable difficulty and unavoidable delay. It returned to the Abri du Crochet, and from there the Varennes road was taken. In Varennes an officer reported to 157th Field Artillery Brigade Headquarters for instructions and was directed to take the main army road to Baulny. From here on the march was a succession of exasperating delays caused by the almost hopeless congestion of traffic on the army road. The column was split into several parts by convoys of trucks. The march from a point just south of Baulny to l'Espérance was under continuous shell fire. The net result of the combined adversities of the night was that it was 5 hours 20 (October 7) before the first battery commenced firing and 8 hours before the last battery came into action. The total distance marched from the Four-aux-Moines was 20 kilometers.

The 319th Field Artillery, at the rear of the column, started the movement about dark. It was after daylight before the first batteries were extricated from the tangled confusion of traffic on the army road and placed in position between Baulny and Charpentry. One battery of the 1st Battalion started firing before 7 hours and was soon joined by the remainder of the 1st and 2nd Battalions. The 3rd Battalion moved into position the following night.

There had been no time on the daylight hours of the 6th for the selection of observation posts. Having come into position after dark, and with visibility in the early morning very poor, it was only with the greatest difficulty that the batteries were oriented. Not only the batteries but the messengers carrying the firing orders to the regiments and battalions were delayed by darkness and traffic jams, and it was 5 hours 40—40 minutes after "H" hour—before batteries of the 320th, the first in position, were able to start firing. The rolling barrage ordered for "H" hour (5 o'clock) was to be fired by the 320th, the 321st and the 6th Field Artillery of the 1st Division. It was to begin 200 meters west of the railroad, west of Aire River, and progress at the rapid rate of 100 meters in three minutes to the first objective of Cornay and Hill 223. This line was to be reached on schedule by about "H" plus 30, the barrage standing on this line. It was on or near this line, therefore, that the first firing by the 320th and 321st was done. This ceased at "H" plus 1 hour 15 minutes, when searching fire was executed until "H" plus 3 hours between the first objective and the Corps objective, along the Decauville Railroad. The batteries were in action intermittently all day long in response to calls from the Infantry. The 319th placed heavy concentration near Châtel-Chéhéry and on Cornay and other enemy positions. At 18 hours, the 321st and the 2nd Battalion of the 320th, at the request of the Commanding General, 164th Inf. Br., executed a barrage on the west slope of Hill 223 to oppose a German counter-attack. The Infantry reported the following morning that they found two companies of Boche had been practically annihilated. Defensive barrages and harassing fire on enemy sensitive points were delivered during the night.

On the morning of the 7th observation posts were established on Hill 224. Liaison officers were sent by the artillery regiments to the Headquarters of the 164th Brigade and to the 327th and 328th Infantries, and telephone communication was established with the 164th Brigade as well as within the artillery brigade. It being realized that the regiments could not lay telephone lines back to the artillery P.C. at Varennes, Lieutenant Watts, the Brigade Telephone Officer, established a forward Brigade central at Baulny.

For the attack of October 8 a rolling barrage from just in front of the infantry jump-off line to the Decauville Railroad was fired by the 321st and the 2nd Battalion of the 320th, while the 1st Battalion of the 320th and the 219th R.A.C. (French) fired a standing barrage along a 2 kilometer east-and-west line just north of Cornay, to protect the right flank of the 327th Infantry. The 319th fired concentrations on Cornay, the southern slopes of Champrocher ridge, Marcq, and battery positions and sensitive points to the north and west. Cornay, however, proved a stumbling block to the infantry's advance and just before 11 hours a heavy concentration of almost the entire Brigade was placed on the town and the heights overlooking it. This fire silenced machine guns and trench mortars in the town and enabled the 327th Infantry to enter it. Throughout the day the wooded slopes west and southwest of Cornay which sheltered the machine-gun nests that were playing such havoc with our infantry were deluged with fire. Harassing fire again continued throughout the night.

The attack of the 326th Infantry, which had relieved the 28th Division, on October 9th was supported by the 53rd Field

Artillery Brigade, while the 320th and 321st fired a rolling barrage for the attack of the 327th and 328th Infantries. A heavy concentration on troublesome machine gun nests on the top of the Champrocher ridge, just southwest of Cornay, was fired between 11.45 and noon. It was on this afternoon that a vigorous German counter-attack from the north resulted in the recapture of Cornay.

Two hours of preparation fire preceded the Infantry advance of October 10, when the 325th Infantry relieved the 327th and 328th, and, with the 326th on their left, attacked at 7 hours behind a rolling barrage. Advancing with little resistance to the ridges north of Cornay, in the course of the afternoon their patrols reached the Aire and the enemy was definitely cleared from this portion of the Argonne.

In the course of the 10th instructions were received for preparations for the attack of the 11th, when the Division sector was shifted eastward astride the Aire River. Up to this time the batteries had remained in the positions occupied on the morning of the 7th. The direction of attack, however, had now been changed from due west to due north and a rapid advance was expected to result from the attack of the morning. Reconnaissances were conducted, accordingly, for new positions farther to the north. During the night of the 10-11th the 320th Field Artillery moved by battalions to the ravine west of Exermont, while the 321st took up new positions in the east and west ravine, just southeast of Fléville. The 1st Battalion of the 319th took position near Apremont, the 2nd and 3rd Battalions going to Châtel-Chéhéry. The next morning the 1st Battalion took position near Exermont. Division Field Order No. 23 of October 10 for the attack of the next day ordered the artillery:

"To keep harassing and interdiction fire in front of the advancing infantry and to fire on all towns and important cross roads and special targets. Artillery liaison officers with infantry commanders will keep artillery commanders constantly informed of the infantry positions. One regiment of 75 mm. field artillery to be assigned by artillery brigade commander who will support the attack of each infantry brigade. One forward gun will accompany each front line Battalion. Artillery observers will move forward with the advanced infantry line for the purpose of directing fire of supporting batteries. All artillery will open fire at 'H' hour and pass under the control of the artillery brigade commander as soon as the action stabilizes. Full advantage will be taken of the open terrain for advancing by echelon the supporting artillery."

The 320th Field Artillery was assigned to support the 164th

Brigade, and the 321st the 163rd Brigade, and preparations were made for the advance of a portion of the artillery immediately after "H" hour.

The Field Order of the 164th Brigade assigned one battalion of the supporting Artillery, the 320th, to the two Infantry Regiments as accompanying artillery. The first Battalion of the 320th, accordingly, moved forward early in the morning and went into position near Fléville, with two forward platoons nearly a kilometer north of that town. Visibility was poor on account of mist and observation and identification of machine-gun targets was difficult throughout the day.

Not only was no rolling barrage ordered but, as it turned out, it would have been of doubtful value, the infantry meeting serious resistance from south of the assigned jump-off line. The heavy machine-gun fire which the infantry suffered from the vicinity of St. Juvin, outside of the Division sector, resulted in an increasing amount of fire being diverted to this vicinity and Hill 182 to the north, where 60 per cent. of the fire for the day was delivered.

Frequent reports were received during the day that friendly artillery was falling on the ridge at 85.5 and causing losses to our infantry. Though this was carefully checked up in the 157th Field Artillery Brigade and it was made certain that no batteries were firing in this vicinity at the times indicated, the reports continued with such persistence that in the evening all firing was stopped within the Brigade for one hour and a thorough investigation was made in the Divisions on both flanks and in the Artillery farther to the rear, with the result indicated in the following messages, copied from the G-3 dossier:

Telephone message from Albany A-1 (Commanding General, 157th Field Artillery Brigade) at 21.20 o'clock, 11 October:

"During the preceding hour none of the Regiments under his command has fired a shot. At same time a message from Anson 1 (C.G. 164th Brigade) states that during same period the fire on troops of Anson 1's command was continued unabated. This seems to prove conclusively that the fire on our own troops was not done by artillery of the 157th Field Artillery Brigade. The Brigade Commander requests that this vindication be given the same publicity which was given to the memorandum complaining of hostile fire."

Extract from Message to Colonel MacArthur at 20.20 o'clock, 11 October (from Division Headquarters).

"In regard to statement that our troops were being fired on by friendly artillery, please notify all concerned that the matter has been carefully checked right and left and all the way to the rear, and none of our artillery is firing in that region. Troops were suffering under enemy shell fire unquestionably."

Excellent work was accomplished on this day and the days following by the forward gun from Battery E, 321st F.A., under 1st Lt. Prentiss S. Edwards. He took position on the early morning in an orchard about 1200 meters south of St. Juvin and on a road just east of Marcq. Three important machine-gun targets were successfully attacked during the morning. During the night of October 11-12 the gun was withdrawn to a position on the reverse slope of the crest where the road runs west from Martincourt Farm. This gun remained at work continuously until about October 22, changing position frequently. Close liaison was maintained with the 326th Infantry, but the majority of targets fired on were obtained by direct observation and a post which was maintained at the Division O.P. near Marcq. At least eight machine-gun targets were destroyed. On one occasion a small ravine into which twenty Boche were seen to enter was taken under fire. Only five Boche left the ravine. On October 19 fire was directed at four machine gunners standing beneath a small tree. A direct hit was obtained on the tree and all four men either killed or disabled. Much sniping fire was executed on groups of men and wagons on the road running north from Champigneuelle. A total of 657 rounds were fired by this piece.

The infantry devoted the 12th to the consolidation of their position on Ridge 85.5. Most of the artillery fire for the day was on crossroads and suspected machine-gun positions. New O.P.'s were established, P.C. moved forward, and defensive barrages were adjusted in front of the infantry line. Throughout the night of October 12-13 a number of small patches of woods west of St. Georges and along the Ravin aux Pierres and the Fishhook Ravine were heavily gassed and in the morning the same areas were harassed with H.E. and shrapnel. In the afternoon of the 13th the Brigade was ordered to make six 25-meter openings in the enemy barbed wire protecting the Kriemhilde Stellung. This mission was assigned to the 238th R.A.C. (French). The cutting had hardly begun when the Boche put on a spectacular counter-attack, supported by a heavy barrage. On the call of the infantry both the 320th and 321st responded with a defensive barrage 200 meters in front of the infantry line. It was afterward reported that this barrage was extremely effective, resulting in the repulse of the attack.

During the afternoon and evening the 2nd Battalion of the 320th Field Artillery, less Battery E, moved forward to positions south of Sommerance. The movement of Battery E was delayed by the counter-attack. A heavy program of harassing fire and gas on wooded areas was maintained throughout the night.

On October 14 a general attack was made by the First Army in an attempt to carry the Kriemhilde Stellung positions. The attack, which began at 8 hours 30 minutes, was preceded by two hours of combing fire on enemy works, assembly areas and communications. Visibility was fair and considerable shrapnel was used. The rolling barrage for this attack, which was fired by the 320th, 321st, and the 238th R.A.C. (French) over a 2½ kilometer front, moved at a rate of 100 meters in six minutes, the rate of 100 meters in three minutes which had been ordered in all previous attacks having been proved much too rapid. About four o'clock in the afternoon the 320th fired a 30-minute defensive barrage along the Ravin aux Pierres. A forward gun under the command of 2nd Lt. Edward F. Gunter, 320th F.A., during this attack destroyed two pill boxes. Heavy fire on woods, back areas and communications was continued throughout the afternoon and night. On the afternoon of the 14th the 319th and 321st Field Artillery and the remaining batteries of the 320th moved forward to the Ravine which runs from Fléville to Sommerance.

On the 15th the attack to break through the Kriemhilde Stellung was continued. Artillery preparation started about midnight October 14-15. It covered crossroads and other sensitive points, while woods and ravines known to be occupied by the enemy were gassed with non-persistent gas at "H" minus 4 hours. "H" hour was 7.30. A barrage similar to that of the preceding day was placed in front of the jump-off line at "H" minus 5 minutes, advancing with the infantry at "H" hour. Very heavy enemy resistance was met, particularly in the Ravin aux Pierres, and after a short advance the entire attack was held up. The artillery had been moved up close to the infantry for this operation and suffered severely from gas and shrapnel. In the afternoon the 325th Infantry made a second unsuccessful attack to cross the Ravin aux Pierres behind a barrage fired by the 321st and the 328th R.A.C.

The attack was continued on the 16th, the preparation fire and rolling barrage being almost a repetition of those of the previous two days. A heavy German counter-attack was made at 11 hours which was broken up by a rapidly delivered artillery barrage. A Boche plane was brought down in flames near Sommerance in the afternoon of the 16th by machine-gun fire from a battery of this Brigade. Battery C, 320th F.A., and the batteries of the 2nd Battalion, 321st F.A., all claim the honor of having fired the winning shot.

There was very little activity on the 17th. A defensive barrage was put down just south of parallel 88 on the Division front. Most of the fire of that day was delivered at the request of the infantry on machine-gun nests and wooded patches. The 238th R.A.C. (French) was relieved by the 219th (French) Portée. On this day, Lieutenant Durrett, 320th F.A., was killed by shell fire at the echelon, this being the only death of an officer that the Brigade suffered at the front. During the nights of October 17-18 and October 18-19 heavy concentrations of both mustard and non-persistent gas were placed on Champigneulle in connection with the attacks on the Bois des Loges by the 78th Division, which had relieved the 77th Division on our left.

In the meantime it was realized that the Kriemhilde Stellung could only be broken through by a heavy and coordinated attack in force by fresh divisions, and our infantry were organizing their positions for defense. The Brigade had suffered numerous casualties in their advanced positions and, on the night of October 21-22 the 1st Battalions of both the 320th and 321st were withdrawn to positions farther in the rear. From this time until the offensive of November 1 conditions for the artillery closely approached those of stabilized warfare. Light harassing schedules were fired at night and close and constant liaison was maintained with front line infantry battalion commanders, at whose call numerous missions were executed, the targets being, for the most part, machine-gun emplacements. On October 23 another attack by the 78th Division was supported by this Brigade, by fire on the Bois des Loges and Hill 214, the 219th R.A.C. (French) laying down a smoke screen. Between October 18 and 31 numerous attempts were made to carry out adjustments with aeroplane observation, but the results were very disappointing, only one fairly successful reguage being secured. The 319th Field Artillery, however, obtained very satisfactory results from adjustments by balloon observers. A balloon from which Maj. John H. Wallace, commanding the 1st Battalion, 319th F.A., was adjusting fire, was shot down by a Boche plane, Major Wallace making a successful descent by parachute.

On October 26 the Brigade received advance information of the general attack on November 1 and work was begun on the plan of employment. In preparing for this attack one gun from each battery of the 75 regiments was moved forward several days before to positions later to be occupied by the entire Battery, and adjustments for the Battery were carried out with this gun. The movements were made at night and the guns were carefully camouflaged.

Brigadier General Rhodes was promoted to the rank of Major General on October 16 and on October 25 was transferred to the 42nd Division. Colonel Pearce of the 319th again assumed command of the Brigade, a position which he held until the arrival of Brig. Gen. Daniel F. Craig on November 3.

On October 30 the 82nd Division, less the 157th Field Artillery Brigade and the 307th Ammunition Train, was relieved by the 80th Division, which the excepted organizations remained in line to support. On the night of October 30-31 the batteries were moved forward to positions close behind the infantry. The Brigade was assigned two batteries of the 69th C.A.C. (9.2 inch), six batteries of the 247th R.A.C. (French) and the 219th R.A.C. (French). The 247th was attached from "H" plus 2 hours on "D" day to 0 hour, "D" plus 1 day.

The attack of the First Army on November 1 was intended to break the enemy's last line of resistance south of the Meuse. It was to be an enveloping attack from the right, the Fifth Corps on our right leading the 80th Division, while the 78th Division, on the extreme left both of the 1st Corps and of the 1st Army, was to make but a small advance on the right of its sector on the first day, advancing with the balance of the line, however, on the following day. The first objective of the 80th Division was the high ground between Imécourt and Alliépont, a commanding height known to be heavily infested with machine-gun nests. The Corps objective was the high ground to the north of Sivry-lez-Buzancy. The 160th Infantry Brigade, consisting of the 319th and 320th Infantries, was the attacking Brigade. The Artillery plan for the attack was quite elaborate. Batteries E and F of the 321st Field Artillery were assigned as accompanying batteries, one accompanying gun being assigned to each of the two infantry regiments. The fire of the remainder of the Brigade was divided into three phases.

"Phase A," the preparation fire, began at "H" minus 2 hours (3.30 hours), and for the first hour consisted of harassing fire on roads, sensitive points in the rear areas, machine-gun nests, and woods. From "H" minus 1 hour to "H" hour the woods north and northwest of Imécourt were heavily gassed, while the 219th R.A.C. (French) fired a smoke screen on the woods and heights along the first objective.

"Phase B" was scheduled to begin at "H" hour (5.30 hours) and consisted of accompanying barrage fire in support of the initial infantry attack. This fire was not to be delivered over the whole area in front of the infantry advance, but only in certain zones where serious resistance was expected. The rate of advance was 100 meters in six minutes to the first objective, at which time the 247th R.A.C. (French) came under the command of the Brigade and, with the 219th R.A.C. (French), fired a box barrage in front of this objective.

"Phase C" was planned to support the infantry attack from this point to the second objective, and again consisted of an accompanying barrage over selected zones. Forward movements by battalions were scheduled, the 320th making the first move at "H" plus 3 hours 15 minutes to positions south of Imécourt.

This fire was not delivered without incident. The advance of the 320th Infantry and that of the 77th Division on the left were halted by machine-gun fire in the difficult terrain around the Ravin aux Pierres, and it was not until early afternoon that the Ravin aux Pierres was actually crossed. The advance was again held up by machine-gun resistance from the woods on Hill 214. As a result of these delays the advance of the barrage fire was held up on infantry request for a total of 190 minutes, which was added to the time schedule of Phase C. The forward movement of batteries was similarly delayed and they finally moved to positions north of St. Georges in the afternoon and during the night of November 1-2. Meanwhile, the 319th Infantry, in liaison with the 2nd Division, had moved forward rapidly and combat liaison between the 319th and 320th Infantries had been lost and a large gap had developed between the two regiments. It was in this gap that the batteries of the 320th Field Artillery and 321st Field Artillery, and part of the 319th Field Artillery, in the darkness, unknowingly took position. During the night all these batteries suffered from heavy artillery and machine-gun fire, and battery anti-air craft machine guns were used to cover the gap. This situation was relieved by the rapid advance of the infantry the following morning. The accompanying guns were placed in position on the night of October 31-November 1. Close liaison with the front line battalion commanders, by telephone and runner, was established, an observer being kept with the battalion commander for the purpose of adjusting fire. No targets were assigned, however, and no requests for specific fire were made during the first two days. Neither were the accompanying batteries really used as such, though the two battery commanders established their posts of command with the respective infantry regimental commanders to whom they were assigned, maintaining direct liaison with their batteries by telephone and runners.

On the morning of November 2 the attack was resumed at 8 hours. There was no artillery preparation, but the barrage was fired from a point just north of Sivry, following a general northerly direction into Buzancy. The barrage was preceded by concentrations of both heavy and light artillery on enemy sensitive points. By this time the enemy was in full retreat and all artillery moved forward. Before the next morning the entire Brigade had come into position in the vicinity of Imécourt, commanding officers of all three regiments having P.C.'s in that town. In the course of the night contact had practically been lost with the enemy. Owing to the congestion of the roads and their terrible condition from shell fire it was impossible to supply more than one regiment with ammunition. Accordingly, the 321st Field Artillery, with the 3rd Battalion of the 319th attached, was assigned to support the Divisional infantry, which on November 3 consisted of the 159th Brigade. A conference was held between the Regimental Commander of the 321st and the Infantry Brigade Commander. The only artillery support that the latter desired was two accompanying guns with each of the two infantry regiments in line. These guns were furnished from the Second Battalion and accompanied closely the infantry advanced on the morning of November 3, at times preceding the first wave without encountering serious enemy resistance. Difficulty in obtaining targets, however, was again experienced. On November 4 the infantry continued to advance with but little rear-guard resistance from the rapidly retreating enemy. Orders were issued to each of the artillery battalion commanders to follow with his batteries at a distance of from 2000 to 3000 yards behind the infantry front line, maintaining close liaison with the infantry commanders and going into position in case the advance should be held up.

During the night of November 3-4 harassing fire was directed on the edge of woods north of Les Taronnes Farm, and on the following morning some very effective observed fire was executed on enemy machine guns in the vicinity of La Polka Farm. The Brigade P.C. moved to Buzancy in the afternoon. No telephone lines were laid due to the extremely rapid advance of the infantry. The 219th and 247th (French) reported that they were unable to advance with the Brigade due to the state of their transportation, and were relieved. One battalion of French 105 guns, horse-drawn, was assigned to the Brigade, but due to the congestion on the roads this unit was also released by the Division Commander. Great difficulty was experienced in getting up ammunition. One trip from Buzancy to Apremont by the Ammunition Train required thirty-six hours.

The 320th Field Artillery, who, in the meantime, had been in reserve, moved on November 3 to positions north of Sivry-lez-Buzancy. This Regiment again moved forward on November 4. At about 11 hours it was found that the infantry advance had been held up along the ravine southwest of Sommauthe by machine-gun fire from Ferme Polka, Ferme d'Isly, and the woods along the ravine Pré Billet and around Source Grosjean. The Regimental Commander accordingly ordered the 1st Battalion into position and, about noon, Battery C fired on these machine-gun positions. This fire was observed and adjusted. At 15 hours the 2nd Battalion also went into position, and at 16 hours the entire regiment, on request of the 318th Infantry, fired a rolling barrage in support of the infantry advance. This fire was continued for 80 minutes, 2600 rounds being expended. At about 17 hours fifty rounds of "D" shell were fired on Stonne at a range of 10,500 meters, word having been received that that town was congested with German troops. No more "D" shell was available.

On the morning of November 5 the 320th Field Artillery, with two guns per battery of the 3rd Battalion, 319th F.A., attached, relieved the 321st Field Artillery in support of the entire infantry of the Division. This was the last day in which any considerable firing was done by this Brigade. The entire Regiment moved forward in the morning in close support of the infantry, the 1st Battalion on the left and the 2nd Battalion on the right. In the afternoon Battery B went into position just south of the Stonne-Beaumont Road and fired on the village of Yoncq. At 11 hours the 2nd Battalion went into position 1½ kilometers southwest of Beaumont and fired at the request of the 317th Infantry on machine-gun nests near La Thibaudine Ferme and La Harnot Erie Ferme. After nightfall, at the request of the 2nd Division, 500 rounds were fired on Yoncq.

In the afternoon of November 5, 1st Lt. George S. Blair took forward an accompanying gun which fired effectively on machine-gun nests. On the following morning he took this gun forward with the 18th Infantry, which had relieved the 318th Infantry, and placed it in position on the southeastern slope of Mont de Brune, which point marked the farthest advance of any unit of the Brigade during the operation. From this position between 9 and 12 hours November 6, direct hits were scored on a church steeple in Mouzon in which machine guns were located. Enemy observation posts across the Meuse River were also fired on. This was the only firing executed by the Brigade on November 6. In the afternoon this gun was heavily shelled by an enemy battery. On being bracketed for range Lieutenant Blair withdrew his men. The gun and one caisson were struck, the gun being rendered unserviceable.

On November 6 the 80th Division was relieved by the 1st Division and on November 8 and 9 the 157th Field Artillery Brigade proceeded to the area Sivry-Imécourt-St. Juvin. On November 10 the Brigade marched to the area of Montblainville-Apremont, and continued the march the following day to the neighborhood of Les Islettes, where news of the armistice was received. The Trench Mortar Battery which had remained at Fléville rejoined the Brigade at this time. It had not served as a unit but had rendered excellent assistance to the Ammunition Train in the arduous operations of that organization during the preceding weeks. Details were also sent from this Battery at various times to take over captured Boche artillery and ammunition and turn them on their former owners.

The Brigade remained near Les Islettes until November 18, and then moved to the vicinity of Ste. Menehould to await orders to rejoin the 82nd Division. These orders did not arrive for nearly a month and the Brigade finally arrived in the Tenth Training area and rejoined the Division on December 17.

The work of the Artillery Brigade while with the 80th Division had in the meantime been commended in the following terms:

HEADQUARTERS EIGHTIETH DIVISION AMERICAN EXPEDITIONARY FORCES

FRANCE, 12th December, 1918.
From: Commanding General, 80th Division.
To: Commanding General, 82nd Division.
Subject: Commendation of Artillery Brigade.

1. I desire to convey to you recognition of the excellent service done by the 157th Field Artillery Brigade while serving with the Division east of the Argonne, November 1 to 6, 1918.
2. The efficient coöperation with the infantry, extending to its

OFFICIAL HISTORY OF 82ND DIVISION 245

close support by guns, batteries and battalions pushed well to the front, contributed the full artillery share to the successful operations of the Division, and maintained the high standard of the 82nd Division and of the Field Artillery.

3. It is a pleasure to acknowledge this service.

S. D. STURGIS,
Major General.

1ST IND.

Hq. 82d Division, American E. F. France, 21 December, 1918—To Commanding General, 157th F. A. Brigade.

To note and return. The Division commander notes with pride the excellent work of the Brigade.

By Command of Major General Duncan:

R. L. BOYD,
Major, A.G.D., Adjutant.

2ND IND.

Hq. 157th F. A. Brigade, American E. F. France, 24th December, 1918—To Organization Commanders.

1. In forwarding an official copy of the above letter to organization commanders the Brigade Commander wishes to add his appreciation of the splendid zeal and fighting spirit of the 157th throughout the Meuse-Argonne offensive. His pleasure and pride in the above commendation is increased by his knowledge that although the Brigade had been in the line without an hour's relief since October 6th it found no difficulty in matching the energy and determination to advance of the fresh division it was called upon to support.

(Sgd.) E. D'A. PEARCE,
*Colonel, F. A., U. S. A.,
Commanding.*

* * * * * —— * April, *1919.

We, the commanding officer and Historical Officer of the Artillery units of the 82nd Division, certify that we have read the history of operations of the 157th Field Artillery Brigade, prepared for the 82nd Division History by Capt. J. G. Pennypacker, F.A., and that this is an accurate statement of those operations.

E. D'A. PEARCE,
Col., 319th F.A., for 319th F.A., and 157th F.A. Brig.

H. C. WILLIAMS,
Cmdg. 320th F.A.

SAMUEL R. DIGHTON,
Capt., 320th F.A., Operations Officer.

JAMES L. FRY,
Major Cmdg., 2nd Bn., 321st F.A., Commander 321st F.A., Mar. 9–Apr. 8, 1919.

JOHN R. SLATER,
Captain and Adj., 321st F.A., Acting Historical Officer.

III

ADMINISTRATIVE AND SUPPLY FUNCTIONS OF THE 82ND DIVISION

CONTRIBUTED BY

MAJOR F. T. ROBSON, ACTING G-1.

The administrative department or section of the General Staff of a Division is in charge of an officer known as G-1. This department is charged with all the administrative and supply functions and correlates the work of the Adjutant's office, Military Police, Billeting, Quartermaster, Ordnance, Engineer, Medical and Signal Departments.

Lt. Col. Geo. W. Maddox, General Staff, was the first G-1. In June, 1918, he organized the department and put it in first class running order. He was with the Division while it was with the British; in the Toul and in the Marbache Sectors. He left in September just after the St. Mihiel drive. Lt. Col. Troup Miller, General Staff, was the next G-1, through the Meuse-Argonne offensive and remained until December 3, when he was sent to the 1st Corps as G-1 there. Lt. Col. J. P. Barney, General Staff, came to the Division as G-1 on December 2, and left on January, 29, being evacuated to a hospital seriously ill. Maj. F. T. Robson, Engrs., who had been Assistant G-1 since June, 1918, was then made Acting G-1.

Roughly the supply system of the A.E.F. is as follows, supplies being divided into four classes:

Class I: Rations, forage, fuel, gasoline, etc. These are known as the daily automatic supplies and G-1 of the Division telegraphs the Army two days in advance giving the required amounts of each kind. Train is then loaded and sent to the railhead of the Division through the Regulating Station. As Divisions are all of the same size the daily automatic supply does not vary greatly. It is customary for the Depot to load what is known as a "balanced train" consisting of rations for 28,000 men, forage for 6000 animals, 3000 gallons of gasoline, 4 carloads of wood, etc., each day.

Class II: Clothing, blankets, etc.

Class III: All other authorized equipment such as Ordnance, Engineer, Signal, etc.

Class IV: Ammunition, construction material and equipment and other things depending upon battle conditions.

When the troops need Class II, III or IV supplies, Supply Officers of the organizations make a requisition and send it to the

A close shave

Church at Sommerance

Chief of the Department from which the supplies are to come. He consolidates the requisition and sends it to G-1 of the Division for approval. After being approved it goes to G-4 of the Army and from there to the Depot that is to supply the goods. After loading the car is sent to Regulating Station to have the destination and route prescribed. The main regulating station for the American Forces has been at Is-sur-Tille. This station was always informed by telegraph as to the location or proposed movements of the troops of the A.E.F. and was thus able to route cars to destination. During battle many changes in location occur after the car has left the Regulating Station and it was usually found advisable to have a convoy with important shipments to minimize their chance of going astray. Upon arrival at the railhead the railhead officer turns over to the Division Quartermaster all goods arriving for that Division. The unloading is done by the personnel of the Quartermaster and the goods taken by trucks of the Supply Train to the distributing point of the Division. Here a segregation is made to the Supply Officers of the various regiments who in turn distribute to the supply sergeants of their smaller units. When a Division is fully equipped and has its complement of animals and motor vehicles from 25 to 30 cars per day are required.

During rest periods and in quiet sectors the G-1 Office is operated in one echelon at Division Headquarters. During offensive engagements, particularly under open warfare conditions, it was found necessary to divide the Office of G-1 into two echelons for effective work. This was thought absolutely essential during the Meuse-Argonne offensive. The second echelon was under control of G-1 with the Adjutant's Department and Trains Headquarters, and remained at or near the railhead properly to control the movement of supplies, replacements, etc., from the rear to this echelon.

An advance section of G-1, consisting in the Meuse-Argonne offensive of Maj. F. T. Robson, a stenographer and an office orderly, was at all times with the front echelon of the Division; their duties being to keep in close touch with the front line and with the rear echelon in order to better control the delivery of supplies and ammunition and to keep informed of changes in the disposition of troops due to necessities of combat.

QUARTERMASTER DEPARTMENT

The Quartermaster Department is the largest of the supply organizations of the Army and is charged mainly with the supply of rations, food, forage, clothing and other articles that have to do with the welfare and comfort of the troops. As the tables of organization do not provide any labor troops for this department it was found necessary, immediately upon arrival in France, to organize a detachment of approximately 100 men and known as the Quartermaster Detachment unassigned. This unit loads and unloads and handles rations and supplies and distributes them to various organizations, etc.

The Officer personnel of the Quartermaster Department of this Division has changed constantly. Capt. A. J. Manning, Finance Branch, and Lt. L. P. Harrell, are the only officers now with the Division who accompanied it from the United States. To these two officers (and to Sergeants 1st Class Warren Merrim, Max Contor and E. H. Ashcraft who maintained an advance Quartermaster dump at Fléville) and to the enlisted men of the Quartermaster detachment unassigned must be given a large share of the credit for the excellent work done by the Quartermaster Department at all times under most trying circumstances.

During the time the Division was with the British and when in the Toul and Marbache sectors troops were practically stationary and the railhead did not change. The problem of supply soon become stabilized and was dependent solely upon the ability of supply depots to furnish the articles requisitioned for. During the St, Mihiel fight this Division acted as a pivot and the troops did not move sufficiently to cause the railhead at Belleville to be changed during the combat. Thus again the problem of supply was not complicated except in so far as the fact that the Division was astride the Moselle River caused inconvenience due to an inadequate system of bridges. In fact, during all engagements of the Division prior to the Meuse-Argonne offensive the supplying of the troops depended very largely upon the ability and initiative of the supply officers of the various regiments.

On September 24 the Division moved to the vicinity of Triaucourt by motor bus and the supply system became much more complicated. A vast concentration of American troops in a small area had been made in preparation for a battle which was to commence on September 26. Railroads were taxed to their utmost capacity to bring in the rations, forage, ammunition and other material required for the offensive. Railheads were very congested and trains were late in arriving. Roads were blocked with traffic and the weather was rainy and cold. Road circulation was limited by the desire for secrecy.

OFFICIAL HISTORY OF 82ND DIVISION 249

The first distributing point in this area was at a triangle formed by roads just west of the town of Froidos. This was used successfully until October 4 when an advance division dump was located about 1 kilometer west of Varennes on the Varennes-Four-de-Paris Road. This dump was within 4 or 5 kilometers of the front and in an exposed position, but it was the only available place where road circulation was obtainable. It was under constant enemy observation and shell fire. The Quartermaster personnel lived in German dugouts in the vicinity that had just been captured. Most of the distribution of rations had to be done during the night. It was at this period that the railhead of the Division was changed almost daily. No information could be obtained as to where the railhead of the Division would be the next day and frequently the entire supply train would go to a railhead to find that it had been changed. The supplies had to be drawn somewhere else. This necessitated a great loss of time and the tying-up of motor transportation which was a serious matter where there was none to spare. However, we always managed to get our supplies in one way or another and the Division was always promptly fed. As the troops went forward the distributing point at Varennes was too far in the rear and on October 12 it was moved to Apremont, at that time only about 3 kilometers behind the line, and in plain view of the Germans down the Aire Valley. All but one company of the 307th Supply Train was moved to this point also and the constant circulation and parking of trucks caused nightly shelling and air raids. A day or two later advance dumps for one infantry brigade and machine-gun battalion was established at Fléville.

It was about this time that Maj. Catchings Therrell was appointed advance representative of the G-1 office to correlate the supply of the troops in the front line and as the front line had become more or less stabilized, to look after the comfort of the men. Major Therrell took charge of this work in an energetic and capable manner and soon had old German baths at Fléville and Sommerance in operation; also rest rooms where the men of the reserve battalions could get a change of clothing and a dry, warm place to sleep. All this while fighting was going on a few kilometers in advance. He also moved up and pooled the kitchens and operated them day and night, sometimes within a kilometer of the front line.

The 307th Supply Train, a motorized unit, furnished the delivery system of the Quartermaster Department from the railhead to the distributing point, and all hauling for the entire Division. This supply train with its repair shop, the 340th Service Park Unit, functioned in a most admirable manner throughout. Although they were never assigned their full complement of trucks and with spare parts and supplies for motor equipment extremely hard to secure, yet there never was a time when the Division was required to call for outside help to transport its supplies. This was due solely to the high grade of the personnel and the untiring efforts of the officers and men of these organizations. To one who is not familiar with road conditions during the Meuse-Argonne offensive it is impossible to describe fully the hardships and difficulties under which trucks had to operate. It would have been bad enough in daylight but with darkness and shell fire added it is utterly inconceivable how heavy trucks can be operated at all, much less reach their destination, sometimes over roads utterly unknown to drivers, and with insufficient data as to the route.

Short of motor equipment themselves the 307th Supply Train had to help the Ammunition Train haul ammunition and the Sanitary Train haul wounded, due to a like shortage in these organizations.

The road from Clermont to Varennes and northward was at all times congested with traffic and hours were consumed in traveling a distance of a few miles. The Germans had blown two immense craters in this road and proper time could not be given to fill them. A one-way turn-out was operated that caused delays of hours. Hauling of rations and supplies went on by day as far as was consistent with secrecy and the same trucks with a change of drivers hauled ammunition all night. A shortage of ambulances made it necessary to haul wounded and sick men by trucks night after night. In fact a truck was hardly ever parked.

Under all of these trying conditions the men of the 307th Supply Train can point with pride to the fact that during the entire offensive not one of their trucks was so seriously injured or broken by careless driving or accident as to be left on the road and abandoned.

On the afternoon of the 29th of September a rush order was received for a regiment of infantry to reinforce the 28th Division which was then hard pressed. From 6 to 8 o'clock that evening 88 trucks were loaded with men of the 327th Infantry at a point on the main road just west of Rarécourt and despatched over the Clermont-Varennes Road to a point of debarkation near

Charpentry, a distance of 15 miles. Due to road congestion and circulation requirements some of these trucks did not report back until late the next afternoon. This is but a sample of what was done day after day.

SALES COMMISSARY UNIT No. 30

This unit was attached to the Division when in the Marbache Sector but received no supplies until sometime in September shortly before the move to the Argonne. Thus from May to October the Division depended upon the Y.M.C.A., the K. of C. and the Salvation Army for canteen service. During the Meuse-Argonne offensive several carloads of supplies came in and trucks were sent out with these supplies to distribute them as close to the front line as possible. Breakfast food, soup, chocolate, etc., were furnished in large quantities to a Field Hospital which the Division erected at Apremont. After return of the Division to a rest area the Sales Commissary continued to exercise its normal duty until the Division was ordered to entrain to the Bordeaux Area when this unit was detached and sent to the Le Mans Area.

ORDNANCE DEPARTMENT

The Ordnance Department furnishes most of the equipment required for fighting. A certain amount of ordnance personnel is scattered throughout the Division, being attached to the various units. But one small unit, consisting of an officer and about 50 men to repair and replace equipment, cannon and machine guns, functions under Division Headquarters. It is known as the 307th Mobile Ordnance Repair Shop.

The 307th Mobile Ordnance Repair Shop, while small, is an extremely efficient organization with technical personnel. Due to its excellent functioning and to the work of Division Ordnance Officer little real difficulty was encountered by the troops in obtaining needed equipment. To perform its duties properly the Mobile Ordnance Repair Shop was at all times working within range of enemy guns and operated its repair trucks there. On October 12, 1918, it moved with the Quartermaster Department to Apremont where an advance ordnance depot was established to reequip men returning from hospitals or who had lost their equipment under battle conditions.

The Ordnance Department has done its work excellently, due to the good training given by Col. P. H. Worcester in the United

States and France and to Capt. A. C. Jones who succeeded him as Division Ordnance Officer on August 27, 1918.

In connection with the Ordnance Department but coming more directly under the Artillery Brigade Commander and the Division Munitions Officers, Lt. Wm. F. Holland and Lt. Charles L. Andrews, was the 307th Ammunition Train, commanded by Lt. Col. C. W. McClure. This consisted of a motorized and a horse-drawn battalion.

The supply of an Artillery Brigade with ammunition is roughly as follows: 3 days' fire are to be kept at the guns or at least with the Divisions. Reports are made to the Corps Ordnance Officer daily of amounts fired during the preceding 24 hours and allocations made to replace this and any additional amount that may be required for a "show" that may have been ordered "pulled off." These allocations state the kind of ammuntion and number of rounds and the location of the dump where they can be secured. As soon as this information is received it is up to the Ammuntion Train to immediately get the ammunition. Theoretically, the motorized battalion procured the ammunition from the specified army or corps dump and delivered it on the main road as close to the battery position as possible. Here the horse-drawn battalion took it direct to the battery positions, because of lack of animals in the artillery regiments.

This at least was the plan decided upon, but the shortage of animals in the entire A.E.F. and the continued loss by shell fire and by sickness caused by working 24 hours a day put a much greater burden on the motor transportation. Trucks furnished were in many cases old and worn out and numbered only about 50 per cent of the authorized quantity. Thus it came about that the trucks of the Ammunition Train were compelled to go farther and farther toward the front over almost impassable roads and direct to battery positions under the most severe enemy fire and the most trying conditions of road congestion, always under the cover of darkness and without lights of any kind. When it is remembered that not only is the chauffeur compelled to operate his truck or a driver his caisson over a road known to the enemy artillery and under shell fire and with the contents of his load highly explosive in nature, too much credit can not be given to the work of the Ammunition Train of this Division.

This Office does not know of a single instance when cannon of the Division were silent because of lack of ammunition. This was not the case in many other Divisions. The 82nd Division is proud of the work of its Munitions Officers, its Ammuntion Train, and not only of the chauffeurs and drivers, but also of the mechanics who kept things in repair. These men, with the assistance of the 307th Supply Train in time of unusual demands, always got the ammuntion where it was needed and in sufficient time.

MOVEMENT BY MOTOR BUSES

On two occasions this Division moved a distance of about 100 miles by motor buses, a system of locomotion developed by the needs of the Allied armies and used in times of railroad congestion or when the transportation lines were controlled by, or under fire of the enemy. The motor buses were American White trucks with a capacity of from 18 to 20 men each and driven by Chinese chauffeurs. The trucks were operated in companies of about 50 trucks each with 4 companies in a section. Immediately after the St. Mihiel drive, on September 24, 1918, the Division was moved from the vicinity of Marbache to Triaucourt by these motor buses; about 1200 buses were required for the movement.

Many new problems in the supply of a Division were presented by such a move. When a Division moved by rail all the equipment accompanied it; when by bus, none of the animals could be moved in this way, nor could the artillery. The distance of this move was approximately 100 miles which is a 5-day trip for the horse-drawn vehicles. Water-carts and rolling kitchens are necessary for the troops at all times in order that warm meals may be given. The Division did not have sufficient motor equipment in its Supply and Ammunition Trains to move these vehicles nor are the bodies of many trucks large enough to accommodate a rolling kitchen. This meant that a survey of rolling kitchens and water-carts had to be made to see what could be handled by the motor equipment. Those that would go in the trucks were selected and the balance sent overland with the horse transport. The kitchens remaining to be loaded on trucks had to do double duty for the 4 or 5 days that the horse transport was on the road.

A road circuit for the buses had to be found and the troops brought to these embusing points, numbering two or three for a division; the troops loaded and started on their journey. These bus columns then traveled over a road designated in advance and under the same general methods that would govern the handling of railway traffic. Travel was by night as the front lines were approached. As trucks broke down or were overturned they took their places in rear of the column. This resulted in some confusion. It is an expeditious method of transporting troops but the supply problem is exceedingly hard until the horse transport reaches the Division again, and takes its proper place with the various organizations.

ENGINEER DEPARTMENT

The Engineers of a Division are organized both as Engineer and as fighting units and in this Division not only performed the work of Engineers in the construction of required structures of all kind, keeping open the lines of communication, etc., but were actually put in the line in numerous instances. As a supply department their main problem was to furnish material for field fortifications and the construction of buildings for the housing and comfort of troops and maintenance of the lines of communication. This work was exceedingly well done under the most trying circumstances. It is more fully set out in another chapter devoted to the history of the Engineer Regiment and Train.

BILLETING

When Americans arrived in France it was necessary to adopt the French system of quartering troops in billets. This system consists in quartering men, animals and materials in houses, buildings, stables or any other shelter, belonging either to private individuals or to the Government. Officers are provided with rooms in the homes of the inhabitants. The French law requires the municipal authorities to prepare and submit to the military authorities a list of such available accommodations and, with a few exceptions, it requires the inhabitant to give over any part of his property not in daily use. The law also provided that the troops will share, in common with the inhabitant, lighting and heating facilities, and water supply. These accommodations are furnished at the rate of one franc per day for an officer, five centimes per day for a soldier, and five centimes per day for an animal.

Although fifteen officers who spoke French had been sent to France in advance by the 82nd Division to familiarize themselves with this system, they had been so scattered that their services did not become available for some time after the arrival of the Division. It was therefore necessary to detail other officers as Billeting Officers and Acting Town Majors, to quarter the troops, keep a record of billets occupied and adjust any claims for damage which might arise. 1st Lt. Stuart W. Goldsborough, Division Headquarters, was put in charge of this work for the Division.

The instructions for the preparation of billeting records and for the settlement of claims were incomplete and were constantly changing during our first few months in France. They were not stabilized until August 31, 1918, when a Manual was issued by the Services of Supply, for the use of Renting, Requisition and Claims Officers.

The system of billeting contemplates having the areas divided into various zones (each of which will accommodate a Division) with officers permanently in charge of each zone, having complete information as to the available accommodations, a list of towns, maximum capacity of each in officers, men and animals, and any other facilities for the troops. It was only after the Division had withdrawn from the Argonne, however, that we made the acquaintance of such an officer, known as an American Zone Major. It had, therefore, been necessary to obtain all such information from the French; or, if that was impossible, by personal reconnaissance.

The difference in language and customs and the fact that the system was entirely new to Americans had led to many minor misunderstandings and claims by the French. Almost invariably an investigation of such claims showed that they were justifiable and they were promptly adjusted. The few instances of exorbitant claims, as well as complaints of extortionate prices having been charged, can usually be attributed to the impression given by many Americans that they were able to pay and must have the best of everything at any price. It was the constant endeavor of the officials of the Division to promote and maintain cordial relations with the inhabitants and it is a source of considerable satisfaction that the Division left France with the entire good will of the French people with whom it has been billeted. This good will was properly reciprocated by the men of the Division, because of the courtesy and kindness of the French, and their unfailing willingness to share the comforts of their homes with the Americans.

82ND MILITARY POLICE COMPANY

When the Division sailed for France, the Military Police was organized under the old tables of organization. There were two companies of one hundred and fifty men and three officers each, and the same Headquarters which served for the trains was employed as Battalion Headquarters for the Military Police. However, shortly after the arrival in France, B Company was placed on detached service, thus cutting the working strength in half.

The weeks spent with the British were used mainly in the study of the British traffic rules and their methods of handling the police situation and the working out of the necessary changes due to our different customs and regulations.

On the Toul sector, the Military Police work covered a wide area, for the sector was large and for the most part under direct enemy observation during the day. This fact compelled the installation of many posts to regulate the passage of vehicles and individuals. All movement in and out of the area was restricted and examination posts kept to prevent unauthorized travel. Details were also stationed in both Toul and Nancy to police those cities. Many A.W.O.L.'s from other divisions as well as our own were handled in these places. At Ménil-le-Tour, a Divisional Guard House was established and maintained.

B Company joined the Battalion when the Division entered the Marbache sector but during the St. Mihiel drive, A Company was detached and placed at the disposition of the 1st Army.

Details were again scattered over the Divisional Area for the regulation of traffic and circulation. Advance straggler posts were maintained close behind the lines and aided in directing the wounded to dressing stations as well as apprehending stragglers.

In Nancy a strong detail was required and often as many as one hundred A.W.O.L.'s or deserters were apprehended in a 24-hour period. These were marched to the Divisional Guard House at Belleville, where they were worked on the roads by the Military Police until called for by their units. A force was also maintained in the evacuated city of Pont-à-Mousson to prevent looting by our troops.

When the Horse transportation moved from the Marbache sector to the Argonne Forest, a detachment of Mounted Military Police served as an advance party, selecting camp sites and posting the road. This movement was made entirely at night and without mishap.

With the entry into the Argonne territory, one hundred men and two officers were transferred to the 1st Army, C.R.A., and one company of five officers and two hundred men was organized according to G.O. 180, 1918.

In the Argonne Forest offensive, our straggler posts were busy, and constant liaison maintained with the Divisions on our right and left made possible to effect more efficient straggler lines. Details were kept at both Infantry Brigade P.C.'s, which conducted the prisoners of war to the Division P.C., where they were turned over to the Corps Military Police.

The traffic in the Forest was very heavy and only by strong road details was it kept under control. The Division Military Police were required to handle the Corps road from Varennes north for several weeks, due to the shortage of Military Police at Corps Headquarters. Each traffic post was supplied with a location list of all units, dumps and railheads of our own Division and the most important ones of the neighboring divisions. In addition, a road map was in the possession of each sentry, with which to direct convoys, troops and individuals to their proper destinations. These aids often proved invaluable to truck drivers, who had been sent out with too little information.

Upon the relief of the Division in the Argonne, the Military Police force was divided into three sections. One went ahead to the staging area and assisted the placing of units when they arrived. Another handled the roads between the two areas, while the third remained in the old area to collect stragglers and material left by the department troops. This last detail was also instructed with the embussing of the troops at the concentration points.

Captain Gordon D. Palmer has been in command of 82nd Military Police Company since its organization.

Y. M. C. A.

The Y.M.C.A. has been operating with the Division ever since its organization. After arrival overseas and while located in Northern France the Division was served by the British Branch of the Y.M.C.A. After the movement of the Division to the Toul sector the American branch of the Y.M.C.A. served the Division and at this time the personnel were assigned to sectors and so continued until major operations began when a permanent personnel was attached to the Division and moved about with it. From the date the Y.M.C.A. first joined the Division they have done much for the welfare and comfort of the troops in the supply of tobacco, candies, cakes, etc., as well as various kinds of athletic equipment. In addition many buildings were built or leased and tents erected in which there was always ample writing facilities as well as the necessary equipment for entertainment in the way of moving pictures, music, and groups of entertainers, who traveled from place to place.

During the Meuse-Argonne offensive this organization did excellent work in the distribution of supplies to the fighting troops and much credit is due Mr. P. H. Gossom, then Divisional Secretary for the 82nd Division, for his untiring efforts and efficient handling of his organization for the benefit of the fighting men.

With few individual exceptions the personnel attached to the Division have been of high type and satisfactory. In certain cases they have been of exceptionally high type. There were many instances of bravery, devotion, and self-sacrifice on the part of both men and women workers and the following were cited in Division orders for their meritorious service:

> MISS BERNETTA A. MILLER
> MISS SUNSHINE SWEENEY
> MISS MARY SWEENEY
> MR. H. B. MCAFEE

IV

307TH ENGINEER REGIMENT OF THE 82ND DIVISION

CONTRIBUTED BY

LIEUTENANT COLONEL H. C. MOWER, 307TH ENGINEERS

1. The officers of the 307th Engineer Regiment reported for duty at Camp Gordon, Ga., 27 August, 1917, in compliance with S.O. 186, 11 August, 1917; they were technical men who had been trained at the Engineer Training Camps at Washington and Bellevoir, Va.

2. The enlisted personnel of this regiment was drawn from the same localities as the men who filled the other regiments of the Division. The organization was trained in infantry combat and in military engineering. Schools were conducted in fourteen subjects and every platoon contained specialists in bridge carpentry, rigging, mine and gallery construction, mapping, obstacles, demolition, revetments, highway and railway construction.

3. The Regiment and Train left Camp Gordon for overseas service 8 May, 1918; sailed from Hoboken 19 May and arrived at La Havre via Liverpool, Winchester and Southampton 3 June, 1918. Col. J. L. Schley, Corps of Engineers, commanded.

On 25 June the command rejoined the Division in the Toul sector and relieved the 101st Engineers.

4. The companies were distributed on the line of resistance of the sector and were employed on field fortifications: dugout, wire, pill box and dugout construction, operation of sawmills and engineer dumps. On 4 August two officers and 48 men of this regiment accompanied a raiding party of about 500 men from the 326th Infantry who entered the German lines opposite Noviant. Wire entanglements were shot out where necessary and concentrated charges were used in mopping up dugouts. 1st Lt. I. F. Witherington and four of his men were wounded.

5. On 7-8 August the 82nd Division was relieved by the 89th Division and moved south of Toul. After seven days in Bicquelay this regiment marched into the Marbache sector and relieved the 2nd Engineers, the command passing on 18 August. Four engineer companies were put on the resistance lines; one position was organized through Forêt de Facq and the work started by the French on the second position, running over the mountain south of Ste. Géneviève, was continued. One company completed the erection of barracks for the 328th Infantry, organized the "barrage position" near Liverdun and took charge of all mined bridges over the Moselle River. The sixth company was employed on camouflaging roads and the care of all division, corps and army dumps and sawmills in Marbache and Dieulouard.

6. Here, as in the Toul sector, field fortifications were directed by the French Army Engineers and all pneumatic and electrical plant employed on dugout construction was furnished by them. The position through Forêt de Facq was organized with wire, emplacements and shelters; the one farther south was an elaborate system of dugouts, and galleries through the mountain with wire and trenches on the north slopes and across the river valley.

7. Colonel Schley, who had been injured near Toul before the regiment entered the sector, rejoined and resumed command on 30 August.

8. Upon receipt of orders for the St. Mihiel offensive A Company was attached to the 163rd Infantry Brigade, F Company to the 164th Infantry Brigade and C Company to the Artillery Brigade. Three companies were held by the Division Engineer for work on lines of communication, care of bridges and for other engineering service.

9. On 12 September D Company opened a sheltered road run-

ning to Norroy from the Pont-à-Mousson. On the 13th all obstacles were removed from the main roads to Norroy and Vandières. F Company sent one platoon with the 328th Infantry to cut wire where necessary; the two platoons not attached to first infantry lines were kept busy clearing *chevcaux de frise* and wire from lines of advance. On the night of the 15th, B C and E Companies were taken from the roads and organized the high ground west of the river from Pont-à-Mousson to the hill west of Vandières which had become our exposed right flank. A Company was held in readiness on the east side of the river; they kept patrols out, built a foot bridge and restored the demolished stone arch bridge of Port-sur-Seille.

10. The platoons of D and F Companies, held at Norroy, opened up roads to the north through the woods and on the night of 15 September brought in to our dressing station 120 infantrymen and machine gunners who were given first aid and evacuated by our battalion surgeon. Among those found in the woods was Lieutenant Colonel Pike, D.M.G. Officer. Although still limping from the effects of his injury Colonel Schley managed to spend most of his time with his foremost units. The regiment lost during the five days, 2 killed, 22 seriously wounded and 43 slightly wounded and gassed.

11. This command was relieved on the west side of the river 17 September by the 315th Engineers and on the east side 20 September by the French engineers. Animals and animal drawn transportation started for Auzéville on the east edge of the Argonne Forest 20 September and the regiment followed in French lorries on the 24th; the entire command arriving and going into camp that night (24-25).

12. The 82nd Division was designated as Army Reserve upon arrival at the new station; the engineer regiment was temporarily detached from the division and charged with the repair and upkeep of the Clermont-Varennes and the Vraincourt-Neuvilly roads, also the opening of and removal of barriers from the forest roads in the vicinity of Les Islettes and Four-de-Paris. On 29 September while planking over the detour around one of the mine craters in the Neuvilly-Varennes road D Company was "shanghaied" by the 28th Division without the knowledge or consent of our regimental, division, corps or army engineer; they were taken from the army work and sent out in front of the 28th Division's outpost line to organize and hold a quarry north of Apremont in the face of an imminent counter-attack. They broke up the attack, captured 11 prisoners

and killed over 200 of the attacking party. Lt. S. H. Andrews and eleven men were wounded, four were gassed and one was missing when the garrison was relieved. This regiment was not permitted to bridge the two mine craters that caused the disastrous congestion in traffic between Neuvilly and Varennes, but with teams and scrapers built a fill bypass to the second or northern crater.

13. On 3 October the regimental P.C. was moved from Grange-le-Comte Farm to a captured German camp southwest of Varennes and on the 5th the 82nd Division was made corps reserve and established its P.C. in Varennes. The 1st Battalion of this regiment was charged with the repair and removal of barriers and road mines from roads in what had been No Man's Land north of Four-de-Paris and the connecting-up of German 60 cm. track in the forest.

14. Orders (82nd Division Field Order No. 20) were received at 20 hours 6 October, for the attack across the Aire River from La Forge to Fléville at 5 hours, 7 October. F Company was loaded on trucks at Chêne Tondu at 22 o'clock with orders to locate and mark any fordable places in the river between La Forge and the Fléville-Cornay bridge. The trucks could not get into Varennes on account of the congestion on the roads, due to troop movements and F Company detrained and marched arriving in time to take all soundings, locate and mark the ford at La Forge, the only site where infantry could cross. The 327th Infantry went over at this point at H hour. On the night of 7-8, F Company built a foot bridge across the Aire River just above the ford, to carry infantry and machine-gun carts; the ford was paved with stone and ramps were dug making the crossing open to trucks and artillery. The shell and machine-gun fire upon this point was very heavy through the night; the crew was forced to leave the work three times and Lt. E. S. Allen and six men were wounded, Lieutenant Allen going to the hospital with his second wound. The 2nd Battalion, commanded by Maj. C. F. Lewis, was stationed near Charpentry.

15. Company E held an outpost in Châtel-Chéhéry through the night of 9-10 and F Company opened the road through Apremont and paved and dug ramp approaches to a ford below the demolished steel bridge at that point. E Company put a light bridge across the Aire at Fléville on the night of the 10th over which two battalions of infantry crossed to attack on the morning of the 11th. They also prepared a ford at this point for heavy traffic, and corresponding crossings were pro-

vided over the millrace and road-mine craters on the Fléville-St. Juvin and Fléville-Cornay Roads. A C.P. for the 164th Infantry Brigade was prepared in Sommerance and engineer dumps were started in Cornay, Fléville and on the Sommerance-St. Juvin Road. The engineer train operated from Le Ménil Farm.

16. In the meantime the 1st Battalion, under Maj. Eugene Kelly, was working roads, removing barriers and road mines following the advance of the 163rd Infantry Brigade in the woods west of the river. On 10 October A Company undertook the repair and operation of the 60 cm. German railway north out of Varennes. They repaired the demolished joints and extended the line into Cornay by setting over one rail of the standard gauge to 60 cm. gauge. Rations and ammunition were handled by this "307th Limited." B Company reconnaissance patrol into Chevières on the 10th found the town in flames, deserted by German troops and no American troops present; patrols also reached the river through Marcq and Cornay.

17. One platoon of B Company was ordered to report to a guide at Marcq on the night of 10-11, no mention being made of the character of service required. The platoon reported without tools, was taken to the demolished steel bridge south of St. Juvin and directed to have the bridge ready for infantry assault at 5 hours next morning. They tore plank from German sheds at the station and with gun slings as lashings put in a floor system. It is worthy of note that the hostile fire on this point was suspended from the time our men went to work; a H.E. shell tore part of the floor up about an hour before daybreak but this was repaired. When our infantry started across at H hour a terrific fire was opened on the assaulting troops forcing a retirement. Captain Catchings, commanding B Company, was the only casualty among the engineer troops.

18. It was reported on the 14th that the last machine-gun clips available for the Division had been drawn. C Company was put on salvage and turned in 80,000 M.G. clips and 2,600,000 rounds of ammunition salvaged from the path of advance. Lt. J. H. Claxon was killed while removing road mines in the path of our infantry advance on the Sommerance-St. Juvin road, 14 October. In compliance with oral orders from the Chief of Staff the 2nd Battalion moved into the support position north of Sommerance at midnight 15-16 October and the following night the 1st Battalion moved up and organized a reserve position southwest of Sommerance. the 2nd Battalion at the same time changing position 500 meters forward and west to the

Fléville-Buzancy road. Here they dug in on the reverse slope and organized a position on the forward slope with trenches and wire.

19. The regimental P.C. was moved to Fléville on the 16th. By the night of the 18th the incessant rains and heavy traffic were making the roads in the divisional area impassable, and the 1st Battalion was put back on lines of communication; roads were repaired, temporary light bridges were reinforced or replaced by permanent heavy structures and A Company resumed the operation of the "Limited" from Varennes to Châtel-Chéhéry. The regimental P.C. was moved to La Forge on the 18th.

20. The engineer train suffered several losses in handling engineer materials from the big St. Juvin dump which was shelled several times a day. Men while in the line were served two hot meals daily from the kitchens which were sent to their station.

21. The 1st Battalion relieved the 2nd on the night of 22-23. The 21st Engineers took over the operation of the "Limited" on the 23rd. The 2nd Battalion began the organization of the position of security north of Fléville under the corps engineer but the orders were changed and on the 28th the 2nd Battalion and Engineer Train moved to the new location of the line of security for the 82nd Divisional sector and with one battalion of infantry and one M.G. battalion began the organization of the ground west of Cornay.

22. Major Kelly was relieved from command of the 1st Battalion 23 October by Capt. H. B. Baird and on 26 October Col. J. L. Schley was made Corps Engineer 5th Corps, and turned the command over to Lt. Col. H. C. Mower.

23. The 1st Battalion and Headquarters were relieved 30 October by the 305th Engineers and moved to the rear. The 2nd Battalion was relieved on 3 November by the 318th Engineers of the 6th Division and overtook the rest of the regiment at Florent. The losses of the regiment in the Argonne were:

1 Officer and 14 men killed in action.
3 Officers and 71 men wounded.
7 Men gassed.

24. The service of the Engineer Regiment is necessary to the proper functioning of the Division and involves the same hardships, long marches and hard work as does that of the other branches of the service; indeed, the two weeks in support line proved a welcome change. While our scattered companies were usually "among those present" near the front lines and, inci-

dentally, always proud of what the rest of the divisional family was doing, they had to work under shell fire and sleep in fox holes without the inspiration and satisfaction of contact and combat with the enemy.

V

HISTORY OF THE MEDICAL DEPARTMENT OF THE 82ND DIVISION

CONTRIBUTED BY

LIEUTENANT COLONEL FREDERICK G. BARFIELD, DIVISION SURGEON

Sanitary detachments of four Infantry, three Artillery and one Engineer Regiment, together with the personnel of one Field Hospital and one Ambulance Company were sent from the Medical Officers' Training Camp, Ft. Oglethorpe, Ga., August 26, 1917, to Camp Gordon, Ga., as a nucleus of the Medical Department of the 82nd Division. By a Division order, September 2, 1917, these detachments were assigned to the various Regiments of the Division, part of their personnel having been withdrawn for assignment to Train Headquarters and Military Police, Signal and Machine Gun Battalions and Ammunition Train. From time to time the commissioned personnel of the regimental and separate organization detachments was increased by the addition of newly arriving medical officers. Enlisted personnel was increased in proportion as the organizations grew. Likewise, from time to time, medical officers and enlisted men were added to the Sanitary Train. No care was taken to select men suited for duty in the Medical Department, and it was soon evident that if the sick and wounded men were to be properly cared for, quite a change would have to be made in the personnel of the Medical Detachments and the Sanitary Train. This fact was constantly presented to the proper authorities and after several months a number of men of the Medical Department were exchanged for those more suited for this kind of work.

While the Division was being trained in military duties, the Medical Department was likewise undergoing intensive training in its special duties, in addition to its work of caring for the sick, administering typhoid vaccine and, where necessary, vaccinating against smallpox. This work was considerably increased by the sending away of practically all of the enlisted men of the Division in October and the receipt of a similar number of men from other camps. These men arrived with their records in very poor shape and it was a very difficult matter to find out those who had been protected against typhoid and those who had not. It is believed, however, that eventually every man of the Division was protected against typhoid fever and smallpox. The training of the Medical Department of the Division was under the direction of Lt. Col. C. E. Koerper, M. C., Division Surgeon, Maj. William T. Cade, Jr., M. C., Division Sanitary Inspector, and Maj. Frederick T. Jenkins, M. C., Division Medical Instructor. Instruction was vigorously carried out until the departure of the Division for France. During its stay at Camp Gordon the health of the Division was very good. As was to be expected, there were numerous cases of mumps and measles. There was some pneumonia complicating with measles, and a few sporadic cases of epidemic meningitis. There were no cases of typhoid fever. Camp Gordon ranked as one of the most healthful camps of the U. S. Army.

The Division, less the Artillery and Sanitary Train, arrived in France during the month of May, 1918, and were with the British in the Somme area. The sick and wounded of the Division were cared for by the British Medical Department, and the training of the Medical Department of the Division was vigorously pursued. Medical supplies were also obtained through the British. This experience was very valuable, especially the training in sanitation, at least one officer and two enlisted men spending one week at the British School for Sanitation at St. Valery-sur-Somme. The health of the command during this period was excellent and nothing of unusual interest occurred. It was very unfortunate that the Sanitary Train did not accompany the Division to this area, for valuable training was missed during this period.

The Division was moved to the Toul sector the latter part of June, and was joined by the Sanitary Train, the medical units of the 82nd Division relieving and taking over, unit for unit, the positions of the 26th Division. The Ambulance Section had assigned to it eight G.M.C. and twelve animal-drawn ambulances. The Division was entitled to forty-one G.M.C. ambulances, but repeated efforts to obtain them were in vain. However, S.S.U. Unit No. 647, with thirty Ford ambulances, was attached to the Division and served with them throughout their front-line activities. The general plan for the evacuation of the sick and wounded was from regimental and battalion aid stations to ambulance dressing stations, thence to field hospital, acting as a triage, or sifting station, and from the triage to other field hospitals or to evacuation hospital. It was the policy of the Division Surgeon to use the Sanitary Train as a replacement unit for medical detachments of the line organizations, so that at all times the organizations were kept at full strength in both commissioned and enlisted personnel. In training areas and in comparatively quiet sectors such as the Toul sector it was the policy to keep one motor ambulance, usually a Ford, and one animal-drawn ambulance for each regiment or separate battalion, while the G.M.C. ambulances made daily rounds collecting the sick and wounded. Preparatory to any action, the motor ambulances were recalled and stationed at points as the need indicated. As a rule, Ford ambulances were used to carry the injured from regimental or battalion aid stations to ambulance company dressing stations, and the G.M.C. from these points to the divisional triage. The patients were then evacuated from the triage to the rear by Evacuation Ambulance Companies (Corps troops). When necessary, trucks were called into service to evacuate patients both from the front to the triage and from the triage to the rear. In the Toul sector the 325th Ambulance Company was stationed at Minorville with a dressing station at Noviant, the 326th Ambulance at Menil-la-Tour with dressing station at Rehannes Woods, Ambulance Company 327 was stationed at Rongeval Abbey with dressing station at Raulecourt, and the 328th Ambulance Company in reserve at Menil-la-Tour. Field Hospitals 325 and 327 were stationed in large barracks at Toul and really operated as base hospitals. Field Hospital 326 was stationed near Royameix and functioned as a triage for the right half of the sector and as a gas hospital. Field Hospital 328 was stationed at Rongeval Abbey and served as a triage for the left half of the sector. This comparatively quiet sector furnished an excellent opportunity for training of the Sanitary Train.

During the period spent in the Toul sector there were only two occasions during which anything out of the ordinary was done by the Medical Department—one, the raid put over by the 326th Infantry, at which time about seventy casualties were handled, and the other occurring during the relief of the 82nd Division by the 89th Division about August 6. The Germans launched a gas attack which resulted in about 750 casualties, a vast majority of which were from the 89th Division. The Sanitary Train of the 82nd Division had not been relieved by that of the 89th, so all these cases were handled by the 307th Sanitary Train through the 326th Field Hospital near Royameix. These cases were all treated for gas and evacuated to Toul within thirty-six hours—a splendid achievement for the 326th Field Hospital. While in this area utmost attention was paid to sanitation under the supervision of Capt. Charles B. Hollis, Division Sanitary Inspector, and the health of the Division was excellent.

The Division moved from the Toul sector to the Marbache sector about the middle of August, 1918, the Sanitary Train of the 82nd Division relieving that of the 2nd Division, with Headquarters at Millery. Three Field Hospitals, the 325th, 326th and 327th, were established at this place in an excellently equipped French hospital. The Division occupied both sides of the Moselle River and this necessitated a plan for the evacuation of the sick and wounded on both sides of the river in case bridges should be blown out; therefore dressing stations were established at Pont-à-Mons by the 325th Ambulance Company, on the right side of the river, and by the 327th Ambulance Company at Blénod-les-Pont-à-Mousson, on the left side of the river. The Headquarters of this company, together with the 328th Field Hospital, which acted as a triage for the left side of the river, was located in an old tannery at Dieulouard. Preparatory to the St. Mihiel drive, one medical officer and sixty men were sent to each infantry brigade and these, together with twelve men from each company of line organizations who had been specially trained as litter bearers, were used to aid medical detachments in evacuating the sick and wounded; also officers and non-commissioned officers were sent to brigade and regimental headquarters as medical liaison officers. The principal casualties of the St. Mihiel drive were sustained by the 328th Infantry on the left bank of the river and were evacuated through the triage at Dieulouard.

The selection of the tannery as a location for a triage was an unfortunate one. It was just in the rear of a large naval gun and had absolutely no protection from enemy shell fire. It was shelled for four consecutive nights. On the morning of September 17, 1918, it was hit by an enemy shell and six men were killed and four wounded. Fortunately, there were no patients at the Hospital at this time, and the highest type of discipline and courage was shown by the officers and men.

The evacuation of the wounded during the St. Mihiel drive proceeded in an orderly and efficient manner from the front line to the dressing stations at Blénod-les-Pont-à-Mousson to the triage at Dieulouard, thence to the group of hospitals at Millery and thence to the Evacuation Hospital to the rear. The

Medical Department was by this time well trained and fully capable of proper functioning.

The Sanitary Train, with S.S. Unit No. 647, moved by French trucks from the Marbache to the Argonne sector the latter part of September, 1918. The Train had been splendidly equipped in the Marbache sector, having everything necessary for the full performance of its duties, except ambulances, and this deficiency was overcome by S.S. Unit No. 647. On account of lack of transportation, a large part of this equipment was left at Millery, so when the Sanitary Train began to function in the Argonne Forest it was very short of equipment in the medical supplies. Later on a few trucks were sent back for a part of the supplies left at Millery and others were obtained by the energetic work of Capt. William F. Coleman, S. C., Division Medical Supply Officer, so that the Sanitary Train was again able to function with a higher degree of efficiency.

While the Division was in reserve in the Argonne Forest various dressing stations and field hospitals were established to meet the medical needs of the Division. On October 6, 1918, Field Hospitals 326 and 328 were moved to crossroads near Varennes, the former to act as a Gas Hospital and the latter as a triage. Field Hospital 325 was held at Clermont as a hospital for ordinary sick and exhaustion cases, while Field Hospital 327 was held in reserve. At this time ambulance dressing stations were established at Montblainville and L'Espérance. Practically all of the wounded up to this time had been handled through the dressing stations at L'Espérance, a very few coming through the station at Montblainville. On the night of October 8, 1918, the dressing station at Montblainville was moved to Apremont. Almost immediately it handled a large number of wounded from the 328th Infantry. The evacuation of the wounded was very heavy through this station all the time it was located at Apremont. The village was repeatedly shelled. On one occasion a shell fell about twenty feet from the door of the dressing station, killing two men and slightly wounding one officer and one enlisted man. On October 12, 1918, a dressing station was established at Pylône, in the rear of the 326th Infantry. On the same date the dressing station at Apremont was moved to Châtel-Chéhéry. Most of the wounded on the left side of the Aire River were collected at Pylône, and as the road between Pylône and Cornay was impassable, it was necessary to evacuate these through the dressing station at L'Espérance, the bridge across the river at Apremont having been

OFFICIAL HISTORY OF 82ND DIVISION 269

completed at this time. About October 12, 1918, all field hospitals of the Sanitary Train were moved to a German hospital site near Apremont and here, using buildings and a large amount of tentage, was established a hospital section with a capacity of 1000 patients. On the night of October 14, 1918, as the Division had been steadily moving forward, ambulance dressing stations were established at Fléville and Pleinchamp Farm. On account of almost continuous shell fire and the decreased number of casualties due to the more or less stationary position of the Division at this time, the ambulance dressing station at Fléville was abandoned on October 22, 1918, the dressing station at Pleinchamp Farm being capable of handling all wounded; and all Ambulance Company personnel, except that directly concerned with the evacuation of the wounded, were sent back to the Field Hospital Section near Apremont. The Division having had long continued front line service was greatly depleted by the evacuation of both sick and wounded. At the direction of the Commanding General, those suffering from colds, exhaustion and diarrhœa were held at the Field Hospitals, given baths, proper food and medical care and were returned to the front line in from three to seven days, fully equipped with ordnance and quartermaster property. The Field Hospitals were caring for over 800 patients, with shells falling in the vicinity of the hospitals day and night and with nightly bombing activities going on. The care of this number of sick so near the front line, and sending them back to duty fully equipped, is believed to be a unique experience in divisional medical history in the American E. F. To Capt. Catching Therell of the Quartermaster Department and Capt. A. C. Jones, of the Ordnance Department, as well as Lt. H. M. Comer, Military Police, is due much credit for the prompt return of men from the hospitals to their organizations. While here the Division triage cared for the sick and wounded of the 78th Division for over forty-eight hours, the Sanitary Train of this Division having been separated from it.

On October 27, 1918, the Division Surgeon, Col. C. E. Koerper, M. C., was relieved from duty with the Division and was succeeded by Maj. Frederick G. Barfield, M. C. On October 28, 1918, Lt. Col. L. H. Reichelderfer, M. C., was relieved from duty as Commanding Officer of the 307th Sanitary Train and succeeded by Maj. O. O. Feaster, M. C., Capt. Duncan M. Draughn, M. C., succeeding Major Feaster as Regimental Surgeon of the 325th Infantry. The Field Hospital Section was operated with great success, returning a large number of men to the front line until the Division was relieved from front line duty November 1, 1918. The Regimental and Battalion Aid Stations rendered excellent service and were moved from time to time as the needs of the situations demanded. It is obviously impossible in an article of this length to give their various activities. It is sufficient to say that at all times the commissioned and enlisted personnel of the Medical Department gave their best services, and it is believed that the sick and wounded underwent no suffering that could be relieved by their efforts. The Division triages handled the following number of cases, by sectors:

Toul Sector	2,532
Marbache Sector	1,807
Meuse-Argonne Sector	9,964
Total	14,303

In the evacuation of the sick and wounded from the ambulance dressing stations to the Division triages all forms of transportation were used—motor ambulances, animal-drawn ambulances, ordinary trucks and ammunition trucks; while from the triages to the evacuation hospitals assistance was rendered by Corps ambulance companies.

The Division moved by stages, from the Argonne Forest to the 10th Training Area, and the Sanitary Train established headquarters at Prangey. Field Hospitals were established near Prauthoy to care for the ordinary sick and venereal cases of the Division, while Camp Hospital No. 10 cared for the other sick of the Division.

S. S. Unit. No. 647, under command of Lt. Leroy Smith, who had rendered excellent services during the entire front line activities of the Division, was now relieved from duty with the Division and the Sanitary Train received 27 Ford ambulances, which enabled it to handle the sick of the Division.

While in this area the Medical Department, as well as the rest of the Division, continued training and special stress was laid on sanitation. The health of the Division while in this area was excellent. However, the only cases of typhoid fever in the Division since its formation occurred in this area. Seventeen cases of typhoid fever occurred in Battery E of the 321st F. A. These cases occurred in three series and, in all three, were traced to typhoid carriers working in the kitchen. Energetic sanitary measures were adopted and the incipient epidemic was checked.

OFFICIAL HISTORY OF 82ND DIVISION

The Division moved, in early March, from the 10th Training Area to the Bordeaux Area, and from this time until embarking for the United States the care of the sick was in charge of area organizations. While in the 10th Training Area and in the Bordeaux Area numerous changes occurred in the commissioned personnel of the Medical Department of the Division. Some officers were sent to schools, some to the United States for discharge, and some to other organizations in the American E. F.

The Dental Corps of this Division rendered praiseworthy service, both in the front line and in training areas. In the front line they acted as assistants to the Regimental and Battalion Surgeons and in training areas they were busily occupied improving the dental condition of the Division. From May, 1918, till the end of March, 1919, 7400 teeth were extracted, 9232 teeth were treated and a total of 40,062 dental operations were performed by the dental staff of the Division, which consisted on the average of 21 dental officers.

Hqrs. 82nd Div., D. S. O., American E. F.
April 27, 1919.

VI

DATA CONCERNING
ADJUTANT GENERAL'S DEPARTMENT, 82ND DIVISION

BY

LIEUTENANT COLONEL R. L. BOYD, DIVISION ADJUTANT

When the Division was formed, the Adjutant's office was organized, with Maj. Charles F. Thompson as Division Adjutant, 1st Lt. L. W. DeMotte as Statistical Officer, and Capt. R. L. Boyd as Personnel Officer; and, inasmuch as the present general staff organization was not then in force, much of the work, which later devolved on the several chiefs of staff, was performed by the Division Adjutant. Owing to the delay in receipt of orders from Washington a thoroughly organized Personnel Section did not come into being until some time after the organization of the Division, consequently the select men were received and assigned by the Statistical Section, under the direction of Lieutenant DeMotte; and due to a lack of time and an accurate knowledge of the occupational qualifications of the newly arrived recruits they were assigned with little regard for suitability for service, this being most noticeable in the case of the Divisional Engineer Regiment, which, as first constituted, was made up almost entirely of farmers and laborers with practically none of the specialists required by such a technical organization.

Shortly after the organization of the Division the occupational census was inaugurated, but before it was completed all of the enlisted personnel of the Division, with the exception of 863 men, were transferred to the National Guard of the States of Georgia, Alabama and Tennessee, and immediately the Division was refilled by transfer of men from the various National Army cantonments throughout the United States. In practically no instance did the qualification cards accompany the men so transferred, consequently they were again reassigned without proper attention being given to their qualifications.

During the latter part of November a large personnel section was organized and an occupational census of the men of the Division taken. It was completed about January 1, 1918, when almost immediately requisitions began to come in from Washington calling for high grade specialists, which resulted in approximately 3000 of the best men of the Division being transferred elsewhere, and a promise given that when the Division received orders to proceed overseas they would be replaced by specialists from other cantonments. However, this promise was not lived up to, for when it was seen that the Division would proceed overseas at an early date a requisition was placed for the necessary specialists needed by the various organizations, and the reply received from the Adjutant General's Office was to the effect that it was impracticable to furnish these specialists, and that the shortage in the Division would be filled by the "run of the draft." After arrival overseas further requisitions were placed for these specialists but they were never furnished, from which it will be seen that the Division was never adequately supplied with the necessary specialists; and insofar as this Division is concerned this much advertised personnel assignment system proved to be very much of a detriment rather than a help.

In November, 1917, Major Thompson was appointed Assistant Chief of Staff (G-2), and Maj. Troup Miller was appointed Adjutant. Just prior to the departure of the Division for services overseas Major Miller was appointed Assistant Chief of Staff (G-1), being succeeded as Adjutant by Lt. Col. John R. Thomas, and at the same time the Statistical Section was merged with the Personnel Section, and at the time of embarkation the commissioned personnel of the Adjutant's office consisted of Lt. Col. John R. Thomas, Adjutant; Capt. George C. Woodruff and Capt. Harry C. Kaefring, Assistant Adjutants; Maj. R. L. Boyd, Personnel Officer; 1st Lt. W. B. Sparks, Jr., and 2nd Lt. James H. Fee, Assistant Personnel Officers.

On June 13, 1918, Lt. Col. Thomas was relieved from duty as Division Adjutant and sent to the Army Staff College as a student, and Major Boyd was assigned as Division Adjutant, and 1st Lt. Sparks assigned as Personnel Officer, and his title changed to Personnel Adjutant under G. H. Q. orders.

While in training with the British Army the necessity for dividing Division Headquarters into two or more echelons arose, and the Adjutant's office was assigned to the second echelon. When an active sector was reached it was found that one of the most important and interesting features of the Adjutant's office was securing and forwarding replacement personnel, which work did not assume very large proportions in either the Toul or Marbache sectors, and replacements were handled through the Trains Headquarters under the supervision of the Adjutant; however, when the Division entered the Meuse-Argonne offensive it was seen that replacements in large numbers must be handled, consequently Division Headquarters was divided into three echelons, the Adjutant's office in the third echelon, which, during this entire offensive, remained at Grange-le-Comte Farm, where it became necessary to establish a large replacement camp, under the command of the Division Adjutant, where replacements were received and held in this camp until they could, under cover of darkness, be forwarded to the units needing them. At one time this replacement camp had as many as 2500 men in it.

During this same offensive it was found that the usual plan of handling battle casualty statistics and reports was not feasible, as company clerks who remained with their organizations were being killed and records lost, so the revolutionary plan of moving all company clerks and company records back to Division Headquarters was decided on, which resulted in relieving the company commanders from making reports to Division Headquarters, and instead Division Headquarters furnished the company commander with all statistical figures and records needed by him. This necessitated securing all information relative to men killed and wounded from the Division triage, where a representative of the Adjutant's office was placed, and daily reports of the men passing through were forwarded to Division Headquarters, and each day the company commander was furnished with the names of his men who had been evacuated, and in a similar manner information was secured from the burial parties as to the men killed.

This plan enabled a much more accurate compilation of casualties, and at the same time relieved the company commander of practically all paper work at a time when it was necessary for him to devote his attention to battle activities.

When the Division went into the training area, after the armistice, the company clerks were returned to their organizations, and the former method of paper work was resumed.

At the time the Division received orders to return to the United States the commissioned personnel of the Adjutant's office consisted of the following:

Lt. Col. R. L. Boyd, Adjutant; Maj. George C. Woodruff, Assistant Adjutant; Capt. Willis B. Sparks, Jr., Personnel Adjutant; 1st Lt. R. M. Bush, Assistant Personnel Adjutant; 2nd Lt. James H. Fee, Assistant Personnel Adjutant; Capt. Robert H. Diamond, Officer in charge of casuals; and 2nd Lt. Joseph M. Austin, Division Postal Officer. However, owing to many changes in commissioned personnel the Division arrived back in the United States with the following officers on duty with the Adjutant's office:

Lt. Col. R. L. Boyd, Adjutant; Maj. Joseph F. Muldrow, Assistant Adjutant; Capt. Ira N. Sprecher, Personnel Adjutant; 1st Lt. R. M. Bush, Assistant Personnel Adjutant; 2nd Lt. Robert E. Cox, Assistant Personnel Adjutant; and 2nd Lt. Joseph M. Austin, Postal Officer.

VII

HISTORY OF THE 307TH FIELD SIGNAL BATTALION

CONTRIBUTED BY

DELLMAN O. HOOD, CAPTAIN SIGNAL CORPS, U. S. ARMY

The 307th Field Signal Battalion, of the 82nd Division, National Army, was organized and trained at Camp Gordon, Atlanta, Ga. The battalion was first commanded by Maj. John E. Hemphill, of the Regular Army. Major Hemphill continued in command, in addition to performing the duties of Division Signal Officer, for several months, until Capt. Kilberth D. Schaefer, at that time in command of Company B, was promoted to the grade of Major and placed in command of the battalion.

Major Hemphill left Camp Gordon early in April, 1918, with the advance party of the Division for France. Upon arrival overseas he was promoted to the grade of Lieutenant-Colonel.

OFFICIAL HISTORY OF 82ND DIVISION 275

With very few exceptions, all of the officers and enlisted men were men of many years practical experience in telephone, telegraph and radio communication work. About 60 per cent of the enlisted personnel were men who had enlisted in the Signal Reserve Corps. The majority of these men came from the Middle Western states of Illinois, Wisconsin, Missouri, Indiana and Ohio. The Radio Company was made up largely of men from the radio class, Beloit University, of Beloit, Wisconsin. All of these men had taken special courses in radio telegraphy at this university and had enlisted in the Signal Reserve Corps.

The Wire and Outpost Companies had on their rosters a large number of men from the large commercial telephone, telegraph and railroad companies, who had enlisted in the Signal Reserve Corps.

The remainder of the enlisted personnel were drafted men from practically every section of the United States. Upon reporting at Camp Gordon these men were classified according to qualifications, those with previous telephone, telegraph and radio experience being assigned to the Signal Battalion. Thus, the battalion was an organization of picked men.

Thanks to the untiring efforts of Lt. Col. Hemphill, much telephone, telegraph, radio and optical equipment, of the type to be used in France, was procured. With this equipment a number of day and night maneuvers were conducted at Camp Gordon.

Lieutenant Defert and Sergeant Pazin of the French Signal Corps were attached to the Battalion as instructors and remained with the organization until its arrival in France. These two gentlemen had seen two years' active service at the front with the French army and were a valuable asset in the instruction of the Battalion.

A Division signal school was organized by the Division Signal Officer with Lieutenant Defert, Sergeant Pazin and personnel from the Signal Battalion as instructors. Telephony, buzzer telegraphy, radio, optical and other means of signaling were taught to officers and men from the infantry signal platoons, artillery and machine-gun signal details. Many practical maneuvers in signal work were conducted for the benefit of these students. The elaborate system of trenches at Camp Gordon was completely wired up by the Signal Battalion under the direction of Lieutenant Defert and Sergeant Pazin, exactly as was being done at the front in France.

On May 9, 1918, the Battalion left Camp Gordon for Camp

Mills, Long Island. After a few days' rest at Camp Mills, the Battalion embarked on the 18th of May aboard the British ship *Virginian* for overseas. On May 31 the Battalion disembarked at Liverpool, England, proceeding from there by train to Winchester, England, from which place it proceeded across the English Channel to Le Havre, France, arriving June 4, 1918. From Le Havre the Battalion was ordered to Rougeux, Haute-Marne. Here the Battalion rested a few days until orders were received to proceed to Toul, arriving June 28. The following morning the Battalion began moving into the Lagny sector, north of Toul, to relieve the 101st Field Signal Battalion of the 26th Division.

This had been known as a so-called quiet sector, but due to the activities of the American troops, characterized by the raids at Seicheprey and Xivray, it was fast becoming semi-active. Previous to our arrival the German artillery fire had been at times rather heavy and it was decided to establish Division Headquarters at Lucey instead of Boucq, which had been the Division P.C. of the 26th Division. This change necessitated much readjustment in the communication system with the establishment of several new trunk, and many local telephone lines.

Despite the fact that our battalion had had no previous experience in the lines, and no training in France, the relief in this sector was accomplished with despatch and without a hitch in the plans.

Another point worthy of mention is that of the close liaison established with the French artillery, which had relieved the 26th Division Artillery—our artillery being at that time in training in Southern France. Our operators quickly acquired a working knowledge of the French language and telephonic liaison with the French was handled with remarkable despatch. Joint French and American switchboards were established at all important posts. Our men and the French Signal men worked in perfect harmony and soon became real "buddies."

Shortly after moving into this sector it was decided to move back several of the Regimental P.C.'s. During this movement about five miles of buried cable—30 pair, were laid from the regimental P.C.'s to within a short distance of the front line. A mechanical trench-digger was used for this purpose, details of men following the trench-digger laying the cable, and other details filling in the trench. Near the front lines the work was carried on at night, but a little farther back where the route extended through woods it was possible to work during the

OFFICIAL HISTORY OF 82ND DIVISION   277

day without detection by the enemy. No work was left uncovered during the day—that is, all unfinished work was carefully camouflaged, in order to prevent the enemy aeroplanes from making photographs of the project.

This being a fairly quiet sector, an extensive optical system was operated with a considerable degree of success. This system, however, was not needed for practical use and was maintained merely as an emergency means of communication.

T. P. S. (Earth Telegraphy) was installed and used between Regimental and Battalion P.C.'s. Radio communication was established between Regimental and Brigade P.C.'s, and from Brigades to Division. Buzzer-phones were used between Battalion and Company P.C.'s. An E-3 radio set was installed at Division Headquarters and used for listening-in on German radio stations. Every radio station, in fact, listened-in and copied all German messages, which were turned in daily to our Intelligence section. The telephone, however, was our practical means of communication, all other methods being maintained as emergency means and for test purposes.

On the night of August 4, 1918, the German lines north of Flirey were raided by the 326th Infantry. The Signal detail attached to the Regiment from the Outpost Company and commanded by 1st Lt. Glenn S. Matthews, went "over the top" with the infantry and maintained telephonic communication throughout the raid, despite the heavy and almost continuous counter-barrage laid down by the Germans. The wire used was No. 22 twisted pair, or better known as small "outpost twist." It was carried forward on spools containing about one kilometer of circuit and each spool transported by two signal men. Details of two men each were dropped about every hundred yards or more to test in and repair breaks. During this operation the Signal Battalion had three men wounded.

On the night of August 8-9, during the relief of the 82nd Division by the 89th Division, the German artillery filled the valley around Bayard, north of Noviant, with a high gas concentration. Without a thought to their personal safety, Corporals McClendon, Aikens and Grubbs, and Privates Evenson, Fenn, Hendrix, Blanco and Taylor remained at their posts repairing broken lines and putting through telephone calls for ambulances, and medical aid and transmitting important orders. Some of these men worked with their gas masks on for eight continuous hours, and every man stuck to his post until completely overcome by the gas and had to be evacuated to hospitals. All were more or less badly gassed and burned with mustard gas, Private Taylor dying from injuries received. Nevertheless their devotion to duty was not in vain, for thanks to the valor of these men, it was possible to summon ambulances promptly and evacuate the wounded with very little delay. While the casualties were very heavy, 701, to be exact, there were very few deaths because the wounded were able to be evacuated without delay and receive prompt treatment. A new and inexperienced division was coming into the lines for the first time, and but for the bravery and cool-headedness of this small detail of Signal Corps men, it would have been several hours before word could have been sent to the rear and assistance rendered. This is a fair example of the type of men the Battalion was made up of, and the importance of their work on the front.

During our stay in the Lagny sector, the Germans attempted several times to tap our telephone and buzzer-phone lines in and near the front-line trenches, coming out for this purpose during the night. They succeeded in making an actual tap one night near Xivray, but fortunately the tap was soon discovered by one of our linemen patrolling the lines, and removed.

A thorough code system was used in this area for both telephone and other means, and was very satisfactory for a time, but it was extremely difficult to hold the line officers down to using the code when making calls, and prevent them from talking "in the clear." It was quite evident that the Germans were provided with a very efficient listening-in system, and there is no doubt but that they were able to pick up our telephone conversations at times. This was evident from the way in which they shelled the roads leading up to our trenches on practically every night our troops made a relief. The gassing of our lines on the night of the relief by the 89th Division is another good illustration.

On the morning of August 10 our Battalion was relieved by the 314th Field Signal Battalion of the 89th Division.

Outside the trenches in the Lagny sector our telephone lines were run on stakes, and farther back it was possible to have pole line leads of iron and copper wire. The majority of the wire used, however, was No. 17 twisted pair, which stood up better under all conditions and gave very satisfactory transmission. The small No. 22 twist was very good for raiding parties where it was only intended to be used for a few hours, but is not practical for permanent or even semi-permanent use, as it will not function during wet weather and is easily broken by concussion from shells.

It was also decided during our stay in the Lagny sector to make some changes in the distributions of our Signal personnel. Originally, each regiment was assigned a platoon from the Outpost Company under command of a Signal Corps lieutenant; small details from the Wire and Radio Companies were assigned to each Brigade P.C. under command of a B Company lieutenant, the remainder of A and B Company personnel working out of Division Headquarters. It was soon discovered, however, that the greater part of the maintenance and operations of the telephone net fell to the lot of Company B, which operated from Division Headquarters inclusive to Regimental P.C.'s exclusive. This is a small company of 75 men, which was found inadequate to handle the work properly in so large an area.

To strengthen these details, each Outpost Platoon detailed six men to its respective brigade, giving each brigade twelve men from the Outpost Company, eight from the Wire Company and ten from the Radio Company. In addition, there were generally six to eight men available from the Brigade Headquarters Infantry detail. One Signal Corps truck was assigned to each brigade. Each regiment furnished their Signal Corps detail one G.S. wagon, and in some cases the battalion details were furnished an ammunition cart to transport their signal property. Communications from the Regimental P.C.'s forward were handled by the Outpost Company platoon attached to the regiment. The Radio Company assigned one non-commissioned officer to each infantry regiment, he being in charge of the radio, T. P. S. and optical liaison within the regiment. The Infantry Signal platoon under command of an infantry officer worked in conjunction with the Signal Corps platoon.

This distribution of personnel remained unchanged during the remainder of the operation of the 82nd Division at the front.

From August 10 to August 17 the Signal Battalion was in training at Blénod-les-Toul, from which place it was ordered with the Division to the Marbache sector, north of Nancy, where we relieved the First Field Signal Battalion of the Second Division.

The Marbache sector was also known as a quiet sector and the signal work was of a similar nature as of that in the Lagny sector. Much work was done, however, in improving the existing buried cable and aerial telephone lines, many of which had been in existence for four years, having been constructed by the French and now in very poor condition. This work was in preparation for the offensive of the American First Army, which had for its purpose the elimination of the famous St. Mihiel Salient.

This was a favorite sector with the Germans for air raids— the towns of Marbache (Division Headquarters), Dieulouard and Millery generally being the targets. One night during the early part of September all trunks from Division Headquarters forward were put out of commission for a few minutes as a result of several large aerial bombs dropped by enemy aeroplanes. Although these bombs exploded fully 200 feet from our telephone lines, which were on standard poles, yet the concussion was sufficient to break every line on both forward leads.

It was in this sector that the Divisional Artillery, the 157th Field Artillery Brigade, joined the Division, relieving the 15th Field Artillery Brigade, of the 2nd Division. The Artillery Signal details connected their units with all Signal Corps switchboards and maintained their own telephone lines. In addition, they also operated their own radio and projector stations. 1st Lt. Walter C. Kiesel was detailed from the Signal Battalion as liaison officer with the artillery brigade.

The Signal Corps and artillery worked in close cooperation, each using the other's lines in cases of emergency. This proved to be a very convenient and valuable arrangement for both.

In the St. Mihiel offensive on the morning of September 13, the Signal Corps men went over the top with their "doughboy" comrades; 1st Lt. Clayborne Arthur and the Fourth Outpost platoon of the Signal Battalion were attached to the 328th Infantry Regiment. Shortly after the troops arrived at Norroy, Lieutenant Arthur had his telephone line into the town and ready to flash back the information that Norroy had been taken. In this advance Lieutenant Arthur used the small No. 22 twisted pair. The circuit worked fairly well for a short time, but a heavy rain started and the line was soon unserviceable. To overcome this, a buzzer-phone was connected to the line and fairly good transmission obtained by buzzer telegraphy. A new line of No. 17 twisted pair was laid the following night and telephonic communication reestablished. During this offensive the Signal Battalion lost two men killed and more than a dozen wounded.

On September 20, the 90th Division took over the position of our troops on the left bank of the Moselle River and the French the position on the right bank. Our Division came out of the lines and withdrew into the area just north of Nancy, Signal Battalion Headquarters being established at Liverdun. Orders were received on September 22 to proceed to the Argonne Forest, where our real work was to begin.

During the stay of the Division in the Marbache sector, a radio station was established on Mousson Hill, in addition to the Division, Brigade and Regimental stations. Several optical stations were also established at observation posts along the front lines. It was not possible to make much use of the optical stations, however, as they most invariably drew fire from the German batteries. The optical station at the Port-sur-Seille observation post rendered excellent service on several occasions in sending back warnings of gas attacks. It was an easy matter for German aeroplanes to come over and locate the position of these optical stations, thereby disclosing the location of our O.P.'s and other important posts.

In addition to the Division, Brigade and Regimental switchboards, relay boards were located at Pont-à-Mousson, Millery and Belleville.

Shortly before the Battalion left the Marbache sector Lieutenant Colonel Hemphill was transferred to the Eighth Army Corps as Corps Signal Officer, being relieved by Lt. Col. George E. B. Daily. It was with profound regret that the 307th said good-by to Lieutenant Colonel Hemphill. He was idolized by every officer and man in the Battalion. Though possessing an extremely stern personality and always insisting upon the strictest discipline, his heart was of gold and the 307th Field Signal Battalion was always uppermost in his thoughts. Everyone felt that his transfer was a serious loss to our Battalion.

The Battalion moved into the Argonne Forest on the night of September 25, Battalion Headquarters being established in the woods about 500 meters southwest of Rarécourt. On October 4 the Battalion moved up to Varennes which had just been captured by the 35th Division. Division Headquarters were established at Varennes the same day. Both the 163rd and 164th Brigades were located in the woods west of Varennes with both Brigade Headquarters in the old German rest camp at Champ-Mahaut. Two lines were laid from this point to Varennes—the circuits being tied-in on trees where possible, and across open fields it was laid out on the ground. All four regiments and the three machine-gun battalions near by were given telephonic communication. In addition a line was put in from the joint brigade board to the 77th Division Headquarters board at

Champ Mahaut. This gave us an emergency outlet to Varennes via the 77th board and the Corps line.

On the night of October 6, the 327th and 328th Infantry regiments went into the lines along the Aire River east of Châtel-Chéhéry and the following morning went over the top.

Our No. 17 twisted pair was now getting scarce, and most of our new supplies of wire was P. O. D. twist, which although a little smaller than No. 17, was of much better grade than No. 22.

The difficult task of carrying the telephone lines forward with the attack of the 164th Brigade was accomplished by Company B as far forward as the Regimental P.C.'s and from there forward by the Outpost platoons assigned to the 327th and 328th Infantry regiments. Capt. William T. Busch, then in command of Company B laid two axis lines forward from Varennes to Chaudron Farm where 164th Brigade Headquarters and the Advance Information Center were established. This work was accomplished in a driving rain and during the night which was pitch dark. In addition to this handicap, the men were forced to work along roads badly congested with truck trains and artillery moving up to the front. These two circuits from Varennes to Chaudron Farm were laid out by truck part of the way and the remainder by wire carts. The wire was reeled off the rear of the truck by placing the wooden spools upon a digging bar placed across the rear of the truck. As the wiring party neared Baulny and Chaudron Farm they were subjected to heavy artillery fire.

The work of maintaining lines from the 164th Brigade P.C. to the P.C.'s of the 327th and 328th Infantry regiments was in charge of 1st Lt. Clarence G. Shriver, 164th Brigade Signal Officer. His task was extremely difficult. His route extended across fields that were a sea of mud; in many places it was necessary to cross the Aire River and other smaller streams swollen by the heavy rains. His men were continually under shell fire, which also wrecked his lines at times almost as fast as they could be laid out or repaired. In addition artillery pieces and ammunition carts were continually moving over the telephone lines and breaking them. The work was being done in pitch darkness. It was impossible of course to use trucks so near the front lines and the spools of wire had to be carried forward by hand. This was usually done by a detail of four men, with from four to six men additional to work shifts in carrying the wire and to replace casualties. It was not altogether a satisfactory method, but the best that could be done under the circumstances, as all of our equipment was for trench warfare and practically no equipment for open warfare, excepting wire carts, which were as useless as trucks near the front line. And our Brigade P.C.'s were generally quite near to the front lines. We made considerable use of our wire carts as far up as was possible to take them, but their value was considerably cut down due to the small amount of circuit that could be carried on the cart drums. These carts were built to hold five miles of single wire, or two and a half miles of metallic circuit. This wire was not very good for metallic circuits, however, due to induction and cross talk. A further handicap was the difficulty in carrying food for the animals and the congestion of the roads.

Maintaining communications in open warfare under these conditions therefore was an enormous task. Stringing lines on poles, stakes or trees was out of the question. First, the infantry advanced too rapidly. Second, there were no poles, no stakes and in many places no trees. Details followed up, however, readjusting the lines and getting them off the roads and tying in on trees where possible. In order to keep up with the fast moving infantry it was necessary for the advance wiring parties to lay their lines out on the ground as they advanced. In this manner we were able to keep up telephone communication as far forward as regimental P.C.'s practically without interruption. The lines were continually being broken of course by the enemy shell fire and our own artillery pieces and ammunition carts moving over them, but by stationing details every few hundred yards along the route, repairs were made almost instantaneously.

Communication from the regiments forward, however, was a different question. It was almost impossible at times, but most of the time the regimental commanders were able to communicate with their battalion commanders by telephone. This work was in charge of 1st Lt. Clayborne Arthur with the 328th Infantry and 2nd Lt. Harvey E. Hannaford with the 327th. Lines were carried forward by hand the same as from brigade to regiments. Their task was all the more difficult as the men had to work through machine-gun fire as well as artillery fire and gas. The lines were shot out more frequently and the Battalion P.C.'s were changing continually; the supplies of wire ran out rapidly and it was difficult to bring up fresh supplies. In spite of these handicaps, Lieutenants Arthur and Hannaford rendered excellent service, going out personally with their men and making repairs themselves. Too much credit can not be given to these regimental and battalion signal men; their work was hazardous; in fact they were under fire and working through gas practically all of the time; they had no time to seek shelter; their work lay in the open.

A division axis was always the first thing to be established, extending from Division Headquarters along the line of advance as far forward as the wires could be carried. One main axis line was carried forward from division to each brigade, two extra lines laid as soon as positions could be consolidated. We also carried one line forward on the axis for use by the artillery brigade. The latter maintained their own lines within their own units. Artillery regiments and brigade were also connected with the nearest Signal Corps switchboard. This work was done by the artillery and Signal Corps detail jointly. Small details were placed along these axis lines at frequent intervals to test in and repair breaks.

We had received a few replacements after reaching Varennes. Lieutenant Matthews was missing in action. 2nd Lt. Timothy J. Murphy reported to us at Varennes on October 3 and was assigned temporarily to Company B.

On the night of October 6, Lieutenant Murphy was given a detail of 12 signal men and ordered to lay a line from Chaudron Farm, which had just been taken by the First Division, to an O.P. location, well out in front and to the top of Hill 224. Although it was Lieutenant Murphy's first experience at the front, he set out with his little detail and the wire was laid during a high gas concentration and through heavy machine-gun and shell fire. Two of his men were killed outright and two wounded. A Y.M.C.A. man from the 1st Division who had volunteered to direct Lieutenant Murphy toward the location was also killed. Several times this detail of men were completely covered with earth from exploding shells. Returning from this duty about dawn, he carried another line to the First Division advance P.C. and another to the 164th Brigade P.C. of our Division, which was then making its famous flanking attack across the Aire River against Hills 180, 223, La Forge Farm and Cornay.

On October 8 Lieutenant Murphy was transferred to the Outpost Company, and assigned in command of the Second Platoon attached to the 326th Infantry of the 163rd Brigade, who were going in to relieve the 28th Division on the left side of the river. 1st Lt. John O. Burnette was in command of the First Outpost Platoon attached to the 325th Infantry, and Lt. Dellmann O. Hood, who had the previous day been promoted to Captain, was the 163rd Brigade Signal Officer. This relief of the 28th Division was made during the night in a driving rain storm on roads and across fields that were a sea of mud. About this time the 325th Infantry was detached from the 163rd Brigade and attached to the 164th Brigade, which had suffered heavily in casualties. Lieutenant Burnette was seriously wounded on October 9 and evacuated. Sergeant First Class James M. Davis assumed command of the platoon, and since has received one Division, and one Regimental citation for the excellent manner in which he handled it.

The 326th Infantry jumped off at La Pelette Ravine, Signal Corps men going over with them and installing lines from this ravine forward with the advanced attacking elements. The brigade detail under command of Captain Hood followed upon the heels of the regimental details establishing communications from brigade to regiment. The work of keeping the brigades connected with Division Headquarters was being carried out by details from Company B in command of Captain Busch. It was possible to do this work with the use of trucks and wire carts.

This work carried us through the very heart of the Argonne Woods, through constant shelling, gassing and machine-gun fire. Rain fell in torrents practically without let up. We were forced to work during the night through pitch darkness, feeling and groping our way along and finding our way as best possible. Our advance was carried forward through Le Chêne-Tondu, La Besogne, Pylône, Marcq, and later St. Juvin and Hill 182. General Cronin, commanding the 163rd Brigade, generally maintained his P.C. at the same place or near by the 325th or 326th Regimental P.C.'s until our movements became more stationary. When this was the case we were able to consolidate more or less regimental and brigade signal details and work both ways. Near Marcq, during the attack upon St. Juvin, it was necessary to filter our signal men across the Aire River to the right, or east side, and follow up the attack from the southeast. The Signal Corps Platoon with the 326th Infantry carried a line from the Regimental P.C. at Pylône down the Decauville railroad, through the woods, and across the Aire River to the P.C. of the 325th Infantry. The maintenance of this line was an example of the courage displayed by our men, it being necessary to work through a river valley filled with gas and constantly under machine-gun and artillery fire, at times amounting to nearly a barrage. Sergeant Arthur De Haven crossed the Aire River eight times on this night before he could complete his line to the 325th. Time and again he went back and forth to make repairs.

The 163rd Brigade was relieved here by the 77th Division, and moved its P.C. to Cornay, the 326th crossing the Aire and taking up a position to the left of the 325th with Regimental P.C. about half a kilometer southeast of St. Juvin.

One of the Battalion P.C.'s of the 326th was located in the town proper. The relieving battalion of the 77th Division came up without a Signal Corps detail, or any Signal equipment. Sergeant Wilbur P. Stanley, of the Signal Corps Platoon with the 326th Infantry, remained with this battalion of the 77th Division and maintained communication for them until their Signal men came up the following day. He was given ten men from his platoon. During this work he lost one man killed and two wounded. In addition, we left two telephones and a four-line switchboard for use by the 77th. They also took over a line for their use, which we had previously put in from Pylône to La Besogne, saying that they expected to establish a Battalion P.C. at the latter place and had no telephone communication.

Division Headquarters had subsequently moved up from Varennes to La Forge, and from La Forge to Chéhéry Farm. We had anticipated taking over the lines laid by the 28th Division but these lines were in such bad condition that we had to lay new lines practically the entire route.

Captain Busch had established an axis up the Châtel-Chéhéry-Cornay Road from Châtel-Chéhéry to Cornay of four trunk lines with a relay board at Cornay. The 163rd Brigade moved into Cornay and took over this board. Two lines had previously been laid from Pylône to Cornay by the 163rd Brigade Signal detail. These lines were now used for lateral communication with the 77th Division. Our axis lines from Châtel-Chéhéry to Cornay were later turned over to the 78th Division and our axis re-run from Pleinchamp Farm, when our Division Headquarters moved up to Fléville. The 164th Brigade Headquarters were now loacted at Fléville. Three lines were carried forward from Cornay to Martincourt Farm by Sergeant First Class Isaac M. Lowry, of Captain Busch's detail, to be used later for the division axis. This was accomplished under a heavy bombardment from German artillery and machine-gun fire. Three lines were

OFFICIAL HISTORY OF 82ND DIVISION 287

also laid from Cornay to Fléville to meet the new division axis there. About October 14 the 163rd Brigade Headquarters were also moved to Fléville, the 78th Division taking over Cornay. One of the Fléville-Cornay circuits was used as Brigade lateral between Fléville and the right brigade of the 78th; another was taken over by the 319th Field Artillery of our Division, at Cornay, to connect with the 320th Field Artillery at Fléville, and the third was used for an 82nd Division O. P. located near Martincourt Farm. From Cornay forward we used one of the axis lines laid by Sergeant Lowry.

327th and 328th Regimental Headquarters were now located at Sommerance, about three kilometers northeast of Fléville; the 325th and 326th along the Sommerance-St. Juvin Road. Operations had settled down to more or less of a waiting game. A joint switchboard for the 163rd and 164th Brigades was established at Fléville with a network of circuits to Sommerance, the 325th and 326th P.C.'s. Relay stations were established at several places along these circuits. Lateral lines were laid between all regiments and even between relay stations. In this manner we established a net whereby we were able to have communication forward with practically no interruption. If one side was shot out, we could get through around the other side or through the middle, and vice versa.

General Cronin, commanding the 163rd Brigade, established an advance P.C. at the 325th Regimental P.C. and General Lindsey, of the 164th Brigade, established his at Sommerance. These two P.C.'s were connected with the regimental switchboards. Although we had now settled down to stationary fighting, our troubles had not ceased by any means. In fact we suffered more casualties in this sector than any of the others. The enemy shelled the area from Fléville forward to the front lines almost incessantly. Fléville and Sommerance were subjected to extremely heavy shell fire and gassing. This of course played havoc with our lines and kept our men out pretty much all of the time. The details were so arranged that when a wire was shot out, a detail would start from each end, clearing trouble until they met or until the circuit cleared.

The advanced signal working parties were supplied with wire and equipment from advance signal dumps, established generally near Brigade Headquarters. The wire and material usually had to be carried from brigade by hand.

Two men of the 307th Field Signal Battalion have received Distinguished Service Crosses, three others recommended and approved; nineteen have received Division citations and fourteen Regimental citations. General Cronin, in a letter to the commanding officer of the battalion, highly commended the work of the Signal detail attached to his Brigade in command of myself. Captain Shriver was likewise highly commended by General Lindsey of the 164th Brigade and our regimental Signal officers commended by their respective regimental commanders for our work during the operations of the Division at the front.

The real credit, however, for the success of the battalion in maintaining lines of information is due the enlisted men of the organization. Our non-commissioned officers were excellent; the morale and spirit of the men admirable. The uppermost thought in their minds at all times was the success of the Division and the Signal Battalion.

I also wish to take this opportunity of expressing my admiration of the excellent work done by the Signal details of our artillery. Their men were equally courageous and were always to be found out on their lines repairing breaks, the same as ours. They kept up their telephone lines and nets in excellent shape and never overlooked an opportunity to assist our men in every way possible. We tried to reciprocate as much as possible, but could not do as much as we would have liked owing to our heavy casualties.

During the Meuse-Argonne offensive we used the radio very little; seldom used the T. P. S., and never used optics. We made some use of our pigeons on several occasions.

It was almost impossible to establish radio stations at Regimental P.C.'s and where they were established the infantry officers did not use them, as all messages had to be enciphered and deciphered, which took up so much time as to render the messages practically of no value—and then, too, the telephone was generally available. The radio details were always on hand, however, ready for use in an emergency.

Soil conditions did not favor the use of the T. P. S. This means of signaling is fairly good in trench warfare, but of not much value in open warfare. Optics are out of the question in open warfare. Furthermore, infantry commanders as a rule will not allow them to be set up near their P.C.'s, as they invariably draw fire.

The telephone was our most useful means of communication and we lent all of our energies toward its maintenance. Our success in doing this will readily be attested to by all line officers of the Division who had occasion to use the telephone.

WE WENT INTO THE FIGHT DETERMINED TO KEEP UP COMMUNICATIONS AND WE DID IT.

VIII
COMPLIMENTARY LETTERS, ETC.
AMERICAN EXPEDITIONARY FORCES
OFFICE OF THE COMMANDER-IN-CHIEF

FRANCE, February 19, 1919.

Major General George B. Duncan,
Commanding 82nd Division. A.E.F.

My Dear General Duncan:

It gives me a great deal of pleasure to extend to you and the officers and men of the 82nd Division my compliments upon their excellent appearance at the inspection and review on February 11 near Prauthoy. It was gratifying to see your troops in such good physical shape, but still more so to know that the moral tone of all ranks is so high. It is hoped that this will continue even after their return to civil life.

Your Division is to be congratulated on its record in France. At the end of June it was placed in a quiet sector of the French line to release veteran divisions for the battle. From the 12th to 16th of September it took part in the first American offensive at St. Mihiel, attacking and occupying Norroy and the heights north and west of Vandières. In this operation it advanced 5 kilometers. In the Meuse-Argonne offensive the Division attacked on October 7th and was engaged almost continuously for twenty-five days. Attacking across the river Aire it assisted the 28th and 77th Divisions in advance, and on October 9, captured Cornay. On October 10, the town of Marcq and on October 16, the strong position of Hill 182 and the town of St. Juvin were also captured, making a total advance of 12 kilometers.

The officers and men of your Division may proudly carry home with them the gratitude of the Allies with whom they fought and the pride of their fellows throughout our forces.

Sincerely yours,
JOHN J. PERSHING.

HEADQUARTERS FIFTH ARMY CORPS
AMERICAN EXPEDITIONARY FORCES
FRANCE

2 February, 1919.

From: Major General C. P. Summerall, Commanding Fifth Army Corps, American E. F.
To: Commanding General, 82nd Division.
Subject: Horse Show and Review.

1. It is with sentiments of pride and pleasure that I communicate to you my commendation of the excellent exhibition of horses and transportation that it was my privilege to witness

290   OFFICIAL HISTORY OF 82ND DIVISION

at the 82nd Division Horse Show on February 1. Not only were the animals and transportation of a very high order, but they gave evidences of such thoroughness and care in preparation, such extraordinary ability and attention to detail on the part of officers and enlisted men, and such devotion, zeal and pride in the Division as to evidence a high standard of morale rarely experienced during my service. I desire to congratulate you and the officers and soldiers of the Division upon the attainment of standards worthy of emulation and imitation. Such troops reflect credit upon the American army and the American people, and they may be relied upon to acquit themselves with honor in peace as to attain their objectives in war.

2. I desire further to express my deep appreciation of the honor accorded me by the review of the mounted officers and soldiers of the Division. The presence of the colors and standards representing all elements of the Division, and of the massed band, which was so ably conducted, was an inspiring sight that I shall never forget. It is an honor to command such troops, and it is with emotions of deep regret that I contemplate their separation from the Fifth Corps.

C. P. SUMMERALL.

HEADQUARTERS FIFTH ARMY CORPS

AMERICAN EXPEDITIONARY FORCES
FRANCE

15 February, 1919.

From: Major General C. P. Summerall, Commanding Fifth Army Corps, American E. F.
To: Commanding General, 82nd Division, American E. F.
Subject: Appreciation of Services.

1. In accordance with orders from Headquarters, American Expeditionary Forces, the 82nd Division is relieved from the Fifth Corps.

2. The Division was assigned to the Corps on November 24, 1918, and since that date it has been constantly occupied with intensive training. While the work has been arduous and at times involved much discomfort in severe cold and inclement weather, the response has invariably been cheerful, zealous and effective. The progress of the Division has been such as to evince a superior state of discipline and morale. At the conclusion of its service in the Corps it is worthy of classification as an assault division. The functioning of the Staff and of the elements of command guarantee success in the employment of the troops.

3. The Corps Commander takes this opportunity to convey to the Division Commander, Major General George B. Duncan, his deep appreciation of the loyalty, cheerful co-operation and marked leadership that he has rendered so abundantly, and to convey to the officers and soldiers of the Division his high commendation and admiration for the manner in which they have conducted themselves while in the Fifth Corps. It has been an honor to command such troops and in the training area,

as well as in the stress of battle, they have shown themselves worthy of the trust reposed in them by their country.

C. P. SUMMERALL.

HEADQUARTERS FIFTH ARMY CORPS
AMERICAN EXPEDITIONARY FORCES
FRANCE

9 February, 1919.

From: Commanding General, Fifth Army Corps, American E. F.
To: Commanding General, 82nd Division, American E. F.
Subject: Corps Horse Show.

1. It gives me great pleasure to express to you my appreciation of the excellent exhibits made by the officers and soldiers of the 82nd Division at the Horse Show of the Fifth Army Corps on February 8. The horses, equipment and carriages gave evidences of the great amount of labor and attention to detail that has been devoted to the preparation of all entries. Not only the exhibits which secured prizes, but the entire representation of the Division, was such as to reflect credit upon the entire command. Such results could only have been accomplished by a prevailing spirit of soldierly pride, marked industry and an intelligent understanding of the standards to which military transportation should conform. The results of the exhibit cannot fail to be far-reaching in enhancing the reputation of the Division and in stimulating the liveliest interest in maintaining the entire transportation of the Division in accordance with the ideas that were manifested at the show.

2. Notwithstanding the fact that the exhibit was held in midwinter, with deep snow and during intense cold, the entire personnel representing the Division showed a keenness and a disregard of the inevitable discomforts that is worthy of the highest praise and that constitutes a further proof of the high standards of morale and fortitude which have distinguished the Division throughout its service.

3. I especially wish to congratulate the Division upon winning the Divisional Trophy. Its success is the more conspicuous because of the high order of entries made by competitors.

4. I wish further to express my appreciation of the active co-operation of the Division Commander and of his Staff, to whom in the greatest measure is due the hearty and active response of the Division.

C. P. SUMMERALL,
Major General.

HEADQUARTERS FIRST ARMY
AMERICAN EXPEDITIONARY FORCES, FRANCE

CORRECTED COPY
GENERAL ORDERS

8 February, 1919.

Pursuant to telegraphic instructions from G.H.Q., the 82nd Division, upon the establishment of its headquarters in the LeMans area, is relieved from duty with this Army.

Beginning August 15, 1918, the 82nd Division relieved the 2nd Division in the MARBACHE Sector astride the Moselle River. While occupying this sector as a part of the 1st Army Corps, A.E.F., the Division was transferred from the command of the VIII French Army to that of the First Army, A.E.F., at 4.00 P.M. of August 30, 1918.

The 82nd Division participated in the following operations of the First Army:

ST. MIHIEL OPERATION

The Division held the right of the line from PORT-SUR-SEILLE to the Moselle River and attacked west of that river in conjunction with the 90th Division. The Division captured and occupied NORROY and the ridge north and west of VANDIERES.

MEUSE-ARGONNE OPERATION

The Division was in Army and Corps Reserve from September 26th to October 6th. On the night of October 6-7, the Division, less one Infantry Brigade, entered the line on the 1st Corps front between the 1st and 28th Divisions along the Aire River facing CORNAY. Early October 7th the division attacked the northeast flank of the ARGONNE capturing Hills 180 and 223, and subsequently the high ground to the west, thus materially assisting in the clearing of the Argonne.

During the period October 10th to 31st, the Division changed direction to the north, advanced astride of the Aire River to the general line east of ST. JUVIN, participated in the general attack of October 14th and several local attacks against CHAMPIGNEULLES and the hostile defences east of that town. The Division was relieved from the front line and passed into 1st Corps Reserve October 31st.

The Army Commander takes this occasion to express his appreciation of the services of the 82nd Division while a part of the combat forces of this Army, and wishes it God Speed upon the final phase of its participation in the activities of the American Expeditionary Forces.

By Command of Lieutenant General Liggett:

H. A. DRUM,
Chief of Staff.

HEADQUARTERS, FIRST ARMY CORPS,
Sept. 12, 1918.

Commanding General,
82nd Division, A.E.F.

Please convey to the officers and men of your Division my appreciation of the difficult part they had to perform in the highly successful operation of the First Corps to-day. This part they performed to my full satisfaction.

H. LIGGETT.

Received at Hq. 1st Army Corps, September 15, 1918.

HEADQUARTERS FIRST ARMY CORPS

11 November, 1918.

GENERAL ORDERS
No. 17

1. During this pause in the operations of these headquarters, the Corps Commander desires that the units which have contributed to the constant success of the 1st U. S. Corps be informed of his full appreciation of the services each has rendered to the common end.

This appreciation must be extended to every element of Corps and Divisional units for it goes without saying that the work of each man, no matter what his station, has contributed powerfully to the accomplishment of the common aim—the defeat of the enemy.

It is the desire of the Corps Commander that his sincerest thanks, best wishes and assurances of his appreciation reach every member of the units which have contributed to the steady and unfailing success of the Corps.

By Command of Major General Dickman:

MALIN CRAIG,
Chief of Staff.

OFFICIAL:
W. A. HAVERFIELD,
*Lieut. Col., A.G.D.,
Adjutant.*

32ND ARMY CORPS,
General Staff,
3rd Bureau,
No. 3965/3.

HQ. Aug. 4, 1918.

GENERAL ORDER No. 138

The Commanding General of the 32nd Army Corps is glad to congratulate the companies of the 326th Infantry, commanded by Major Watkins, which took part in the raid of August 4.

These companies displayed a vigor worthy of American troops. They attained all their objectives and brought back material and valuable documents.

This first attack of the 82nd Division shows what may be expected in the future, of this splendid Division.

GENERAL PASSAGA,
Commanding the 32nd Army Corps.
Signed: PASSAGA.

OFFICIAL:
The Chief of Staff.

IX
STATEMENT OF THE MILITARY SERVICE OF WILLIAM P. BURNHAM

Born in Pennsylvania	10 Jan., 1860
Cadet M. A.	1 July, '77
to	30 June, '80
Pvt., Corpl. and Sgt., gen. ser. and Co. E, 14th Inf.	26 Apr. '81
to	5 July, '83
2d Lt., 6th Inf.	3 July, '83
Accepted	6 July, '83
1st Lt., 11th Inf.	25 Feb., '91
Trs. to 6th Inf.	20 July, '91
Trs. to 20th Inf.	22 July, '95
Lt. Col., 4th Mo. Inf.	16 May, '98
Hon. Must. Out	10 Feb., '99
Capt. of Inf.	4 Aug., '98
Assd. to 5th Inf.	1 Jan., '99
Trs. to 20th Inf.	8 Apr., '01
Trs. to 9th Inf.	2 Aug., '06
Maj., 20th Inf.	20 Aug., '06
Trs. to 7th Inf.	31 May, '07
Trs. to 20th Inf.	29 Dec., '10
Unassigned	11 Mar., '11
Assd. to 20th Inf.	14 Apr., '11
Lt. Col. of Inf.	2 Mar., '12
Assd. to 10th Inf.	8 July, '14
Unassigned	5 Aug., '14
Lt. Col., Porto Rican Rgt.	1 Oct., '14
Col. Inf.	1 May, '16
Brig. Gen., N. A.	5 Aug., '17
Maj. Gen., N. A.	12 Apr., '18
Discharged as Maj. Gen.	2 July, '19

Joined his regiment at Fort Douglas, Utah, August, 1883, to August, 1887; Fort Leavenworth, Kan., September, 1887 to July, 1889; Fort Lewis, Col., August, 1889, to September, 1889; Fort Riley, Kan., October, 1889, to August, 1890; Fort Porter, N. Y., September, 1890, to (sick March 3 to March 13, 1891) August, 1891; St. John's Military School, Manlius, N. Y., September, 1891, to August. 1895; Fort Leavenworth, Kan., September, 1895, to March, 1898; Mobile, Ala., April, 1898, to May, 1898; Camp Alger, Va., June, 1898, as Lt. Col. 4th Missouri Infantry; mustered out

February 10, 1899; Augusta, Ga., February, 1899, to April, 1899; St. Joseph, Mo., May, 1899, to September, 1899; en route to and at Moro Castle, Santiago, Cuba, October, 1899, to June, 1900; en route to and at Fort Sheridan, Ill., July, 1900, to August, 1900; en route to and at Cabayao, P. I., August 9, 1900, to January, 1901; Vigan, P. I., January, 1901, to April, 1901; Santiago, P. I., April, 1901, to May, 1901; Vigan, P. I., June, 1901, to September, 1901; Tanauan, P. I., October, 1901, to January, 1902; en route to and at Fort Sheridan, Ill., February, 1902, to October, 1903; Rialto Building, San Francisco, Cal., November, 1903, to October, 1905; Headquarters Department of California, San Francisco, Cal., November, 1905, to March, 1906; Presidio of Monterey, Cal., April, 1906, to March, 1907; Headquarters Southwestern Department, St. Louis, Mo., April, 1907, to June, 1907; Headquarters of the Columbia Vancouver Barracks, Wash., July, 1907, to August, 1909; Headquarters, Department of Missouri, Omaha, Neb., September, 1909, to February, 1911; en route to and at Fort Shafter, Hawaii, March, 1911, to September, 1911; en route to and at Fort Douglas, Utah, October, 1911, to (sick November 3 to November 4, 1911) August, 1912; Fort Leavenworth, Kan., September, 1912, to August, 1914; en route to and at San Juan, Porto Rico, September 26, 1914, to May, 1917; en route to and commanding Camp E. S. Otis, C. Z., May 19, 1917, to July 6, 1917; en route to Fort Oglethorpe, Ga., to July 19, 1917; commanding 56th Infantry at that post to August 24, 1917; commanding 164th Infantry Brigade at Camp Gordon, Ga., August 25, 1917, to April, 1918; in addition commanding the 82d Division from September 2 to November 11, 1917, and December 27, 1917, to September, 1918; assigned to command of the 82d Division in April, 1918, and commanded same to September, 1918 in France; on duty at Athens, Greece, to June, 1919; en route to United States to July 2, 1919; on duty at Washington, D. C., July, 1919; en route to and on duty at Fort McDowell, Ga., to date.

X

CRITIQUE ON THE FIGHTING CHARACTERISTICS OF THE 82ND DIVISION

BY

COLONEL GORDON JOHNSTON
Chief of Staff, 82nd Division, during Meuse-Argonne Offensive.

Just before the 1st Division jumped off from the line in which it had relieved the 35th Division I went up to have a look at them. I went to the P. C. of the 1st Brigade, near Baulny, thence to the support battalion, and then on to overlook the front line, and particularly the eastern slopes of the Aire. I was very much impressed with the formidable appearance of the northeast corner of the Argonne forest. The command of that position over the sector in which the 1st Brigade was to attack struck me very forcibly and raised a serious doubt in my mind as to the success of the advance. Being unofficially in this area, I did not feel inclined to obtrude my views, but did make inquiry as to the means for dealing with this menacing position. I was assured that it was to be smeared with artillery fire and felt confident that if any one would do such a job thoroughly it would be General Summerall. Meantime I had been put on duty at the 1st Corps and being occupied elsewhere could not go with the 1st Division in their attack. They made a splendid plunge and then were under such punishment from this very ground (northeast corner of the Argonne) that the hope of reaching the German line in their sector had to be abandoned.

It came to my attention on the 6th of October that the 82nd Division was designated for a flank attack across the Aire to capture this high ground. I was extremely interested in this plan and obtained authority to make another reconnaissance. I went along the left flank of the 1st Brigade to a point about abreast of Cornay. The extremely hazardous nature of this attack was most evident. I asked the battalion commanders if they knew anything about new troops coming in on their left and they did not. I then searched for General Parker and found him at the Division P. C. near Very. He likewise knew nothing of the attack, and we both went in to see General Summerall. He was not aware of the plan. We looked up the location of the 82nd Division on the map and after a bit of calculation, none of us could see how the maneuver was to be executed. We were all under the impression that the assault troops of the 82nd would maneuver in the area of the 1st Brigade and that troops would be formed facing their objectives with the necessary echelons in depth. Neither of the generals had been asked for guides nor had anyone consulted them. General Parker said, "The 1st Brigade couldn't do that in one night and that means no other Brigade in the Army could do it." General Summerall said, "The 1st Division couldn't do that and I wouldn't ask them to." General Summerall then called up the Corps, but whatever the answer was, the conversation didn't last long. I then took it on myself to call up the P. C. of the 82nd Division. Colonel

Sheldon answered. I asked if arrangements for guides had been made with the 1st Division. He replied that he did not know, but that General Lindsey was at the Division P. C. It was then about 3 or 4 P.M. I talked with General Lindsey and urged him to come over to the 1st Division P. C. and discuss matters with General Parker and General Summerall. General Lindsey came over and explained the plan of marching north of the roads and then moving by the flank to attack. When he had gone we were all rather depressed. It seemed that to commit a large body of troops to an assault without thorough orientation, careful placing of troops in position for attack and a thorough co-ordination with artillery presented very grave difficulties. General Summerall said that his Division was being destroyed and that he had begged for fresh troops to make this attack. He felt that no further progress could be made until this high ground west of the Aire was taken.

As a matter of fact, only a part of the 82nd Division artillery got into position in time to lend any assistance. Little help, if any, was given by the 6th Field Artillery of the 1st Division. There was no machine gun support on a general scale. The guides did not function properly and half of the attacking troops were lost at H hour. All of which increases the honor due to the Infantry units which delivered the assault and accomplished their desperate mission October 7th.

Great credit is due to the swift and forceful drive which General Duncan put into the execution of his task, and the cheerful, buoyant spirit of General Lindsey. His confidence of success and keenness for the job, which never abated during the horrors of that forced march on that miserable night of rain and mud on roads already congested to the limit, contributed most materially to the success of the Brigade.

Again Fate was with us in the thick fog which covered the Aire valley that morning. Soon after the jump off, the Boche knew something was doing but not the direction of the attack. I saw his interdiction fire, shells falling at crossroads and searching the ravines east of the main road. As the fog lifted a little on the high ground, I was amused to see him firing furiously at half a dozen old abandoned tanks of ours. The fire was very accurate and several direct hits were obtained. Indeed so accurate was his fire that I felt quite safe within 200 yards of a tank at which he was firing.

I could only follow the fight by the musketry fire, but soon felt that the attack was well under way and realized that a push from the south against the Boche might be very useful. So I hustled back to Corps Headquarters as fast as possible, reported that the attack was well under way, and that troops were across the river and fighting on high ground to the west. I asked permission to go over and stir up the 77th Division. General Craig said that he would start Conger's Brigade of the 28th Division. He had word just before I left that this Brigade was making headway along the La Viergette-Marc wood. At about 2 P.M. I reached the P. C. of 77th Division and told General Alexander (the Lord forgive me) that the 82nd was cutting right through to the Decauville road and driving the Boche back and that the 28th were pushing north on the road through La Viergette, and that now was the time for the 77th to break through also. He sent me on to General Wittenmeyer, who commanded the right Brigade. I caught General Wittenmeyer on the way to his front lines and gave him the same rosy report. He was ready to fight right away and asked if he could use the wood through La Viergette (which was out of his sector) to flank the Boche line. I assumed the responsibility for giving this authority with right of way reserved to 28th. This was reported to 1st Corps and confirmed later in the same day. There is every reason to believe that these efforts distracted some attention of the Boche from Lindsey's Brigade.

The outstanding lesson of this attack seems to me to be that with a worthwhile objective, a desperate and chance attack, if driven with great energy and unswerving determination, promises success in spite of the crudity in details. The failure to make fool proof arrangements regarding guides came very near causing disaster. Lack of traffic control and the fact that troops going into this action had no "right of way" was another near cause of failure.

Full recognition of this attack seems to be very slow in coming from higher Headquarters. I often wondered about this and once asked General Drum directly why it was. He said, "We could never understand why you kept milling around in Cornay. Why didn't you envelop it from the north?" I was astonished at this and asked if he realized that to do this we would have been forced to go a good bit further than the 1st Division had been able to go and that troops executing this movement would have been compelled to progress fighting in three directions at the same time. Cornay was merely in the way to our objective, the high ground beyond, and had to be taken.

I have talked with a number of officers who have made studies on the ground later and the importance of this attack is steadily gaining ground in the minds of all of them.

The 82nd Division made some very material contributions to the science of war. The ideas may not have been original, but their application was. At least, the fact that our lead in these matters was promptly followed by others and adopted by higher formations is a great compliment. The Commander in Chief called at our P. C. about the middle of October and his remarks to General Duncan impressed themselves on my mind so vividly that I feel at liberty to cite them as a quotation. He said, "General, there is no relief in sight for your Division. I know that the men are very much exhausted and the organization reduced in strength, but you must not only hold on but continue to push on. You must remember that war is waged with weary men and that battles are fought by tired and hungry soldiers. It is the same on both sides. It is the normal, not the abnormal, condition of active operations. You must nurse your men all that you can, but not hesitate to demand sacrifices when the time for that comes.

"I want to impress on you the importance of the leaders of smaller units. They must love initiative and must hold what ground they gain to the utmost. It often happens that a Sergeant or even a Corporal may decide a battle by the boldness with which he seizes a bit of ground and holds it. Even if they cannot hold it, if they fight to the last man; it may enable other leaders to gain valuable ground.

"You must impress on all of your officers the desire and determination to get forward without waiting for some one else.

"You must not be unduly influenced by weariness and exhaustion of your men and must impress your Commanders with that fact. These are the natural conditions of war and cannot be avoided."

This visit led to a conviction that it was vital to first check up carefully our resources in man power; second, to check the loss of men from the line; third, to check the loss of physical vigor.

The effort to check up our available man power proved to be a serious problem. The morning reports did not convey anything more than the paper strength. In the sector of the Division there is not only a great number of non-combatants or men engaged on non-combatant duties, but there is also a large floating population for various reasons, much of it quite necessary. The final solution adopted by General Duncan was to count only "fighting effectives." These were defined as soldiers actually present with their *platoon* commanders with weapons in their hands engaged in killing the enemy. That was a pretty drastic cut, but after all that is what all the resources of a Division should be devoted to, to push and maintain weapons on the line. A form was issued and each platoon commander required to make a daily battle report and account briefly for his losses or gains. The strength of all the fighting platoons in a Regiment was the "fighting effective" strength of that Regiment. The consolidation of the first report showed results which gave real concern. However, the attention of every officer and non-commissioned officer was centered on this one subject and the "fighting effective" strength of all organizations showed a constant improvement. When this had gotten well under way, General Dickman called at the P. C. one day and asked for our strength on the line. I asked if he wanted the effective strength and on his reply that he did, gave him the daily report, which showed about 4000 men (our losses then were about 7000). He told me that a neighboring Division Commander had just informed him that he had 22,000 men on the line and wanted to know where the rest of our men were.

Later Colonel Marshall, G-3, 1st Army, came to our P. C. and said he had heard we had a new way of figuring strength and he was on a committee to draft an order on the subject. I gave him our memorandum and forms. Within a few days the 1st Army issued a general order which followed very closely our memorandum.

Then came the drain in man power. It was found that the triage system was responsible for many unnecessary losses. When the ambulances came back, every occupant would be tagged and passed on with practically no plan of retention. A hospital was immediately set up at Apremont, messes were opened, cots and an ample supply of blankets and even some luxuries provided. At the triage strict orders were given that no officer or man should be evacuated who could possibly be returned to any duty within two weeks. Arrangements were made for the retention of 300 beds in a hospital further to the rear with the understanding that patients would be returned direct to our rest camp at Apremont for return to any useful duty. Practically all gas and neurosis cases were stopped here. This checked the loss in man power to a minimum.

Then came the question of retention of physical vigor. At Apremont and in connection with the hospital a "rest camp" was established. In the rest camp convalescents were cared for and all patients capable of light duty were put to useful work, particularly in the care of arms and equipment turned over to them by the salvage officer. Neurosis cases got no coddling and very little sympathy. They were also always in sound of the guns and got a bombing every now and then, or some long range shelling to cheer them up. Their recovery was unusually rapid.

As soon as the flow back to the front line began, regimental surgeons were authorized to send back for four days' rest, officers and men who were most exhausted. These men slept many hours when they first came back. From time to time a bit of soup or coffee was forced into their mouths. On about the third day they were put to light work and on the next day or so were ready and keen for the front line again. In this way we were building up continually from the weakest. This with greater attention to the third line Battalions tided us over the peak of the load until we could hold our own.

General McArthur paid us a visit one day after we had this plan in operation and was so impressed that he carried the system out in the 42nd Division immediately. I have heard that it was recommended to and adopted by a number of other Divisions.

From a technical point of view, the Division was groping its way toward a development which promised to receive confirmation in the use of machine guns. The great fire power of the machine guns of a Division had never been fully co-ordinated.

While stabilized on the St. Juvin-St. Georges front with a wedge thrust through the Kriemhilde-Stellung, we were holding alone four kilos front with about 3000 men. The men were physically weak and at the same time subject to counter attack. We were still trying to gain a bit of ground here and there, but the dangers of an attack in force had to be considered and therefore the necessity for organizing a defense of artillery and machine gun fire to cover them or at least disorganize the enemy before getting to us. A system very much like that of the Coast Artillery was adopted. The ground in front was divided into numbered squares and all firing data prepared so that on the appearance of a target in our given squares all artillery guns and all machine guns (direct or indirect) could open fire immediately. Lines of information reached each battery (artillery or machine gun) so that all could be called at once. The effectiveness of the system was tested when a strong force of Boche formed up north of St. Juvin and made an attack. The machine gun barrage fell in two and a half minutes and practically every battery of artillery was firing in five and a half minutes. The effect was terrific, the enemy formation was smashed to bits instantly and broke to the rear. The howitzer regiment very neatly got behind them with phosgene and finished the job. Prisoners taken later confirmed the damage done.

This work developed a very close relation between the artillery and the machine gunners, each gave targets to the other and mutual lines of information were laid with one set of observers working for both arms. This led to the idea of co-ordinating the work in an offensive action. It was not the idea to take from Brigade Commanders and others the tactical use of the machine gun units, but there are many instances in which the lower formation cannot make the best use of all their ground. In an action, the fullest fire power of the Division must be developed in order to insure the progress of the Infantry at the least cost. No gun can afford to be idle so long as the Infantry is being punished. Therefore, all machine gun and artillery units not actually required and until required should be brought to bear on points where the Infantry might be assisted. So the Machine Gun Officer and the Artillery commander hold the fire power of their unengaged units at the direction of the Division Commander.

In the use of the 37 m/m and 3" Stokes, it seems that our sections followed the "hit and run" principle more than anything else. The idea was to locate a target, go into action and fire as rapidly as possible for several minutes then "beat it" elsewhere before the Boche got on.

XI

82nd Div., U. S.
6 October, 1918.
21 Hrs. 30

SECRET
FIELD ORDERS
 NO. 20.
MAPS: Foret D'Argonne 1/20,000.
 Verdun 1/80,000.

1. Information of the enemy indicates that he is withdrawing to the KRIEMHILDE STELLUNG from the AISNE to the MEUSE. The First American Army and the Fourth French Army resume their attack on the 7th instant. The 38th French Corps attacks the FORET D'ARGONNE in a general northeasterly direction through Lancon. The First Corps (U. S.) attacks on the present front of the 28th Division at 6 Hours, 7 October, 1918.

2. The 82nd Division, less 1 Infantry Brigade, will attack at 5 Hours, 7 October, 1918. Attack will be made by the 164th Infantry Brigade supported by the 157th Field Artillery Brigade.

OFFICIAL HISTORY OF 82ND DIVISION 303

3. (*a*) Sector limits of the attack.
   Right Boundary: FLEVILLE, exclusive—Elevation 151.
   Left Boundary: Ferme De GRANGES—La FORGE—CHATEAU of CHATEL-CHEHERY—Meridian 79.8.

   (*b*) Objectives:
   First Objective will be the line FLEVILLE, exclusive—Cornay, inclusive—Hill 223, inclusive—Point 97.3-79.0.

   (*c*) Corps Objective:
   Same as the first objective to CORNAY—Elevation 151 (½ km. West of CORNAY)—Cote 263 (1½ km. West of CORNAY)—Point 95.5-80.0—To LA VIERGETTE.

   (*d*) 164th Infantry Brigade will relieve the infantry elements of the 28th Division on the line North of La FORGE before 24 hours 6 October, 1918. The leading elements of the Brigade will be crossed over the AIRE River via the Bridge at La FORGE and improvised foot bridges between La FORGE and FLEVILLE and formed along the Railroad track running along the West side of the Aire River before the hour for attack, covered by active patrols. Rate of advance of Infantry units from position of departure 100 meters in 3 minutes. Front line Infantry Battalions will not be reinforced but will be passed through by support Battalions when they are definitely slowed down by enemy resistance. Combat Liaison Detachment consisting of one company of Infantry and 1 Machine Gun Platoon will maintain contact with the 28th Division on our left. One company of Infantry and one Machine Gun Platoon will maintain combat liaison with the liaison detachment of the First Division on our right near the Bridge at FLEVILLE.

   (*e*) ARTILLERY:
   157th Field Artillery Brigade will support this attack. The advancing Infantry will be covered by a rolling barrage moving at the rate of 100 meters in three minutes. Barrage to start at 5 Hours and to be placed within Division sector limits and parallel to the railroad track on the West bank of the AIRE River.

   The initial position of the barrage will be 200 meters West of the track and to advance in a Westerly direction up to a line 200 meters beyond the first objective. At "H" plus 3 hours the barrage will be laid beyond the first objective and advanced at the same rate to a point 200 meters beyond the Corps objective. In addition to this barrage, artillery concentration will be made during the advance on known enemy Infantry and Artillery positions.

   (*x*) Troops will be prepared to advance from the first objective at "H" plus 3 hours. The Corps objective when reached will be organized and held at all costs.

4. Axis of Liaison:
   Axis of the 1st Division to Chaudron Farme, thence L'ESPERANCE—La FORGE—CHATEL-CHEHERY—CORNAY.

   Plan of Liaison, Annex 6 (as amended) to Field Order 17 in effect.

   Plan of communication, supply and evacuation as prescribed in Field Order 17 (Annex 5).

5. Post of Command:
   P. C. 82nd Division VARENNES.
   Advance Center of Information, 82nd Division, CHAUDRON FERME.
   P. C. 163rd Inf. Brigade without change.
   P. C. 164th Inf. Brigade Depot MUNICIONS (00.3-79.3).
   P. C. 157th Field Artillery Brigade VARENNES.

G. B. DUNCAN,
*Major General, U. S. A.,
Commanding 82nd Division.*

SECRET.

COPY NO. 4.

82 DIV., U. S.
9 October, 1918.
2:35 o'clock.

FIELD ORDERS
NO. 21.
MAP: FORET D'ARGONNE—1/20,000.

1. Our attack to-day made substantial gains.
2. The attack ordered by Field Order 68, 1st Army Corps, will be resumed at 8 Hr. 30, 9th October, by the Division and be vigorously pushed.
3. (*a*) The 163rd Infantry Brigade is released from Corps Reserve, and less one Infantry Regiment will relieve in its sector the 28th Division (less Artillery and Engineers), the relief being under the direction of the Commanding General, 28th Division, and will be completed by 4 hours, 9th October.

Present Sector limits of the 28th Division.
   East boundary: Hill 223 (exclusive) Point 96.0-80.5—MARCQ (inclusive), thence due North to AIRE River.
   West boundary: LA VIERGETTE—Point 94.5-80.0—La BESOGNE, CHEVIERES.

Present Sector limits of 82nd Division:
   Eastern: FLEVILLE-BAULNY Road.
   Western: Same as East boundary of 28th Division.

(*b*) The 163rd Infantry Brigade, less one Regiment, will attack in the area of the 28th Division—to the Corps objective, parallel 82. Rate of advance not to exceed 100 meters in 3 minutes.

(*c*) The 164th Infantry Brigade will continue its attack. Rate of advance not to exceed 100 meters in 3 minutes.

(*d*) One Infantry Regiment, 163rd Brigade, Division Reserve—at CHARPENTRY.

(*e*) *ARTILLERY:* The 53rd F. A. Brigade will support the attack of the 163rd Infantry Brigade and the 157th F. A. Brigade will support the attack of the 164th Infantry Brigade. Interdiction fire will be kept in front of Infantry.

Harassing and destructive fire as ordered by Commanding General, 157th F. A. Brigade, under whose orders the 53rd F. A. Brigade comes at 21 hours, 8th October. Upon arrival of the Infantry at their objective, all artillery will be available for harassing and searching fire North of the final objective. This fire must be so regulated by Infantry Commanders and Artillery Liaison Officers as to best protect their troops and exploitation patrols.

(f) 103rd Engineers—Present missions—307th Engineers, Division Reserve.

(g) Signal Troops of 28th Division to be relieved by Signal Troops of 82nd Division.

(h) Sanitary Troops of 28th Division to be relieved by Sanitary Troops of 82nd Division.

(i) Combat Liaison—Combat liaison groups consisting of one Infantry platoon with machine guns detailed from each Brigade will assure contact between Brigades. One of these groups will be detailed by each Brigade for each of its flanks, except that for the right of the 164th Infantry Brigade there shall be one Infantry Company.

(j) *RESERVE:* Division Reserve will be alerted at "H" Hour.

(x) *EXPLOITATION AND ORGANIZATION OF POSITION:* Immediately upon arrival at the objective, the position will be organized in depth as the position of resistance, and exploitation patrols will be sent to the North and West as far as the Aire River, which will be the limit of the outpost position.

4. Administrative instructions are covered in orders to be issued later.

5. Posts of Command:

82nd Division at and after 12 hours, 9th October, La FORGE (02.5-75.2).

163rd Inf. Brigade ....CHENE TONDU
164th Inf. Brigade ....CHATEL CHEHERY

GEO. B. DUNCAN,
Major General, Commanding.

G-I

82 DIV., U. S.,
October 11, 1918.

SECRET
ORDERS
NO. 30.

1. The following administrative instructions are published:
2. RAILHEAD: October 12th—FROIDOS.
October 13th—CHEPPY.

DISTRIBUTING POINTS:

(a) Rations—Commencing October 12th and until further orders, in the forward area, excepting the artillery, will draw rations from this point after 2 P.M. October 12th. Rations will be distributed to the artillery by truck to regiments as heretofore. Troops at GRANGE le COMTE Farm will be supplied by truck from the railhead.

(b) Gas supplies: To be at the Distributing Point at APREMONT.

(c) Gasoline: Gasoline will be supplied at the distributing point at APREMONT.

3. MOVEMENT OF UNITS:

(a) M.O.R.S. and M.S.T.U. will move to APREMONT on October 12th or as soon thereafter as practicable after reconnaissance of that place by the Division Ordnance Officer and Division Motor Transport Officer.

(b) Supply Train to APREMONT.

(c) Medical Supply Depot and Triage at VARENNES will move on October 12th to the German Hospital, one-half kilometer southwest of APREMONT on the lower APREMONT—le CHENE TONDU Road.

(d) Field Hospital at CLERMONT will move to VARENNES on October 12th.

(e) Supply Companies of Infantry and Machine Gun units will move from their present location to the forward area and will be stationed at such places as may be directed by Captain Catchings Therrell of the Division Quartermaster's office. Commanding Officers of Supply Companies will keep closely in touch with their organizations so as to be able to supply them with hot meals whenever possible.

(f) Second Echelon of Division Headquarters (G-1 office, Trains Headquarters, Division Surgeon, Division Inspector) to La FORGE as soon as that place is vacated by the First Echelon.

4. DRESSING STATIONS: PYLONE, l'ESPERANCE, CHATEL CHEHERY.

5. SMALL ARMS AMMUNITION DUMPS: Commencing October 12th.

Farm des GRANGES—99.8-79.8.

APREMONT.

MONTBLAINVILLE (for the 12th and 13th only).

6. The Division Signal Officer will have a telephone placed in the old railroad station near APREMONT.

7. SALVAGE: All property for salvage will be turned in by the field trains at the distributing point, and by trucks to the salvage dump at CLERMONT. All machine gun units will make special effort to salvage their machine gun strips for reloading by the machine gun units, as there is only a limited supply of machine gun strips on hand.

8. The Division Ordnance Officer will keep on hand at the M.O.R.S. at APREMONT a supply of individual ordnance equipment.

9. ENGINEER MATERIAL: Engineer material can be drawn without formality from the following dumps:

> North of MONTBLAINVILLE: Barbed wire, pickets, picks and shovels.
>
> South of APREMONT: Barbed wire and pickets.
>
> North of APREMONT: Lumber, barbed wire, picks and shovels.
>
> Northwest of APREMONT: (Along railroad) German dump not inventoried.
>
> Le MENIL Farm: German dump not inventoried.

(a) Special Divisional Dumps of barbed wire, stakes and sand bags are being established at MONTBLAINVILLE and Le CHENE TONDU. A large dump of all classes of engineer material is in the northwest part of VARENNES. Material can be drawn therefrom on requisition signed by an officer, setting forth the purpose for which needed; approval is effected at the dump.

(b) The Divisional Engineers are located as follows:

Headquarters, 307th Engineers—At La FORGE, just east of CHATEL CHEHERY.

Headquarters, 307th Engr. Tn.—Le MENIL Farm.

(c) The Engineers will construct a brdige as soon as practicable at CHATEL CHEHERY.

BY COMMAND OF MAJOR GENERAL DUNCAN:

GORDON JOHNSTON,
Chief of Staff.

SECRET.

Copy No. 5.

82 DIV., U. S.,
14 October, 1918.
21 Hours.

FIELD ORDERS
NO. 25.
MAPS: BUZANCY 1/20,000.

I. INFORMATION OF THE ENEMY AND INTENTION OF THE HIGH COMMAND.

(a) The Kremhilde Stellung has been breached by the 82nd Division.

(b) The First Army continues its advance on 15 October at 7 hours 30—15 October, 1918.

II. ZONES OF ACTION AND OBJECTIVES. See attached tracing.

III. USE OF TROOPS.

(a) Troops will be formed up for attack at 6 hours, 15th October. Order of Brigades in line same as to-day.

(b) Infantry Action.

Troops advance from jumping off line at 7 hours 30, and continue without halt to the Corps objective. Rate of Infantry advance 100 meters in six minutes for the first 1000 meters.

(c) Artillery preparation will commence at once. Ravines and woods will be strongly gassed with non-persistent gas up to H minus four hours. Routes of approach, cross roads and other targets will be strongly shelled.

A barrage will be placed 300 meters in front of jumping off line 7 hours 25 and held there until 7 hours 30, when it will be moved forward at the rate of Infantry advance for 1000 meters, when this barrage will be stopped. Smoke shells will be included in this barrage.

When barrage stops the fire of the 321st Field Artillery will be at the disposal of the Commanding General, 163rd Brigade, and the fire of one battalion, 320th Field Artillery, at the disposal of the Commanding General, 164th Brigade.

Forward guns—no change.

(d) Upon arrival on the Corps objective the position will be organized in depth, and exploitation made by contact patrols.

(e) *Division Reserve.* One Battalion, 325th Infantry, to be in the vicinity of cross roads at 98.1-85.0, at 6 hours.

(f) *Machine Guns.* One Machine Gun Company will accompany each support and assault Battalion. Long range machine guns will fire in accordance with instructions already given.

The 319th Machine Gun Battalion will form a part of the Division Reserve, and will fire as directed by Division Machine Gun Officer.

(g) Attention is invited to the advisability of covering the advance with scouts separated by wide intervals. In the attack supports and reserves will be kept well echeloned in depth and will advance in lines of small columns. It must be impressed upon all that the wide front the Division is called upon to cover necessitates considerable intervals between Combat groups.

Thickening of front line where resistance is encountered by feeding in supports and reserves must be avoided. Full use will be made of all auxiliary infantry weapons and the forward guns of the Field Artillery.

IV. LIAISON.

(a) Axis of Liaison. See attached sketch.

(b) Combat Liaison: No change except that initial points will be determined by Brigade Commanders after agreement with adjacent Brigade Commanders.

(c) Plan of Air Service. No change.

V. No change in administration details.

VI. *Posts* of command:
    82nd Div.—No change.
    163rd Brigade—98.4-84.9 from 10 hours.
    164th Brigade—SOMMERANCE from 10 hours.
    157th F. A. Brigade—No change.

GEO. B. DUNCAN,
Major General, U. S. A.,
Commanding.

SECRET.

82nd Division, U. S.,
17 October, 1918,
20 Hours.

FIELD ORDERS
NO. 29.
MAPS: BUZANCY 1/20,000.

1. INFORMATION OF THE ENEMY AND INTENTION OF THE HIGH COMMAND.

(a) The 78th Division on our left occupies the Southern edge of BOIS de LOGES.

(b) The attack of the First Army Corps will be resumed at 6 hours 30, 18 October.

(c) 82nd Division will support and protect the right flank of the 78th Division, maintaining contact and advancing with that Division.

2. ZONES OF ACTION AND OBJECTIVE.
(a) Objective—Without change.
(b) Zones of Action.

East Boundary after 5 hours, 18 October—CHATEL CHEHERY (exclusive)—MARCQ (inclusive)—CHAMPIGNEULLE (inclusive)—RESILLE FARM (exclusive).

Boundary between Brigades after 5 hours, 18 October, point 98.5-86.3; 98.8-88.8; thence along Eastern edge of woods between Meridians 97 and 98 and between parallels 88 and 90; thence from the North edge of the woods due North.

3. USE OF TROOPS.

(a) Commanding General, 163rd Brigade, will relieve with one battalion and one machine gun company the 309th Infantry in the area between the present left boundary of the 82nd Division and the boundary as announced in Paragraph 2. Commanding Officer of the battalion to make this relief will report upon receipt of this order to the Commanding Officer, 309th Infantry, at his P. C. at East entrance of ST. JUVIN on the St. JUVIN-FLEVILLE road and arrange relief. Relief will be completed by 5 hours, 18 October.

Patrols from the left Battalion of the Division will constantly maintain contact with the 78th Division and will be ready to move forward with the right of that Division.

Commanding General, 164th Brigade, will make the necessary dispositions in new area assigned him before 5 hours, 18 October.

(b) ARTILLERY: At 6 hours, 18 October, 157th Field Artillery Brigade will place a strong concentration of high explosive shells and gas in CHAMPIGNEULLE and East of the AGRON River, thus supporting the advance of the 78th Division. Artillery will not fire in the BOIS de LOGES. Any known enemy batteries in action will be taken under counter-battery fire.

(c) Division Observers will carefully watch for enemy concentrations that would indicate a counter-attack and report such concentrations promptly. Any enemy machine guns in action will be promptly reported in order that they may be covered by artillery fire.

4. LIAISON—Without change.

5. POSTS OF COMMAND—Without change.

GEO. B. DUNCAN,
Major General, U. S. A.,
Commanding.

XII

DECORATIONS, PRISONERS TAKEN, MATERIAL CAPTURED

DECORATIONS

The number of decorations awarded to officers and men of the division shown below represent the figures obtained from the records prior to the departure of the division from France. Subsequent to that time several additional decorations have been awarded by the War Department and several decorations have been granted by the allied governments.

Kind of Decoration	Number of officers and men decorated.
Congressional Medal of Honor	2
Distinguished Service Medal	3
Distinguished Service Cross	75

DIVISION CITATIONS

There were cited by the Division commander for splendid conduct in action against the enemy, or for conspicuous efficiency in positions of great responsibility, 436 officers and men.

ENEMY PRISONERS TAKEN

During the operations against the enemy there were captured by members of the division the following:

18 Officers
827 Men

MATERIAL CAPTURED

The following represents the material captured by the division in the St. Mihiel and the Meuse Argonne offensive:

	St. Mihiel	Meuse-Argonne
Heavy Machine Guns	2	121
Light Machine Guns		156
Field Pieces 150's		1
Field Pieces 155's	1	
Field Pieces 77's		9
Minnenwefers	3	29
Auto-Tank Guns		3
Aeroplanes		2

In addition to the above, there were captured during the Meuse-Argonne offensive large quantities of railroad and engineering material.

www.ingramcontent.com/pod-product-compliance
Lightning Source LLC
Chambersburg PA
CBHW031940080426
42735CB00007B/205